MY DUEL
WITH THE VATICAN

MY DUEL WITH THE VATICAN

THE AUTOBIOGRAPHY OF A CATHOLIC MODERNIST

BY

ALFRED LOISY

PROFESSOR IN THE COLLÈGE DE FRANCE

Authorized Translation

BY

RICHARD WILSON BOYNTON

With a New Introduction

by

RT. REV. MSGR. E. HAROLD SMITH, M.A., S.T.L.
Pastor, Church of Our Savior, Bronx, N. Y.

GREENWOOD PRESS, PUBLISHERS
NEW YORK   1968

Introduction to the Reprint Edition

On June 1, 1940, a militantly patriotic Frenchman, who for the first half of his scholarly life had been a priest and an outstanding Roman Catholic biblical scholar, and for the second half a secular savant with an international reputation, died in the eighty-fourth year of his age. Those who knew him were thankful that he did not live to see the France of Vichy and Nazism.

Alfred Firmin Loisy was born in 1857. He was ordained a priest in 1879, and studied at the Institute Catholique, beginning in 1881. After taking a theological degree he became a professor there.

Early in Loisy's career, his writings brought him into conflict with his ecclesiastical superiors. As a result of an article on the biblical question and inspiration he was dismissed from his professorship in 1893. He later began to lecture on biblical criticism at the Ecole des Hautes Etudes Pratiques. In 1900 his article on the religion of Israel was condemned by both the Archbishop of Paris and the Pope. In the meantime he had published his *Evangile et l'église*, which he intended to be the Catholic answer to Harnack's *Wesen des Christentums*. Loisy's book was condemned in Paris but Leo XIII declined to condemn *Etudes Evangeliques*, which appeared at the same time.

In 1903 these books, together with two other of Loisy's works, were placed on the Roman Index by Pope Pius X—Leo XIII's successor. Loisy made a partial submission, but it was unacceptable to the Roman authorities. He then retired to his home in

Lorraine. In 1908 he published his now completed *Evangile synoptiques* which embodied the results of the higher criticism. This was followed by *Simples Reflexions*—on the decree "Lamentabile" and the encyclical "Pascendi." The Holy Office pronounced the major excommunication on Loisy in 1908. Modernism as an overt movement in the Catholic Church may be said to have come to an end with Loisy's abandonding of the faith. Loisy became professor of Church History at the College of France the following year. He continued to publish works on biblical criticism and religious subjects in the remaining years of his life.

My Duel with the Vatican is an account, from Loisy's side only, of his differences with the Roman authorities from 1903 to 1908.

Two questions concerning Alfred Loisy deserve some comment here. First, what was this French priest-scholar attempting to do in the field of religion —this was the only field that basically interested him—in the years between 1890 and 1908? He asserts that beginning in his Seminary years he had lived with tension between his scientific and religious beliefs. He had become fully aware over the intervening years that other thoughtful Christians faced this same problem. Hence, during the first decade of the twentieth century he had fashioned a new apologetic for the Christian Faith—a synthesis between Faith and Learning which is demanded by any age of intellectual activity of a new kind. He hoped by this means to resolve the tension between scientific facts and religious truths. A limited number of other clerical and lay Catholic thinkers, principally in

France, Italy, and England (George Tyrrell, an English priest, probably being the best known with Loisy) shared this hope. These persons did not form a unified group nor did they support a unified program. In general their approach was the application of a symbolistic and a radically evolutionary interpretation to Christian and Catholic dogmas.

The "Lamentabili" and Encyclical "Pascendi" promulgated in 1907 list a number of propositions in various parts of the religious sector and condemn them as incompatible with the teaching of the Roman Catholic Church. Most of these condemned statements were taken from Loisy's writings. He had realized since 1904 that unless he were willing to abdicate his intellectual position his usefulness and work in the Church were ended. Thus the last thirty-two years of his life were lived outside the Catholic Church.

Loisy possessed certain attributes both inherited and acquired that shed some light on his intellectual accomplishments as well as on his estrangement from the Church. His peasant birth and upbringing undoubtedly influenced his manner of living. He was an indefatigable worker (as his forbears had been in the purely physical sense), but he was a day-time worker, rising early and early to rest. He had a love for the land, for his garden and his chickens, which were the only diversions from his studies. By temperament and training, he was an ascetic. For social intercourse, convivial dining, witty conversation, he cared nothing.

More important still, Loisy was a lone worker—books and ideas were his life. He knew very few of his progressive or Modernist contemporaries. He never met Teilhard de Chardin, whom he admired and whose optimistic view of the spiritual potential of man he shared. From time to time, he was dominated by the attraction of certain theories of human philosophy. At other periods personal suffering obscured the clearness of his vision. These experiences, joined with his greatest weakness—his inability to accept the rejection or even overt criticism of any of his thought-out intellectual positions—furnish the basis for some of the contradictions that appear in his writings, as well as for some broken friendships, which saddened him to the end.

The general view today is that Loisy's work as an historian has not been surpassed, but that his theological work is passé. He never understood and hence never accepted the theological revolution that began towards the end of his life, and that continues today under both Protestant and Catholic auspices.

Maude Petre, a distinguished English writer on religious subjects and a contemporary of Loisy's, carried on an intellectual friendship with him until his death. She has the distinction of being the only woman whose name appears in the index of any of his works. Among other observations concerning him she offers these: first, he upheld religious values in a time of crisis, and worked for the religious evolution of mankind; secondly, the Loisy at the end was more like the Loisy of his early priesthood.* At the time of his final rupture with the Church, Alfred Loisy wrote: "The Pope has said truly that he could not keep silence without betraying the deposit of traditional doctrine . . . the two positions are taken

. . . the divorce is complete. It is impossible to foresee when and how modern thought and society can be reconciled with the Catholic faith and institution. . . . The wrongs are not all on one side. . . . Time is the great master. . . . We need despair neither of civilization nor the Church but one cannot usefully speak to them of reconciliation at a time when they are turning their backs on one another."

Their backs are no longer turned on each other. Thus Loisy, through his work as an historian, may yet come to have some part in the reconciliation of progress and religion—the goal he set for himself seven decades ago.

— RT. REV. MSGR. E. HAROLD SMITH
Bronx, N. Y.—1968

* Maude D. Petre, *Alfred Loisy: His Religious Significance* (Cambridge: Cambridge University Press, 1944).

AUTHOR'S PREFACE

ONE may all too readily expose himself to ridicule by venturing to appeal to the public in his own behalf; the wisest course, as long as the world shows no disposition to go out of its way on our account, being to leave it in peace, that it may be predisposed to leave us so. But if the world insists on meddling in our affairs, and especially if it tattles about us and, worse yet, puts its hasty conjectures into print, the matter takes on a different aspect. Then it becomes imperative that we should testify in our own behalf, if our past is not to be placed in a radically wrong light. Even the testimony we may offer will not seem to every one conclusive, or avail to defeat calculated misrepresentations. Nevertheless, it becomes an obligation towards those who want simply to know the truth, and who have not made up their minds in advance to a verdict of condemnation.

"O, but they will paint me black!" Renan used to say, when he amused himself by conjecturing the portrait that Catholic theologians would make of him after the lapse of a century or two. Yet there is another who bids fair to go down to posterity in even worse case than Renan, without having, like that brilliant writer, the advantage of being protected by works whose immortality can be measured only by the duration of the French language. Renegade from the Church that he was, Renan was no common heretic; yet he is not, and never will be, reckoned among the heresiarchs. That doubtful honor has already accrued to the writer of these lines; his books are condemned by the same token as those of Luther and Calvin; and his Catholic readers must stand in peril of the excommunication visited upon even the abettors of heresy. Whatever life he may live, or whatever death he may die —unless he shall stultify himself at the last—a sombre legend is destined to attend him. Those who profess to know have already consigned him to the despicable class to which he belongs—that of Judas, forsooth! So it is pertinent to inquire whether the alleged heresiarch has ever dogmatized; whether it was not the so-called traitor who was himself betrayed.

An opposite group of persons, typical of the present age—frank unbelievers, for the most part—are quite incapable of conceiving such a course as leaving the Church without once speaking ill of her. How is it possible, they ask, for a scholar and thinker to refrain from roundly berating that acknowledged enemy of modern science? Does it not argue a want of insight or of candor to wait to be anathematized before abandoning her and, after being made the subject of the most solemn excommunication in her power, to continue to regard her with sympathy and treat her with respect? What is to be thought of a Biblical scholar who nevertheless served a long term of willing captivity within Catholicism, where it has to be maintained that the Bible is without error of any kind, the ecclesiastical tradition infallible, and the decisions of the Pope or of a Commission appointed by him a court of final appeal in the criticism of texts? Must not the scholar in question lay himself open to the suspicion of having temporized to remain in the Church, and of being willing to compromise and suppress his convictions since he has seen its doors close behind him?

It is certain that nothing is to be gained by pleading blamelessness or by suggesting the existence of extenuating circumstances to either group, that of wholly convinced believers or that of irreconcilable free-thinkers. These pages are not written for such absolutists, of one or the other sort. For the first, the "sin of apostasy" admits of neither remission nor pardon; while for the second, there is no freedom of thought outside of what calls itself "free-thinking," implacably hostile to religion, and confronting the fanaticism of traditional belief with a counter-fanaticism bent on its extermination. Any middle way is equally contemned by both. But between these two extremes is to be found a large and increasing group of persons, less confident of themselves and less certain of possessing truth in its finality, who know or suspect the endless complication of human motives and who, in a case like the present, are not obsessed by the passion to judge and to blame but wish, above all, to be told what actually occurred so that they may be free to draw their own conclusions. To such as these the present volume is addressed; and it solicits less their indulgence than their thoughtful consideration.

If there were, in the past which is here to be evoked, nothing but disappointment and disillusion, and if the future were, in fact, securely mortgaged to either of the rigid dogmatisms just referred to, it would be too painful to write these memories and much too futile to publish them. But the reader may look forward to more than mere echoes of a tormented and broken life. He will find here fruitful experiences, wherein exaltations of spirit have mingled with external reverses and internal agonies. And, uncertain as the present outlook may seem, it begins to be evident that the embattled dogmatisms, still as haughty and domineering as ever, are engaged in defeating their own ends; that the general intelligence of mankind is overleaping the bounds of narrow creeds; and that the confining and embittering spirit of hate is gradually being outgrown. One may therefore venture to leave behind him a word of peace and sincerity, at least for those who continue to accept so much of the original gospel as to believe that, in the moral order, truth is reconcilable with goodness and with mutual charity.

The present work is in no sense an apologia. Its author passes no final judgment upon himself, and he inclines to question the right of others to sit in judgment upon him. He is aware of no need for self-defense. In the crucial moments of his life, he was never swayed by low motives. Impelled by the exuberance of a youthful enthusiasm to embrace an ecclesiastical career, the normal evolution of his thought—a result of studies loyally and disinterestedly pursued; of publications in no way designed to promote heresy or schism in the Catholic Church, but rather to bring out the actual incidence of certain historical, theological and ecclesiastical problems; lastly, of official acts of the hierarchy condemning these writings and impressively, even sensationally, expelling their author from the Roman Communion —all this has led to his involuntary alienation from the Church. There is here, surely, no "mystery of iniquity," no dishonor that need crave forgiveness. Explanations are offered that may have their use, but no attempt is made at self-justification, which would be superfluous.

Nor is there here any endeavor to construct a personal life-history, or to furnish data relevant to the religious movements of recent years. The aim is not to afford material for the compilers of dictionaries of contemporary biography or to historians of the Church, or to writers and speakers who may find it worth while to busy themselves with the history, discussion or criticism of Catholic Modernism. Since the author has often, and at times violently, been haled before the judgment-seat of public opinion, he now bears public witness, without anger and without recrimination, to the purpose and meaning of his acts. Some details, that will be liable to misuse in certain quarters, might well have been omitted from these confessions. The impartial reader, who alone merits consideration, is entitled to have before him all the facts.

ALFRED LOISY.

Ceffonds, near Montier-en-Der,
Haute Marne, France, 1913.

CONTENTS

FOREWORD

[BY THE TRANSLATOR]

IN rendering into English the text of this volume I have had in mind a single aim—to present it, with scrupulous fidelity to the meaning of the original, in an idiom that might hope to rise, at least in some measure, above the level of the usual translation-English. To this end no pains have been spared, though it goes without saying that I have found it impossible to retain the full flavor and finesse of Professor Loisy's expressive French style.

The translator is grateful to the distinguished author, first, for permission to offer to the English-reading public this, his spiritual autobiography, which it is hoped may serve as an adequate introduction to his other writings, only two or three of the lesser of which are, as yet, translated;[1] and, chiefly, for the interest and sympathy with which he has followed the work as it advanced. In pursuance of instructions received from the author, one or two slight changes and a significant addition have been made in the text, to enable it to conform to

[1] *The Gospel and the Church,* translated by Christopher Home, New York, Charles Scribner's Sons, 1904. Second edition, 1912, with Introduction by Newman Smyth, D.D.

The Religion of Israel, translated by Arthur Galton, London, Fisher Unwin, 1910.

The War and Religion, translated by Arthur Galton, Oxford, B. H. Blackwell, 1915.

xi

that of the second French edition. A passage of several paragraphs has been transferred from the end of Chapter III to the beginning of Chapter IV, where it seems more properly to belong, and Chapter VI has been slightly recast, to admit of an addition of two or three pages, including the important letter of explanation to Abbé Houtin.

The Index has been especially compiled for this translation, with the intention of showing at a glance how intimately the contents of the book are related to a wide range of burning questions of the moment.

The author's description of his evolution in thought and belief, as well as his discussion of the vexed problems—Biblical, theological, historical and critical—that he encountered in his progress, will be found to bear directly upon the current debate within American Protestantism between Fundamentalists and Modernists. For this reason, the appearance of the book just now seems well-timed.

What is likely to impress an American or British reader is the excess of partisanship and even bitterness with which a great scholar, like Loisy, was hounded by persecution and finally expelled from the Roman Catholic Church. The close connection of religion, in its institutional form, with public affairs and matters of state in a country like France, will doubtless account for the exasperated tone of much of the controversy in which Loisy was perforce engaged, a condition witnessed to by others concerned in the same general movement of reconstruction in religious thought.

As a revelation of the inner workings of the Papal system in its dealings with the Modernist Movement, especially during the reactionary pontificate of the late Pope Pius X, this autobiography of one of the greatest of living critics of the New Testament and historians of religion seems likely to remain a unique document. The translator's estimate of the Catholic career of Alfred Loisy, and of the significant and far-reaching issues involved in it, will be found in the Translator's Introduction, to which the reader is referred. Since Frenchmen, Britons and Americans fought and suffered side by side in the Great War for democracy, it behooves us of the Anglo-Saxon heritage to acquire a fuller appreciation of the leading personalities of contemporary France. This volume is issued in the hope of making one of the most remarkable of living Frenchmen better known to the English-speaking world.

RICHARD WILSON BOYNTON.

Buffalo, New York,
March, 1924

TRANSLATOR'S INTRODUCTION

THE CATHOLIC CAREER OF ALFRED LOISY [1]

IT takes perhaps some boldness of assertion to maintain that the life-story of an author relatively unknown—at least to the English-reading world—deserves to rank with those acknowledged masterpieces of religious autobiography, the *Apologia pro Vita Sua* of John Henry Newman, and the *Souvenirs d'Enfance et de Jeunesse* of Ernest Renan. Renan and Newman were born leaders of men, each drawing after himself a train of zealous disciples, and followed by an admiring public. Both were consummate artists in words, knowing full well how to make the most of the dramatic and human element that chance or their own choice had woven into their careers. Each produced a long row of eloquent volumes, and their writings not only enjoyed the widest vogue in their own day but are among the works of the Nineteenth Century whose significance is still far from being exhausted. Each was a convert—the one into Roman Catholicism, the other out of it—and so their self-revelations appeal to the psychological interest of such a process when the subject of it is a man of genius, and no less to the

[1] Reprinted, by permission of the Editors, from the *Harvard Theological Review*, for January, 1918.

historical interest attaching to any conspicuous individual whose career has become interwoven with the Church of Rome. The *Choses Passées* [1] of Professor Alfred Loisy assuredly did not originate in any conscious imitation of these two famous writers, although both were conspicuous among his formative influences. But his book belongs in the same class with theirs, and in its distinction of style, its dramatic and human appeal, and its psychological and historical interest, as I shall try in these pages to show, falls no whit behind. It is my confident belief, at least, that *Choses Passées* bids fair to become in its turn a classic to be placed beside the *Apologia* and the *Souvenirs* on the shelf of the student of religion, as a document of outstanding significance for the intellectual and religious evolution of the last quarter-century.

Since 1909, Professor Loisy has occupied the chair of the history of religions in the *Collège de France,* made vacant by the death of the lamented Jean Réville. In March of the previous year, on the ground of his obstinate persistence in "modernist" opinions, Loisy was visited with excommunication in its extreme form by the authorities of the Roman Church, in whose unstinted service he had thus far spent his life. The most competent critic of the Bible and of Christian origins yet produced by that Church in any land, he has been as prolific an author as either Renan or Newman. With already twenty volumes to his credit—three of them monumental achievements of exegetical science running close to a

[1] *Choses Passées,* Paris, Emile Nourry, 1913.

thousand pages each—he is still at sixty [1] in full career, except in so far as the war has necessarily interfered with his productiveness. His bi-monthly *Revue d'Histoire et de Littérature Religieuses* has not been issued, for reasons that one can easily conjecture, since the fatal August of 1914. [2] The first overwhelming wave of German invasion reached almost to his summer home at Ceffonds, near Montier-en-Der, Haute Marne, and the present line of trenches runs not many miles away. The past, however, is secure. Neglecting, therefore, his recent work in the general history of religions and in the pagan and Christian mysteries, which presages important results to come, we turn—following his own account of the things that are behind—to his career up to the age of fifty-one in the Roman Catholic Church.

I

Alfred Firmin Loisy was born at Ambrières, in the upper reaches of the Marne valley, on February 28, 1857, of peasant stock which had been on the land and had swarmed into several of the neighboring hamlets for something like two hundred years. Too frail of body to become a tiller of the soil, from an early age he gave evidence of a rare intellectual endowment. When taken to school at the age of four and a half, the timid and sickly child sat for two days mute before the teacher who was trying to instruct him in the alphabet; on the third day, without being asked, he recited all the letters, not wish-

---

[1] Written in 1918. See Supplementary Note, p. 46.
[2] Written in 1918. The *Revue* resumed publication in 1920, but was definitively suspended at the end of 1922.

ing, as he says, to pronounce the names of those strange signs until he knew them perfectly. The incident is typical of his whole later career,—of his marvelous capacity for assimilating languages, ancient and modern, and provinces of learning, one after another; and equally of his sturdy independence and self-respecting pride. In it all, the child was father of the man. His appropriation of Catholic scholasticism and the traditional dogma was so complete as to leave nothing to be desired. But his conclusions, when finally announced, came straight from his own intelligence and conscience. Authority never awed him. A friendly superior, unable to persuade him into the usual smooth and politic ways, characterized his conscience in later years as "perpendicular." If it was not always strictly so, as we shall have occasion to see, the cause may be looked for in the peculiar training he received, and in the deep love he continued to cherish for the Church of his baptism until she rejected him with anathemas.

The Catholic Church hardly has herself to blame for having furnished the future heresiarch with the weapons that he was gradually to turn against her system of dogma. The young Loisy received the usual education, wholly in Church schools, of a French boy destined for the priesthood. From the hands of the village curé he passed to the ecclesiastical *collège* (i.e., high school) at St. Dizier, where he formed a resolve to serve the Church in her sacred ministry. Before he had quite reached eighteen, he entered the diocesan seminary at Châlons-sur-Marne.

His theological course was of a perfectly orthodox mediocrity. His description of his, generally incompetent, teachers, while not unkind, is to the full as diverting as the account of the not much more illustrious masters of the seminary at Issy-sur-Seine, in whose high-walled garden, now invaded by the roar of suburban Paris, the youthful Renan drew in such stimulating draughts of the quiet and still air of delightful studies. The two bright spots in the four years' course were, first, a year in philosophy under the Abbé Ludot, a lifelong friend, who, because of modernizing tendencies, was transferred at the end of Loisy's first year to the obscurity of a village curacy, where he remained until his death in 1905; and secondly, the acquisition of Hebrew, with help from a fellow-student at the outset, and the reading of the Hebrew Bible, in conjunction with the Septuagint, in the spare time of his last three years. In this concrete study of texts, the future critic found his *métier,* and the amassing of positive linguistic and exegetical knowledge brought a solace of mind which his prescribed courses had denied him. The effect on his growing intelligence of the empty abstractions and futile dialectics of the Thomist system of education, still fastened on Catholic seminaries today by the decree of Leo XIII in 1879, was desolating. Of the time given to the study of Christian doctrine, after the Scholastic method, he speaks as "four years of intellectual and moral torture." Even the private research that he found time to bestow on the writings of the great Aquinas not only brought no relief, but rather deepened his

doubts. Thus at twenty-one, having disregarded
the sound advice of his high-school principal, to take
his baccalaureate in arts before embarking on the
ecclesiastical career, he left Châlons, having for mental furnishing only the narrowly traditional teaching
of this provincial seminary, corroded by a secret
scepticism that he was wholly unable to suppress,
and relieved by his independent acquisition of a
knowledge of the Bible in its original tongues.

He was, naturally enough, marked by the head of
the seminary, M. Roussel, for a professorship, and,
with this in view, was presented to the Bishop of
Châlons, M. Meignan—whom we are to meet again
in an interesting connection—for appointment to the
just-established (1878) Catholic Institute of Paris,
to take an advanced course in theology. This is the
sort of good turn that the Catholic Church is capable
of doing for her more brilliant sons. In Loisy's case
the outcome was unlooked-for. He had undergone
a severe inner struggle as to the soundness of his
Catholic faith prior to ordination to the sub-diaconate, when the obligation of celibacy had to be
assumed, and after a few months of hard study in
Paris his always uncertain health gave way. Repair-
ing, after a short rest, to his old haunts at Châlons,
he was there ordained deacon, and, on June 29th,
1879, priest. Two years in the country, in charge of
small parishes, did much to restore his strength, and
in May, 1881, at his urgent request, seconded by
that of his professors in Paris, he was reassigned to
the Catholic Institute. So began a more significant
stage in what he himself calls "my laborious Odys-

sey"—the stage of a dozen strenuous years, that was to end in a serious check to his career, and in his first tragic disappointment with human nature.

The leading spirit in the Catholic Institute was the Abbé Louis Duchesne, well-known as a historian of the early Church and in later years a member of the French Academy. To him Loisy attached himself, and he held a guiding hand over his remarkable pupil until 1889, when a serious breach occurred between them. While engaged in his brief parochial duties, Loisy had kept on with his studies to such effect that within two months after the return to Paris he was granted the baccalaureate in theology. The next fall, owing to illness of the professor of Scriptural interpretation—the diocese of Paris not being prolific in Hebrew scholars—he was made, at the age of twenty-four, instructor in Hebrew at the Catholic Institute. To extend his knowledge, he took courses in Hebrew under Renan at the *Collège de France* and in Assyriology under Arthur Amiaud —he was his only pupil—at the *École Pratique des Hautes Études*. Then, as was inevitable, perspectives of which he had hitherto not dreamed began to open. Renan's informal but searching discussion of the Old Testament text made havoc of whatever was left of his early faith in Biblical infallibility and literal inspiration. The young abbé, who sat taking notes in his corner—and had progressed to the point of laughing with the rest when a tall ecclesiastic suddenly left, slamming the door behind him, on hearing Renan say that Jeremiah might have had something to do with the composition of Deuteron-omy—at first secretly hoped to use the master's arguments some day to refute him. But the cloak of Elijah fell, as of old, on the shoulders of Elisha. A copy of Tischendorf's New Testament, lent him by Duchesne for a summer vacation's reading, was a revelation not only of the endless variations in the manuscripts but also of the serious inconsistencies in the narratives themselves. He saw these with a characteristically French trenchancy and incapacity for self-deception; and thenceforth belief in the Virgin Birth and in the Resurrection rested in his mind on the sandiest of foundations. Even the unsuspecting Abbé Vigouroux, professor of Scriptural interpretation at St. Sulpice—where nothing had been forgotten and nothing learned since Renan passed through its portals thirty-six years before— contributed his full share to the disillusionment. The cautiously apologetic tone of his lectures utterly failed to meet at least one student's keen curiosity and clear perception of the state of the evidence; while an ill-advised course in Biblical rationalism, in which he reviewed the history of critical exegesis, only made matters worse, the professor's attempted refutations of critical results merely bringing out in more glaring fashion the disaccord between the Biblical data and the propositions that Catholic theology professes to derive for them. "I must say," testifies Loisy, "that his instruction and his books did more to turn me away from orthodox opinions in this matter than all the rationalists put together, Renan included." So much for half-measures, and for conventional apologetics, when an eager and penetrating mind is in question!

The inner state of the young instructor was by this time even more perplexed than when he had tried at Châlons to squeeze spiritual nutriment out of the barren logomachy of Thomas Aquinas. With the prevalent Catholic teaching he was deeply disenchanted. Formerly, his religious feeling had been intense and at times ecstatic. Now it had almost entirely lapsed. He saw clearly the flat impossibility of reconciling the position toward which he was tending with the accepted Catholic doctrine. "I had not brought to the seminary (Châlons) the shadow of an idea contrary to the teaching of the Church." But, he now writes in his dairy, "The Church is at the present hour an obstacle to the intellectual development of humanity." A Latin thesis prepared in 1883-84 for the doctorate in theology opened the eyes of the rector of the Catholic Institute, Monsignor d'Hulst, to the total abandonment of the traditional dogmatics on the part of his most promising scholar. Such radical views on inspiration, in the Bible and in the Apostolic Fathers to Tertullian, Loisy was told, it would never do to print; they would only be grazing-ground for the Congregation of the Index. The ideas are obvious enough, but they were not then and are not now Catholic doctrine:

"That the inspiration of the Scriptures, having to do with existing writings, subject to analysis, was a belief to be controlled by the study of the books in question; that the psychology of the inspired authors was visibly the same as that of all men who write; that whatever inspiration might add of the divine, changed not at all the nature of the writings to which it pertained, and did not transform a pseudonymous book, like *The Wisdom of Solomon,* into an authentic work of Solomon; that, if the revelation was contained in the Bible, and without error, as declared by the Vatican Council, it was under a relative form, proportioned to the time and to the environment in which the books had appeared, as well as to the general outlook of that time and environment; that the insufficiency of the Scriptures as a rule of faith resulted from their very nature, and that the magistracy of the Church had for its object the adaptation of ancient doctrine to ever-new needs, in disengaging the essential truth from its superannuated expression; that authors like Irenaeus and Tertullian had anticipated this when they had opposed to the extravagant exegesis of the Gnostics not the letter of the Bible, interpreted by common sense, but the ecclesiastical rule of faith, imposed on the Bible as the rule for its interpretation."

Implied in these conclusions—so arresting, when we consider the environment in which they were matured—is the frankly revolutionary idea of the complete relativity of all doctrinal construction, whether derived from the Bible or formulated by the Church, an idea so incompatible with any vestige of finality or authority in doctrine that comparatively few minds are yet prepared to admit it in its fullness. Loisy says that he nowhere met this idea in his reading. It was not likely that he would meet it there, though hints dropped by Renan may well have helped to form it. Rather, it came to him one night by a kind of sudden illumination. The completely rounded thought was the result of vital fermentation which had long been going on in his mind.

The inner conflict of his Catholic career—which

was to last for twenty-four years longer—consisted, on the one hand, in his heroic effort to win a standing-ground in Roman Catholic teaching for this principle of the complete relativity of ecclesiastical doctrine to the time and conditions of its origin, with the necessary corollaries of a development of doctrine through all the past, and its further progress through all the future; and, on the other hand, in the repeated and at length definitive refusal by the Pope and his advisers to abandon one jot or tittle of the rigid absolutism of the mediæval structure of dogma. To this the Roman Catholic Church, since the opening of the new century, seems to have irretrievably committed itself, largely by way of explicit repudiation of Loisy's conclusions as a critic and a historian of Christianity. The encyclical *Pascendi* of Pius X, and the anti-Modernist oath by which it was followed to ensure its more complete effectiveness, have fastened this Scholastic system on the Catholic Church with paralyzing results, so far as concerns the normal progress of thought. This is the key to the apparently easy repulse of the Modernist movement. The victory was of that Pyrrhic kind which the Church won, with equal ease and self-delusiveness, over Galileo. The parallel occurs more than once to Loisy himself. The phenomena of doctrinal growth and change, throughout the Bible and the history of the Church, are undeniable. The historical method has become as axiomatic to minds trained in the modern point of view as the scientific reasoning based on the Copernican astronomy. It is interesting to speculate on how long the Roman organization can hold back the inevitable admission that the Thomist philosophy, in all its principal assumptions and deductions, is as dead and useless as the Ptolemaic theory of the heavens, with its cycles and epicycles. While this conflict emerges in sharpest outline from conditions that have developed within the Roman Catholic Church since the assertion of Infallibility in 1870, it is also present in slightly different form in the more backward sections of Protestantism, where it will long trouble the spirits of both progressives and conservatives. The profit to be drawn from a study of the Catholic career of Alfred Loisy is so great because there the issue is joined with a clarity and a completeness not elsewhere surpassed if anywhere equaled.

II

In the crisis of doubt which followed the rejection of his thesis on inspiration and which remained more or less acute for several years, Loisy kept unremittingly at work, carrying his studies far beyond the demands of his instructorship. He made it a duty, he tells us, to read through the whole Bible in the original tongues in the course of every year. Thus his ultimate mastery over it was arduously won. Beginning in 1886, he conducted a seminar in Assyriology at the Catholic Institute. His second-year instruction in Hebrew developed into a course in exegesis, to prepare for which he studied the works of Reuss and the best German commentators. Resolved as he was to avoid any closed system, and determined to know all the facts, it was not long

before he had to face squarely the question whether
he could continue teaching as a priest of the Roman
Church, whose fundamental claim—that of the
supernatural character of revelation—he now realized was untenable. His reasons for not seceding
forthwith are significant. The most conclusive was
that in the depth of his soul, notwithstanding all he
had suffered, he remained profoundly attached to the
spirit of Catholicism. Then, as he tried to persuade
himself, his doubts were speculative rather than
material. Even where they touched essential beliefs,
could not these be retained in some symbolic sense,
as having a value not readily to be acquired by new
constructions? If the hope for an intellectual rebirth among the French clergy—which had been the
official reason for the founding of the Catholic
Institute—was no longer his, might he not live
peaceably in the service of the Church, a modest
scholar, confining himself to the minutiæ of philology, and avoiding the perilous paths of theology
and apologetics? This seems to have been for a
time his heart's desire; but circumstances and his
own irrepressible candor made such a program in the
end impossible.

His sympathy for his students, whom he would
gladly have spared such sufferings as he himself had
undergone, furnished the motive for doing what he
could to bridge the yawning chasm between Catholic
tradition and the modern mind. The attempt he
was making, and was to persist in until the Roman
authorities took stringent measures to disown him,
was in line with a notion of Duchesne's, that the

fields of history and of theology could be permanently held apart, without disturbing each other. To this essentially futile endeavor Loisy was to consecrate his remaining years in the Catholic fold. It could not succeed, because, in his professions of loyalty to the Catholic principle, he steadily meant one thing while the official Church meant another. The situation, as we have already seen and as he now admits, rested on a fatal equivocation.

In 1890 he was made assistant to Abbé Vigouroux in Biblical introduction, the larger part of the work falling to his share, while the title, for reasons of policy, went to the older and "safer" man. In the same year he received his doctorate, not without making a solemn public profession of faith, part of which—a promise to teach the Bible only according to the unanimous consensus of the Fathers—nearly stuck in his throat. Soon after, his first book appeared, drawn from the material of his lectures, a *History of the Old Testament Canon* (1890), followed the next year by a *History of the New Testament Canon* (1891). In these works, the dogmatic method was quietly ignored and the historical and critical definitely adopted. His general plan of campaign as an innovator was to attack the less exposed parts of his subject first, in the expectation that a gradual liberalizing of opinion would make it safe to pass on to more debatable topics. In the genial closing years of the pontificate of Leo XIII, such a hope seemed for a time not wholly vain, and was shared by many besides himself. But it was destined to a rude disenchantment.

From 1892, Loisy began the regular publication of his lectures in a little periodical, which had some two hundred subscribers, called *Enseignement Biblique.* This soon brought him into difficulty, and eventually led to his summary expulsion from the Catholic Institute. His works on the Canon, already referred to, had awakened the first of a long series of newspaper polemics; and an article on Proverbs, denying the Solomonic authorship and assigning a post-exilic date to the collection, gave occasion for a denunciation at Rome—by his titular head, Abbé Vigouroux, we are led to infer. There was, on the part of the older man, a touch of professional jealousy as well as of doctrinal suspicion, which a little spice of malice in Loisy's narrative allows to show through. A general taint of heresy began to attach to the young professor's fast-growing reputation. Two articles on the Babylonian myths of the creation and deluge, as related to the Genesis stories, led to his courses being forbidden to the students of St. Sulpice by the superior, Abbé Icard, a strict traditionalist. The same measure of protection from the infiltration of novelties had been taken some years before against certain temerities of Duchesne in the history of the early Church. The latter's prestige, however, as a member of the *Institut de France,* and his strong backing from the laity, as well as a probable dread of his biting invective, had saved his standing in the Catholic Institute. Neither by nature nor by circumstances was Loisy so well protected. Reserved in manner, delicate in health, and so absorbed in his work as to be practically a recluse, he had in his favor, when assailed, only the solid scientific merit of his results—not the most potent recommendation in circles where mundane opinion and ecclesiastical policy had a determining voice over mere considerations of historical and critical accuracy.

'Some day it will be matter for astonishment—at least so I should hope," he writes, "that a Catholic university professor was adjudged a dangerous character, for having said, in the year of grace 1892, that the narratives of the first chapters of Genesis are not to be taken as literal history, and that the pretended agreement of the Bible with natural science is a rather shabby subterfuge."

Loisy was not chiefly to blame for his break with his superiors coming when it did. There had been a lack of accord between the two allied institutions— the Catholic Institute, committed to a mild and circumspect, but in so far genuine, Liberalism, and St. Sulpice, the bulwark of Ultramontanism, upheld by the aged and reactionary Cardinal Richard, archbishop of Paris. On the death of Renan in 1892, Monsignor d'Hulst published in the *Correspondant* an article in which he made the invidious suggestion that if St. Sulpice years before had given Renan the kind of enlightenment now to be obtained, for example, at the Catholic Institute, his great powers need never have been lost to the Church. The well-meaning but imperfectly trained rector of the Catholic Institute appears to have felt vaguely that the time had come for doing something toward bringing the mind of Catholicism more into touch with the living thought of the age. He began, that is, to be haunted by the same dream that had long been in

the mind of his young professor of Biblical introduction. It was not to him, however, that the latter
turned for help in the *impasse* toward which he felt
himself drifting, but to his former patron at Châlons,
Monsignor Meignan, then archbishop of Tours and
on the point of being made a cardinal. To him
Loisy wrote, appealing for a public token of approval and support. The wise old man—a fine type
of the higher French clergy, with no less goodness of
heart than keenness of mind—knew better than to
commit himself on paper in so delicate a matter;
but he invited his former *protégé*, whom he seems to
have sincerely liked, to an interview, which was held
on a late October morning in 1892, at an old Paris
inn in the Latin Quarter. A remarkable conversation it was. The archbishop, who smoked cigarettes
as he talked, was almost, if not quite, as conversant
with the state of critical learning as his companion.
On that score, they frankly stood together. But
when it came to publishing critical results, the
would-be cardinal bluntly declared that the intoler-
ance of the Jesuits set rigid limits to what Catholic
scholars could safely avow, and their power and
vindictiveness were to be feared. He instanced the
example of the Oratorian, Richard Simon, crushed
by Bossuet, saying, "Our theologians are ferocious;
they put us on the Index for nothing." A free criticism, he held, never had existed and never could
exist in the Roman Catholic Church, and he warned
Loisy that even those who thought in their hearts
as he did would not uphold him in a crisis. All
this was shown in the sequel to be true. They must

be advocates, sincere advocates, he urged repeatedly, of tradition. Nothing else would serve.

From the point of view of worldly policy, this was sound advice; and if Loisy had been the time-server that most of his liberal friends and colleagues showed themselves to be—anxious above all for preferment and the rewards of an ecclesiastical career—he would have gone back to his textual criticism and Assyriology, leaving others to burn their fingers on more dangerous topics. Writing, years afterwards, to one of his associates who had gained some of the kingdoms of this world—becoming at last, by an un-faltering compliance with the Papal tactics of repres-sion, Rector of the Catholic Institute in Paris,—he sketched the lines on which his own life might have moved serenely to the end:

"If I had been willing to imprison myself in Oriental-ism, I should still be teaching Hebrew and Assyriology under you; as Rector of the Catholic Institute, you would sing my praises in your annual reports to the assembly of bishops; I should be cited as an example of the harmony between science and faith, precisely because I had occupied myself only with science and had never spoken of faith. I should probably be an honorary canon of Notre Dame. And that is how I missed being happy in this world!"

That was not to be the kind of obscure, untroubled happiness appointed for Alfred Loisy. It was, how-ever, no false step on his own part, but over-eager-ness of the superficial and at bottom timorous Mon-signor d'Hulst to be a leader of Catholic thought that brought on the catastrophe. Flattered by the acclaim that had greeted his article on Renan, and sincerely concerned to protect his professor of Biblical introduction, the Rector launched a second article in the *Correspondant,* this time on a more perilous theme—the Biblical question.   It was the product of a tactician, not of a scholar.   Under the caption of the *école large,* which he was pleased to contrast with the traditional and the mediating schools—the last being the position he assumed for himself—the Rector outlined what was taken at Rome and elsewhere to be an authoritative statement of Loisy's principles. The *école large,* as a matter of fact, never existed, except as a diplomatic fiction.   The writer had no grasp of exact scientific method and was incapable of comprehending Loisy's guiding conception of the complete historical relativity of doctrine.   The plump admission, in behalf of the mythical *école large,* of errors in the Bible, shocked the Ultramontane theologians, while the counter-claim that, notwithstanding acknowledged mistakes in science and history, the *école large* held the Bible to be inerrant in faith and morals, offered no adequate compensation.   The sensation was great.   After a show of resistance, Monsignor d'Hulst, thoroughly alarmed for his own future and that of the Institute, bent before the storm.   A visit to Rome convinced him that no headway was to be made on the line he had chosen, and he was persuaded that his young professor—whom he had meanwhile done nothing to disentangle from the compromising connection in which he had placed him—would better be relieved of his chair of Biblical introduction.   This was accordingly done, and Loisy submitted to go back to his Hebrew and Assyriology, on the condition that his scientific results in exegesis should continue to be published. The compromise was not destined to last long.

In the closing lecture of his course, in June, Loisy felt himself entitled, in self-justification, to define his actual position on the Biblical question and on inspiration. His lecture, when published in his review the following November (1893), a fortnight before the annual meeting of the episcopal protectors of the Catholic Institute, created a scandal. The permanent acquisitions of an unfettered criticism were summed up in five propositions. The first denied the Mosaic authorship of the Pentateuch. The nied the Mosaic authorship of the Pentateuch. The opening chapters of Genesis. The third declared that the Biblical books should be subject to the same processes of interpretation as other writings. The fourth established a real progress of doctrine, in all its branches, within the Bible itself. The fifth asserted that, as regards natural science, the Scriptures do not rise above the opinions of the time in which the various books were composed. These elementary statements of critical certainties seemed to the traditionally minded Cardinal Richard to be damnable heresies of the most pernicious kind. He had never encountered the like. He lost no time in bringing the case before the assembly of bishops, and they voted, with only four protesting voices, to dismiss Loisy from the post where he had labored so abundantly, though not without serious searchings of conscience, for twelve fruitful, if troubled, years. It was a heavy blow. He naturally felt himself to be on the point of exclusion from the Church, and long afterwards he seems to have wished that the authorities might have signified to him then that his tendencies were those of a lay scholar, and given him back the freedom he had pledged to the Church that could only spurn his talents.

III

Man proposes, but God more wisely disposes. The next stage in the career of this much-buffeted Ulysses was an unlooked-for haven of rest, where for five pregnant years he found external peace, a not uncongenial task, and abundant incitement to continue the researches into Biblical and Christian origins, for which the work already done had laid so solid and durable a foundation. Cardinal Richard, who was not unkindly disposed toward him personally—although their total dissimilarity of outlook made their few interviews very distressing to Loisy—appointed him, in September, 1894, chaplain to a convent of Dominican nuns at Neuilly. His task there was to give daily instruction in the catechism to young girls of secondary grade. Nothing could have seemed more innocuous, and so the Cardinal doubtless felicitated himself. But nothing could have been more nicely calculated to set the future "Modernist" forward on his way. He had an ample margin of free time for his chosen studies, which he employed to the fullest advantage. His whole mind was now concentrated on the problem of adapting the teachings of Catholicism to contemporary thought.

In 1893, he had made the acquaintance of Baron

Friedrich von Hügel, and at his suggestion had taken up the study of Newman, especially the *Essay on the Development of Christian Doctrine.* Those were significant years in the world of Protestant theology. Not long before, Harnack had published his great *History of Dogma.* In 1894, appeared Wellhausen's *History of Israel and Judah,* while the year 1897 was marked by the publication of Auguste Sabatier's *Outlines of a Philosophy of Religion,* Heinrich Holtzmann's *New Testament Theology,* and Albert Réville's *Jesus of Nazareth.* These great works Loisy also studied and meditated, while as a reviewer for the *Revue Critique* he was in the habit of receiving current publications in the history and philosophy of religion, the history of dogma, and church history. His activity as a reviewer has always been phenomenal. In 1896 he established, with the aid of friends, the *Revue d'Histoire et de Littérature Religieuses,* which continued, with a short break, until August, 1914. While at Neuilly, he was laying the foundation for the elaborate commentaries on the Fourth Gospel and the Synoptics, which appeared in 1903 and 1908 respectively. But his most absorbing task in this safe retreat was the writing of a long historical and philosophical apology for Catholicism, in contrast with the Protestant masterpieces just named, and largely in obedience to the impulse to demonstrate to himself that he could still remain a Catholic. Personally unable to accept literally any single article of the creed—unless it were that Jesus was crucified under Pontius Pilate—he was yet sincerely devoted to the Catholic Church, which he believed might have a future as glorious as her past, if she could only learn to use the language of living men. A deep distress was afflicting the inner life of the Church and it was not only in relation to Biblical questions that there was need of rejuvenation. Preparing his daily lessons in the catechism for his young hearers with these preoccupations in mind, Loisy devoted himself to the composition of a book in which he unfolded his conception of a reformed Catholicism. From this large work, in twelve chapters, of which he gives a most suggestive outline in *Choses Passées*, were drawn parts of the famous "little orange-colored books," to the first of which we shall soon come in describing his decisive conflict with the Papacy.

A severe illness, which carried him within a handbreadth of death itself, led in the fall of 1899 to his resignation of the appointment at Neuilly. As his strength came back, he continued the publication—part of the time over pseudonyms, to throw inquisitors off the track—of articles dealing with such themes as the origin of the New Testament, Catholic opinions on the Pentateuch and the Papal brief of September, 1899, on the studies of the French clergy. An exceptionally frank discussion of Biblical questions at the congress of Catholic scholars in Freiburg, in 1897, in which Loisy's friend Baron von Hügel took a leading part, had quickened his hopes, notwithstanding the discouragement that had resulted from the encyclical *Providentissimus Deus* in 1893. His endeavor was to claim a place for free and fearless criticism within the Catholic system, largely as a means of meeting Protestant contentions, which he felt—as he sought to demonstrate in *L'Évangile et l'Église*—to be fallacious. If his dismissal from the Catholic Institute might be considered merely a stroke of policy, the authorities showed themselves to be on the alert by an official censure which he now received. The first of a series of articles in the *Revue du Clergé Français,* on the religion of Israel, was disapproved and the continuation of the series forbidden, by Cardinal Richard, proving how little the hierarchy was yet prepared for any advance in this direction. Loisy now felt, even more than when he had been expelled from the Catholic Institute, that he was being singled out as a heretic and as a spreader of heresy. In order not to sacrifice his independence, he declined to be longer the recipient of a small pension, which had been granted him during his illness, from a fund for infirm priests.

At this juncture, as later at a more important moment, help came to him unexpectedly from the lay element in French society. Through Monsieur Paul Desjardins, with friendly aid from Professor Albert Réville, he was appointed lecturer in the section of the science of religion at the *École pratique des Hautes Études,* and assistant in the preparation of the *Corpus inscriptionum semiticarum,* and in December, 1900, he began a series of public lectures on the Babylonian myths and the first chapters of Genesis. On the death of Auguste Sabatier in the spring of 1901, Loisy hoped to succeed him in the chair of early Christian literature, but the fact that he still wore the habit of a priest stood in the way. In the year 1901-02 his lectures were on the criticism of the Gospels, in 1902-03 on the Galilean, and in 1903-04 on the Jerusalem ministry, thus continuing the work that was to issue in *Les Évangiles Synoptiques.* Loisy believes that Cardinal Richard was from this time determined to suppress all overt utterance and publication on his part, but did not clearly see his way to do it. There was much consultation of the authorities behind the scenes, though no action, and Loisy tried through Cardinal Mathieu to make his position understood in high Roman circles. He felt, beneath the *régime* of rigid repression, a growing intellectual anarchy among the Catholic clergy. Many besides himself were infected with the new ideas, some of them his own pupils, and his responsibility for these kindred spirits worked strongly to keep him within the Catholic fold, long after his own conviction and convenience would have impelled him to withdraw.

Two otherwise unconnected events came together to mark the end of the year 1902—Loisy's presentation as a candidate for the bishopric of Monaco by Prince Albert, who was out of favor with Rome, and whose three candidates were summarily rejected; and the publication of his most noted volume, *L'Évangile et l'Église,* the first of the "little orange-colored books," together with a foretaste of his synoptic commentary in *Études Évangeliques.* The latter work was perhaps too technical in character to attract wide attention, but the former marked a date, not only in its author's personal career but in the progress of Catholic Modernism.

In form, a reply to Harnack's *Wesen des Christentums* (1900), of which a French translation appeared early in 1902, and received warm approval in Catholic as well as in Protestant circles, in fact *L'Évangile et l'Église* was a discreet yet frank plea for the more progressive Catholicism of which its author felt called to stand forth as sponsor. The book has thus two aspects, of nearly equal significance. The more obvious is the orderly and explicit refutation of Professor Harnack. His "essence" appeared to Loisy to be that of Liberal Protestantism, rather than of Christianity as the scientific historian must conceive it; a dogmatic construction, therefore, resting on an inadequate understanding and an imperfect analysis of the Christian origins. As a living faith, carried on by actual men in the bosom of existing society, Christianity must needs have a body as well as a soul. It cannot be summed up in a formula so simple as inward trust in the loving Father revealed by Jesus. Its essence, so far as the term can be made to apply, must be found in its total life, advancing with constant change and ever-new formulation down the centuries, while still loyal to the initial impulse given it by the Founder. "Why must we consider the essence of the tree as contained in a particle of the germ from which it sprang, and why may it not be as truly and more completely realized in the tree than in the seed?" he pertinently asks. "Professor Harnack," he adds, "does not conceive of Christianity as a germ that has developed, at first potentially and only later really a plant, identical with itself from the beginning of its evolution to the stage it has now reached, and from root to topmost branch; but as a ripe, or rather damaged, fruit, which must be peeled to reach the untainted kernel. And Professor Harnack peels so industriously that it is a question whether in the end he has anything left." Attractive as Harnack's thesis is, and useful as has been on the whole its influence as an antidote to the older Protestant dogmatics, still an open-minded reader can scarcely set his book and Loisy's side by side without feeling that the latter proves himself to be the more penetrating critic of the Gospels and the sounder historian of early Christianity. He is successful in showing that the Roman Catholic Church as a doctrine, as a life, as an organization, and as a worship—widely as it has departed in externals and at times in spirit from the gospel of Jesus—has yet held true to the "notes," as Newman would say, of primitive Christianity. It is an impressive demonstration, to which Protestant students would do well to pay more heed. This criticism of Liberal Protestantism—represented not only by Harnack, but also by Auguste Sabatier, as too subjective, abstract, and out of touch with historical religion, which has always been a communal rather than an individual affair—seemed to Loisy later to be the most valuable part of his work.

IV

When we consider *L'Évangile et l'Église* in its second aspect, as a plea for a new and progressive Catholicism, able and willing to admit to the full the results of a criticism of the Old and New Testaments as radical as Loisy's, and prepared, moreover, to concede the complete relativity of its own doctrines to the times and circumstances of their origin, we are confronted by an irrepressible conflict which could hardly issue otherwise than in the excommunication of the intrepid scholar. "Admitting," as he says, "that the tradition is sacred and immutable, any word derogatory to the tradition is reprehensible." In Tyrrell's terms, it was Mediævalism pitted against Modernism. Whatever Loisy might say in defense of Roman Catholicism as the legitimate product of a long historical evolution, by the end of the Nineteenth Century it had become in government and in doctrine a rigid absolutism. The last faint stirrings of national independence, in Gallicanism, had been effectually suppressed, and Ultramontanism was everywhere triumphant. After the promulgation of Papal infallibility in 1870, Döllinger and the Old Catholics were scarcely able to make a ripple in the general current of Catholic life, which flowed on as if unconscious of any inner conflict. The vigorous effort of Lord Acton in England to impart an intellectual stimulus to Catholicism, met with a discouraging response. "It is incontestable," writes an authority, referring to the situation in France, "that Catholics, on the average, have not in the least assimilated the intellectual movement of the last four centuries, although a small *élite* of Catholics is at the forefront of the movement."

After the encyclical *Providentissimus Deus* (1893), on the study of Holy Scripture—which, Loisy tells us, did not expressly condemn the idea of a truly critical and historical exegesis because its existence was then not even suspected at Rome—he had taken the advice of a friend in the priesthood and written the Pope a letter of filial submission. Like his attitude in general during those earlier years, his letter was scarcely ingenuous in its attitude toward the Roman authority. This was perhaps inevitable, yet it brings out vividly the ineradicable weakness of the Modernist position. One cannot have his cake and eat it too. Loisy frankly stated his critical principles, but at the same time avowed his wish to remain an obedient son of the Church. So long as he held to this equivocation, he was neither happy nor free, nor had he even the power to aid those who thought and suffered with him. Largely for their sakes he clung to it until it was made no longer a tenable position within the pale of the Church.

"Called, four years ago, to occupy the chair of Biblical exegesis in the faculty of theology at Paris," thus he wrote to Leo XIII in 1893, "I have wished to pursue in my lectures the accord between faith and science in the field of Scripture. . . . In questions of history, I have sought to resolve, by an attentive scrutiny of the means employed by the sacred writers and of the end which they had in view, the contradictions which seem to exist among them. It appeared to me necessary, in response to the needs of the present time, to make a prudent application of the critical method, so far as might be legitimate, to the study of Holy Scripture, and thus to meet the adversaries of the Bible with their own weapons."

After alluding to his dismissal from the Catholic Institute—which the Pope and his advisers had thought a trifle abrupt—he concludes:

"It is a severe trial for a priest whose life has long been devoted to Biblical studies to find himself thus held up to general reprobation as a disseminator of dangerous opinions, in advance of any judgment by the Apostolic See. But I now find much consolation in attesting to the Vicar of Jesus Christ, in all simplicity of soul, my most entire submission to the doctrine promulgated in the Encyclical on the Study of Holy Scripture. The objections which the enemies of the Church already raise against this admirable document have suggested the idea of a memorial, addressed in lowly homage to Your Holiness, as a witness to my perfect submission to the instructions of the Holy See, to the good-will with which I have hitherto served the Church, and to my hope of further service in conformity to all the directions of the magnanimous Pontiff, Leo XIII."

This overunctuous epistle is probably best explained by the hope of the writer, shared with reason by many others, that Leo XIII was really on the side of progress. Appended to it was a longer statement in which "with an audacity equalled only by my candor," as Loisy now declares, he more fully explained his critical procedure. The Pope read both documents and returned word by Cardinal Rampolla that, while appreciative of the expressions of fidelity to the Holy See, he advised the writer, "owing to circumstances and in his own interest," to apply his talents to another kind of studies. Loisy thus received the plainest of hints from the highest authority in the Church. It was his own responsibility if he did not choose to take it, but persisted in his reforming efforts until another pontiff, of a different calibre and more direct methods, came upon the scene.

Mention was made earlier of the suppression by Cardinal Richard of the first of a series of articles on the Religion of Israel. In the spring of 1901, Loisy was denounced before the Holy Inquisition, but he was still writing as a scholar for scholars and nothing came of it. *L'Évangile et l'Église*, which was his first appeal to a wider public, gave the signal for a storm of criticism and abuse in the Catholic press. Loisy intimates that personal enemies, who are perhaps to be sought among his former associates at the Catholic Institute, egged on his persecutors. He was made to appear as a deliberate troubler of the faith of simple Catholics. He hints at a persistent campaign of calumny, motivated by the bitter hatred of some one in a place of influence. Cardinal Richard at once took official action. On January 17, 1903, he issued an ordinance forbidding the reading of the book by the priests or faithful of his diocese, for the reason that it appeared without the usual *imprimatur*, and was "of a nature gravely to disturb the faith of believers in the fundamental dogmas of the Catholic teaching." Like action was taken by the titular heads of a number of other French dioceses. Loisy deemed it prudent not to resist this prohibition, and held up the second edition of his book, already in the press.

"My intention," he writes, "was to go no farther in the way of concessions. Just as I had kept silent before the condemnation in 1900 of the articles of 'Firmin' (one of his pseudonyms) I meant to say nothing before the censure placed upon *L'Évangile et l'Église.* This was the best posture I could assume, and the most sincere, because within myself I had no real respect for the archiepiscopal sentence, and I could not make a 'submission' except by adding reserves that would render it unmeaning or equivocal."

Nevertheless, on hearing from his friend, Archbishop Mignot of Albi, that Leo XIII expected his formal adherence to Cardinal Richard's decree, he wrote the Cardinal a letter in which occurs the following sentence:

"It goes without saying that I condemn and reprove all the errors that have been deduced from my book by those who place themselves, in interpreting it, at a point of view wholly different from that which I necessarily occupied in composing it."

The equivocation here leaps to the light, and naturally his subtle meaning was totally misconstrued. Loisy regrets having taken this step. In the hope of clearing himself, he wrote again, this time telling the Cardinal:

"I reserve, certainly, my personal opinion on all that has occurred in connection with this work of history in which it pleases some to hunt for errors in theology."

This is the last trace we can find of the dubious influence over him of Duchesne's sophistical dualism. At last comes the sincere note of personal revolt. It was time. The situation was inherently false, and needed clearing up. Between papal Rome and the unfettered reason no truce can be made, at least until Rome lays aside its pretense to sovereign infallibility and adopts a radically different conception of the

seat of authority in religion.   Of Loisy's initial good
faith and entire loyalty in striving for a gradual low-
ering of the papal claims, there can be no question.
But he was now at the parting of the ways.   Either
Rome must bend, or he must end his career as a
priest of the Catholic Church.

Rome was not preparing to bend.   As long as the
politic and crafty Leo XIII had been at the helm,
Cardinal Richard and others might rush to the Vatican and clamor eagerly for lightening the barque of
Peter by throwing overboard the Jonah who was
troubling its peace; still nothing was done.   But in
July, 1903, Leo XIII passed to his reward, and a
month later Pius X reigned in his stead.   The change
was almost instantly felt.   Now Cardinal Richard
had his chance, and he hastened to use it.   One of
the last acts of the old Pope had been to refuse to
sanction the placing of *Études Évangeliques* on the
Index.   The new Pope was told that the younger
clergy were losing respect for tradition, and disdaining the Scholastic system and the two great councils
it had inspired, that of Trent and that of the Vatican,
and that Loisy was largely to blame for this.   Meanwhile, Loisy's own spirit was growing firmer and
more resolute.   His extended commentary on the
Fourth Gospel was finished, and its printing had
begun.

"In it," he says, "I formulate conclusions unheard of
among Catholic exegetes—the unauthenticity of the
book, which cannot be attributed to the apostle John;
the symbolical and factitious character of the narratives,
in accord with the theology of the discourses, which do
not reflect the teaching of Jesus; and that the Fourth

Gospel is a product of Christian faith, not a history of Christ himself."

At the same time, he decided to issue an explanation and defense of *L'Évangile et l'Église*, with replies to some of his critics. This was the second of the "little orange-colored books"—*Autour d'un Petit Livre* (1903). Following an extended introduction, the volume consists of seven letters, in part to friends by way of explanation, and in part to opponents by way of rebuttal. The subjects of the letters are— (1) the origin and object of the "little book" *(L'Évangile et l'Église)*, (2) the Biblical question, (3) the criticism of the Gospels, and especially of John, (4) the divinity of Christ, (5) the foundation and authority of the Church, (6) the origin and authority of dogmas, and (7) the institution of sacraments. The recipients of these epistles are described in the book as first issued by title only—as, "To a Cardinal," "To the Superior of a Seminary"—but in *Choses Passées* their names are given without reserve.

Autour d'un Petit Livre only deepened the offense given to the Ultramontane circle by *L'Évangile et l'Église*. The first of these little books had been a defense of progressive Catholicism against Protestant subjectivism and individualism; the second was an impassioned defense of the author and his critical freedom against Catholic Scholasticism and excess of Traditionalism. It is a magnificent outburst of consciously righteous wrath against entrenched Scholastic dullness and haughty obscurantism in the Church of his birthright. More incisive and brilliant, more solid and convincing polemical writing than these ringing chapters cannot be found, so far as I know, in the long record of theological "wars of the Lord." They vibrate with personal emotion, showing not only the scholar, but also the man. Nowhere has Loisy better displayed the resources of his immense learning, the strength and firmness of his historical method, the trenchancy of his critical intelligence, and withal the play of his biting wit and lambent humor. Nothing but the fact that mankind is solicitous for anything and everything except searching out the truth about its own gravest concerns, and that the debate was in a region remote from the external passions of the moment, kept this from being a shot heard around the world. But the fortunate few, who have had the intellectual, yes, the spiritual, joy of reading it, must feel that a new Erasmus is here, equal in culture and more than equal in courage to the gentle dreamer of Rotterdam. "After all, it does move!"—this is the challenge that he seems to hurl in the name of modern scholarship at the sealed doors of the Vatican. After all, modernism, progress, reliance on reason, is the spirit of the age in which we live. A Loisy may be excommunicated, as a Galileo was silenced; but that settles nothing. The world goes its way, and an institution —even if it be as ancient and august as the Roman Catholic Church—which refuses to move with it, is left behind. However, the old Church is wiser than any one pope or any single generation of her doctors, and the story of Catholic Modernism is not yet a closed book.

"*L'Évangile et l'Église* was written to show how the Catholic principle, in virtue of its inexhaustible fecundity, is able to adapt itself to every form of human progress. But the adaptation in the past has never been made without effort; it will be the same in the future."

That effort cannot be said to have more than begun; but unless Catholicism is to belie its past, its hour and Loisy's full justification will yet come.

V

What Loisy hoped and desired of the Roman Catholic Church was nothing excessive or unreasonable.

"There is a sort of latent incompatibility," he wrote in his sixth letter, "which speedily becomes conscious in a great many individuals, between the general knowledge of the world and man that is acquired today in the most ordinary education, and that which controls, or rather penetrates, the Catholic doctrine. Any substantial change in that doctrine could not be realized and is not required; what is demanded is above all a change in spirit and attitude toward the intellectual movement of our time."

As a historian, he realized that no sudden revolution in the formulas of the Church could take place. Inclined himself toward a theory of critical symbolism in religious belief, he seems to have been willing to leave the Church in possession of her traditional symbols, provided only a new and larger interpretation of the formulas might be permitted where they come into conflict with fact. But the official Church was not receptive to such counsel, and in giving it, Loisy was at last determined to suffer excommunica-

tion rather than sacrifice further his freedom of
conscience as critic and as historian.

Autour d'un Petit Livre and *Le Quatrième Évangile* had not been published a month when Cardinal
Richard was in Rome, bent on securing their author's
condemnation by the Holy Office. In December,
1903, five of his books—*La Religion d'Israel, Études
Évangeliques, L'Évangile et l'Église, Autour d'un
Petit Livre,* and *Le Quatrième Évangile*—were
placed on the Index of prohibited books. Loisy made
up his mind to receive this decree with respect, and
to tender his formal submission, as he had done after
the censure of *L'Évangile et l'Église.* The essential
statements in his reply to the notification by Monsignor Merry del Val, the Cardinal Secretary of
State, are these:

"I receive with respect the judgment of the Sacred
Congregations, and myself condemn in my own writings
whatever in them is reprehensible. . . . I must nevertheless add that my adherence to the sentence of the
Sacred Congregations is purely disciplinary in character;
I reserve the right of my conscience, and do not wish
to be understood, in bowing before the judgment rendered by the Sacred Congregation of the Holy Office, as
abandoning or retracting the opinions put forth in my
quality as historian or as critical interpreter."

There was no chance of this language meeting with
sympathy or understanding from the Roman curia.
In reply, Merry del Val sent to Cardinal Richard a
letter which Loisy describes as "extremely violent."
It was read to him but never put into his hands. It
demanded immediate retractation, without reserve,
of the five condemned volumes and their contents on

pain of a further proceeding of the Holy Office *ad ulteriora*. This, of course, was the expected threat of excommunication. A second letter to the Cardinal Secretary of State, couched in the same general terms as the first, only brought another insistent demand for an unqualified retractation. Loisy seems to have felt it his duty to stay in the Church as long as he could, or at least to do nothing himself to provoke the final rupture, although he felt keenly the absurdity of being required to retract the entire contents of his books, as though all in them alike were untrue. Excommunication now appeared to be imminent. Loisy even prepared the letter that would be expected of him on the publication of the decree. He recognized that his place could only be outside of the Catholic Church as it was then inspired and directed. Suddenly, however, affairs took a new turn, and his expulsion was indefinitely postponed.

What happened was a sudden breakdown, under the intense and prolonged strain, of his physical and nervous forces. He came to shrink from the notoriety connected with excommunication, to dread lest it should turn him aside from his precious work of writing and teaching. Already a curious and unwelcome throng was crowding the lecture room at the *École pratique des Hautes Études,* where his exposition of the Synoptic Gospels was steadily progressing week by week. Also, he dreaded the possible effect of his exclusion on the many who had followed, encouraged, sustained, or protected him in the Church. Above all, his soul was sadly weary of strife. It was, he suggests, a crisis of neurasthenia. He took an impulsive resolve; to let the excommunication come, and then after sentence was passed to write to the Pope, protesting the uprightness of his intentions, declaring that he could not honestly have refrained from making the reservations he did in his two letters to the Cardinal Secretary of State, and witnessing to his good-will for the pacification of spirits by abandoning the instruction he was giving in Paris. After that, His Holiness could judge whether or not to maintain the censure brought against him.

On the advice of two friends, a priest and a layman, he decided to change this plan in one important respect: to write to the Pope before, instead of waiting until after, the sentence of excommunication was decreed. This meant only to prolong the agony. But he was not in a condition to decide calmly. His letter to Pius X began with an appeal to the Pope's goodness of heart. It expressed the writer's wish to live and die in the communion of the Catholic Church, and not to contribute to the ruin of the faith in France. Asserting that it was not in his power to destroy in himself the results of his labors, he yet submitted as much as lay in his power to the judgment brought against his writings by the Congregation of the Index. As a token of his good-will and for the pacification of spirits, he was ready to abandon his teaching and suspend the scientific publications he had in preparation. Early in March, a rumor of his excommunication was printed in the newspapers, and Loisy believes the decree was actually prepared. Then came the most painful of all his encounters with Cardinal Richard. Through

him the Pope sent word that the letter addressed to
his heart had not proceeded from the heart. The
promise to abandon teaching had been acceptable,
but had been spoiled by the words, "It is not in my
power to destroy in myself the results of my labors."
The letter to the Cardinal ended:

"Assuredly, he is not asked to write no more, but to
write in defense of the tradition, conformably to the
words of St. Remy to Clovis: 'Adore what you once
burned, and burn what you once adored.'"

At this, Loisy says, something gave way within
him. He had yet other experiences to undergo to
make him wish to be no longer a Catholic, but this
heartless rejection by the Head of the Church was
the decisive one. By a strange revulsion of feeling,
however, after a tumultuous debate with the venerable Archbishop of Paris, on the same day Loisy
sent him the following note:

"Monsignor—
"I declare to Your Eminence that, in a spirit of obedience toward the Holy See, I condemn the errors which
the Holy Office has condemned in my writings."

This was superfluous, if not actually misleading;
and afterwards he would gladly have recalled it. He
proceeded, however, to resign his chair at the *École
Pratique des Hautes Études,* and his place as assistant in the *Corpus inscriptionum semiticarum,* left
Paris, and went to live in a small cottage loaned to
him by his friend, the Orientalist, François Thureau-
Dangin, in the village of Garnay. There he hoped
to end his days in peace. He had just passed his

forty-seventh birthday, but he seemed to others and to himself an old and broken man.

The "laborious Odyssey" of his Catholic career was to last four years longer; yet not without compensations. The first of these years was occupied in the composition of the magisterial Introduction to his *Évangiles Synoptiques*. Nearly two years more were spent on the revision of the Commentary and the Introduction, while the fourth—from January, 1907, to January, 1908—was consumed in seeing the great work of 1,800 octavo pages through the press. All but the last few months of this quiet and prolific interval were spent in what Loisy calls his "hermitage" at Garnay, the toil of writing and proof-reading being varied by care of his tiny garden and his few fowls. Some sections of the forthcoming commentary were published in the form of review articles, and he continued his activity as a book-reviewer. It is evident that he had grounds for not feeling himself bound by his promise to the Pope to suspend his scientific publications. The Vatican, incensed by an article on John the Baptist's message to Jesus, retaliated by refusing to reissue a permission which had been granted him, owing to his infirm health, to say mass in his room. Thus on the first of November, 1906, he ceased after twenty-seven years to perform this daily service of the Catholic priesthood. During the same month he suffered from severe hemorrhages, and became so ill that he took measures to ensure the publication of *Les Évangiles Synoptiques* in the event of his death. In April, 1907, he removed from Garnay to live with his sister at Ceffonds, having received medical advice that he would be better for living less alone.

That was the period of the mighty struggle of Church and State in France, which ended—chiefly owing to the arrogant and unbending attitude of Pius X and Merry del Val—in the abrogation of the Concordat and in complete disestablishment. Coincident with this, and as a further endeavor of the Vatican to "restore all things in Christ," came the campaign of increasing severity against Modernism. This part of Loisy's career can best be followed in the correspondence which he published in *Quelques Lettres* (1908), extracts from which are given in the later pages of *Choses Passées*. But we must hasten to the long-foreseen conclusion.

In July, 1907, appeared the expected syllabus of Modernist errors, the decree *Lamentabili sane exitu,* and in September the encyclical *Pascendi dominici gregis,* "against the errors of the Modernists." The only comment on these papal pronouncements calling for mention here is that which Loisy made to admiration in *Simples Réflexions sur le Décret du Saint-Office, Lamentabili sane exitu, et sur l'Encyclique, Pascendi dominici gregis* (1908). In the first half of this volume, he shows that practically all of the sixty-five condemned propositions of the syllabus were taken from his two books, *L'Évangile et l'Église* and *Autour d'un Petit Livre,* in a large proportion of cases, however, distorted to suit the systematizing passion of his Roman censors. The second half is given up to a demonstration of the artificiality and injustice of the procedure of lumping together in one sweeping condemnation the extremely various and unconnected efforts of philosophy, theology, criticism, history, apologetics and practical social reform which the official inquisitors saw fit to group together under the rubric of Modernism. Less interesting, because more scholastic in tone, and less personally impassioned, than *Autour, Simples Réflexions* is none the less a document of the first importance for the history of Modernism, and a damaging indictment of the false logic, critical and historical incompetence, and essential superficiality of the reigning Catholic theologians of the beginning of the twentieth century.

The thread was now wearing painfully thin, and the sword of excommunication could not much longer hang over him. There were final vain efforts by Loisy's friends in the Church to persuade him to conform. The Pope even sent a last solemn warning—"in order if possible, to save a soul." The sentence of excommunication (March 7, 1908) was published to the world two months after the appearance of *Les Évangiles Synoptiques,* the two events apparently not being connected, and without its victim being personally notified. It was after all a relief. A few months later, Loisy had the honor of election to a chair in the *Collège de France,* made sacred to him by his early master, Renan. His Catholic career was ended. But its influence upon the Church that so laboriously made him a heresiarch is still to be reckoned with, and can hardly fail of its ultimate, transforming effect.

SUPPLEMENTARY NOTE

Books by Professor Loisy not mentioned in the above Introduction, or published since it was written, are listed below for the sake of completeness.

Leçon d'ouverture du cours d'Histoire des religions au Collège de France (1909), 12mo. 43 pages.

Jésus et la Tradition évangélique (1910), 1 vol. 12mo. 288 pages.

À propos d'Histoire des Religions (1911), 1 vol. 12mo. 326 pages.

L'Évangile selon Marc (1912), 1 vol. 12mo. 503 pages.

Choses Passées (1913), 1 vol. 12mo. x + 398 pages.

Guerre et Religion, deuxième édition (1915), 1 vol. 12mo. 196 pages.

L'Épître aux Galates (1916), 1 vol. 12mo. 204 pages.

Mors et Vita, deuxième édition (1917), 1 vol. 12 mo. 90 pages.

La Religion (1917), 1 vol. 12mo. 310 pages.

La Paix des Nations et la Religion de l'avenir (1919), 12mo. 31 pages.

De la Discipline intellectuelle (1919), 1 vol. 12mo. 192 pages.

Les Mystères païens et le Mystère chrétien (1919), 1 vol. roy. 8vo. 368 pages.

Essai historique sur le Sacrifice (1920), 1 vol. roy. 8vo. 552 pages.

Les Actes des Apôtres (1920), 1 vol. roy. 8vo. 960 pages.

MY DUEL WITH THE VATICAN

CHAPTER I

TOWARD THE PRIESTHOOD

I

THE Marne, after it leaves St. Dizier, bends slightly toward the south, washing the base of the wooded, vine-covered slopes which from this bank rise above the fertile Perthois.   The river then sweeps by the antique chapel of St. Aubin, a place of pilgrimages, where even yet miracles sometimes occur; thence it flows westward to the tiny tower of Neuville-au-Pont, lower than the trees around it; and farther on past the ancient church of Ambrières, which seems ready to slide down the bank on which it stands—widowed of its transepts, lacking its spire, and with its portal mutilated as if by the stroke of an axe.   After a sharp turn toward the village of Perthes, the sluggish stream creeps past the heights crowned by the ancient abbey of Haute-Fontaine and, soon emerging from the barrier of hills, advances peacefully through the broad plains of Champagne.

47

I was born at Ambrières, in the last house in the village. It stands a little apart, not far from the church, in the direction of Haute-Fontaine, with a pleasant outlook over the sinuous course of the Marne and the villages in the valley. Here my ancestors—farmers from one generation to another—had made their home from the earliest years of the last century. For at least a hundred years before that the Loisys had been tenants of the monks of Haute-Fontaine, and their prolific clan had swarmed over into the neighboring hamlets. When the monks were dispossessed, my great-grandfather had a falling-out with the purchaser of the national properties who replaced them, and came to establish himself at Ambrières. It seems that suppleness of character was never the dominant trait of my forebears! Good citizens, hard workers, attached to the soil and skilled in its cultivation, a little proud perhaps for their station—such were my ancestors. I, as it happened, inherited more of their tastes than of their toughness. Like them, I should have loved to till the ground, and even now would never tire of it if my strength were equal to the task. But it never has proven so.

Although, or because, they had been tenants of the monks, these older Loisys seem to have been only lukewarm in their devoutness. Wholly respectful toward religion, they did not practice it, leaving that to their womenfolk. The region was Jansenist in temper, that is, its pastors under the old régime and their successors in the first half of the last century had accustomed their flocks to give serious heed to Christianity, as a wise and stern discipline, always to be esteemed, even when only in part conformed to. A distant cousin of my father's had been a priest, but he was never held up before me as an example.

Quite another tradition prevailed in my mother's family. Two first cousins of her father's had been priests, holding rather important posts in the diocese of Châlons-sur-Marne, following in the footsteps of great-great-uncles who had entered the priesthood before the French Revolution. My mother herself was earnestly devout, but with no special fondness for either theology or mysticism. She was probably just a trifle superstitious. Endowed with an exceptional memory and of an inquisitive disposition, she knew by heart all the old tales that had gone the rounds on winter evenings when she was still young, in the reign of Louis Philippe. She could recall, as well, not a few of the formulas of the popular magic; also signs and portents such as constituted the total science of the peasantry in past ages. These she did not much credit, and never relied on them herself, referring to them for the most part laughingly. For example, she could never be persuaded to recite a magical incantation for the certain relief of horse colic that her grandfather knew; but it was rather because this sort of thing was forbidden by her religion than from entire conviction of its inefficacy. She cherished, however, certain precepts with a moral bearing,—this among others: Never defame a priest, even if he deserves it, because that is sure to bring misfortune. She was convinced that the enemies of religion were always punished in this world, if not in their person, then in their posterity. In proof of this she would cite the fate of those who had demolished the figures of the saints in our church in 1793. Her grandmother had told her their names, and she passed them on to me. The descendants of these profaners had turned out badly!

All this local folklore interested me intensely. My father heard her tales without comment, smiling at the end, but not believing a word. Until well on in life, he gave no evidence of feeling the slightest concern for religion. Its moral precepts he observed, but toward beliefs and practices properly religious he retained a perfectly serene, and one may say spontaneous, indifference; for he had never been beyond the lowest grades in school, had no time to read, and realized his incompetence to criticize in detail the teaching of the priests. Moreover, he would not have wished to do so, being circumspect by nature, and judging severely those who spoke of what was beyond their comprehension. Thus he held his peace, because to him religion was simply meaningless. If I had not taken orders, he would probably have persevered in this attitude to the end. But in his last years, although I had no thought of wishing to change his lifelong habit of mind, he gave a little more attention to the affairs of the church. He came voluntarily to hear the short sermons that I preached to the parishioners of Ambrières in my vacations. Some months before his death, which occurred in 1895, he even consented to make confession to a Jesuit father who had come to hold a mission in our village.

In my childhood, neither my father nor my mother

had the faintest notion of inclining me toward an ecclesiastical career. On the contrary, if the thought could even have occurred to them that one day I might consider such a course, they would certainly have dissuaded me. My early promise as a scholar had given them other ambitions on my behalf. The intelligent and devoted teacher at Ambrières [1] had found in me a diligent, docile pupil, always eager to get my lessons. Indeed, when I was taken for the first time to school, a timid and sickly child of four and a half years, and the master undertook to teach me the alphabet, I remained for two days mute before the blackboard on which the letters were displayed; on the third day I said them all without being asked, not having wished to pronounce the names of these strange characters until all had been mastered. After that I learned whatever was expected of me. In my eleventh year, taking a good rank in a certain competition, something was said about making a scholar out of me. However, this idea would have had no charm for either my parents or myself if there had been any hope that I might some day follow the plough. But I was so frail that this seemed out of the question. An attempt had been made to find easy tasks that I could perform, but entirely without success. I was afraid of the horses I was supposed to lead, my hand being too weak to control them. I did a few chores about the place and tended the cattle in the enclosure when out of school. But that would not suffice to make a

[1] This teacher, M. Alfred Philippe, is still living; he is now (1913) in retirement and mayor of the commune.

farmer of me. My incapacity once conceded, to my keen regret, it was decided that I should enter the high school (*collège*) to continue my studies, being obviously fit for nothing else, and so become what I would or what I could.

This early uncertainty of aim was to have an unfortunate outcome. The only way open to me was to enter the municipal high school at Vitry-le-François, where I was admitted after the Easter vacation in 1869. The war of 1870 and the Prussian invasion, combined with my weakness of constitution, decided my parents to keep me at home during the school year, 1870-71. They also kept me there during the year following, because a young priest, who had become curé of Ambrières, was induced to give me instruction. This arrangement was my own idea, since I found life in a public school intolerable and, without admitting it to anyone, continued to hope that I might still gain strength enough to become a toiler like my father and all my progenitors. There I found awaiting me what, in the language of Catholic piety, is called the grace of a special vocation.

Up to this time I had not shown any precocious piety. My religious education had been what would naturally be expected under the family auspices. My mother directed it. At church, as at school, I was dutiful. Like all the others, I took my catechism literally, and I had made what was called a good first communion. But the aged priest who had charge of my spiritual welfare was a man of the old school, inclined to severity. His method was to instill the rudiments of the faith without attempting

to stir the deeper feelings. I believed in all simplicity, and acquitted myself creditably in whatever
I was told were the duties of a Christian child.
There had been, however, in my general confession,
before the first communion, among the peccadilloes
of childhood, the avowal of an enormous sin. One
day, when eight or nine years old, wandering alone
on the hill-slope in front of our house and reflecting
on the tediums of my petty existence, I had said
aloud, "God is not good." The remembrance of
this had stayed with me. So radical an opinion was
hardly compatible with the curé's teachings, and
besides, one is never justified in losing patience with
the Eternal! So I reconciled myself in all sincerity
to Providence, asking forgiveness of God for having
doubted Him.

From time to time, various persons, noting my
studious application and my distaste for outdoor activities, as well as the sort of preoccupied gravity
which resulted from my weak health, would prophesy
that I should become a priest; but nothing gave me
more displeasure. The priests whom I had thus far
known had inspired me rather with respect than
with admiration. I had felt, indeed, a degree of uneasiness and disquiet before these representatives of
the supernatural. However, on the September Sunday in 1871 when the Abbé Munier was installed
curé of our village, I had a singular experience. The
whole parish was astir. The Mayor and the Council
of Works were in attendance. Even the firemen
were there in uniform, with their chief. I was in
my seat in the family pew, at my mother's right, as

usual. When the priest passed close by us, he seemed to me deeply moved, as was doubtless the case; and the next instant, when he mounted toward the altar, something said to me that some day I too would stand before that altar and say mass in that church. It was a sort of illumination, which I did not in the least take for a sign from Heaven. Yet it was from that very day, in all probability, that I was marked for the sacrifice, and guided almost without realizing it toward the priestly office.

The year ended for me without special incident. My new instructor confined himself to indicating to me the lessons and exercises to be done, in conformity with the program of classes of the fifth and fourth grades. I worked hard, but almost independently of any control by my excellent preceptor. Nothing was said as to my possible future. My mentor was a man of parts, who on this point displayed a tactful reserve. The pastors of the vicinity, whom I encountered at the parsonage, were less discreet; thus, however, only inclining me the less to wear their uniform. Seeing them at close range, they seemed to me rather a poor lot. When I entered the ecclesiastical high school at St. Dizier in October, 1872, not only had I not decided to become a priest; rather I supposed I had decided not to be one.

II

I remained for two years at St. Dizier. The high school was directed by ecclesiastics of the diocese of Langres. All those with whom I came in contact were devout and kindly. My professor in the third grade, the Abbé Thibonnet, was, I believe, the only bachelor of arts in the institution. He was very kindly disposed, and appealed to me from the first; I chose him for my confessor. The spirit of the institution was not that of a seminary for priests; but a certain element of piety was present, to which I freely abandoned myself. The pupils went to confession, following the regulations, once a month. The more fervent confessed at shorter intervals, and it was not long before I ranked among the most fervent. In each division an especially devout group was formed, with meetings of its own. I was elected shortly to that in my division, and even became its prefect, in which capacity I presided gravely at the brief service that we recited weekly in the chapel of the Virgin. All my teachers were satisfied with my progress, but with my fellow-students I was less popular. Taking no part in their sports, and awkward and timid as well, I inspired in the majority a mingled feeling, of disdain for my shabby appearance combined with that naïve admiration felt by the members of a school for one of their number who happens to be distinguished by steady excellence. Even among these youths of my own age, I lived largely by myself, with a few friends of a very pacific temper. From the end of the first year, the general opinion was that I was destined for the priesthood, and the more malicious said among themselves that I was fitted for nothing better.

It was not until the end of October, 1873, that the fatal choice was made. We went into retreat once a year, just before the feast of All Saints. The preacher for that year was a man who acquired a special prestige from circumstances. He was Father Stumpf, a Jesuit, formerly rector of the *collège* of St. Clement at Metz, which had been closed in 1872 by order of Bismarck. Thus our preacher came to us with the halo of persecution about him, as a Frenchman expelled from that Lorraine which had been torn from us by violence. He addressed us as a member of a religious order, with a wide experience of the youthful heart. None knew better than he how to adapt the Spiritual Exercises of St. Ignatius of Loyola to the conditions of a retreat for students. He put before us with supreme clarity the great principles of the faith. In these retreats, all the instruction is made to converge to a single end, leading up to what is called the "election," a personal decision between the world and God. This act of choice, even when it concerns only believers who are not engaged in making a career of religion, has no slight significance, and this fact Father Stumpf knew much better than we did. He made plain to us that not our eternity alone was in question, that the simple resolve to live as good Christians was not all that God expected of us, but that above all we must seek to know what we could accomplish for God in our future in this world.

I was deeply stirred, all the more so because just then my sister's health was giving my parents serious cause for anxiety. The Jesuit made us feel the fragility of everything human; he exalted before us the virtue of sacrifice: God refuses nothing to those who dedicate themselves unreservedly to Him. If I

were to renounce the world—that is to say, all sorts
of things that I knew imperfectly or not at all, and
regarding which I could not know whether it is even
possible to renounce them absolutely—who knows
but God might have mercy on my dear ones and
spare them every mischance? What was to be my
usefulness here below? No one had ever told me that
I was fitted for one occupation rather than another.
I felt no special inclination toward any of those with
which I was acquainted. The idea of consecrating
myself to the disinterested service of humanity al-
lured me. It never once visited my mind that many
and various functions are, or may be made, a service
of this kind, and that the Catholic Church possesses
no monopoly of devotion. Thus my reflections as a
lonely and inexperienced boy led me to take a resolve
that I had not foreseen and against which I should
still have protested only three short weeks before.
It seemed clear that God was calling me; that my
real inclination had always been toward the priesthood; that a mere prejudice had hindered me from
perceiving it; and that those who thought me un-
suited to a lay career were probably right. And
ought I not to rejoice in this incapacity? To serve
the Church, was not this to serve the truth? In any
case, such was the slightness of my hold upon existence that I could offer my life to the Eternal without seriously inconveniencing anyone; let Him draw
benefit of some kind from it before recalling me entirely to Himself!

For the moment, I contented myself with forming
this resolution. I did not confide it even to my con-

fessor, much less consult Father Stumpf on the subject. Today I should be exceedingly curious to know what he might have said to me. Perhaps he would have chilled my enthusiasm. Some time later there came into my hands a medal, given by him to one of my fellow-students, which bore in reverse the monogram of Henry V with the lilies of France. This detail rather surprised me. Doubtless it was quite without significance, and it is highly probable that if I had consulted him, instead of presenting me with his medal we should have talked only of my "election." He could readily have turned my choice toward the Society of which he was a member; or, if not that, doubting my fitness, he might have exhorted me to reflect more seriously before promising my life to God.

An unexpected circumstance made my design irrevocable. That year I happened to be in relations of close intimacy with a fine lad, decidedly original, who believed himself a poet because of the extreme facility with which he composed French verse. Our relations were wholly blameless; but owing to the ill-will of a few of the students, they had the result of arousing the dislike of nearly all. This unpopularity did not disturb me, especially as I had the good-will of our teachers. However, such a situation made it easier to cut short my stay in the secondary school, and to hold fast to my hasty resolution to embrace an ecclesiastical career. One day I confided to my friend my intention to enter the seminary at the end of that year—we were finishing our "rhetoric." He replied that his purpose was the same, and that a place had been spoken for him in the Langres diocesan seminary. I laid my plans before my confessor, who made no objection.

To secure the consent of my family was the real difficulty. My mother was much surprised and not at all pleased when I spoke to her of my determination in the school parlor on a certain May day in 1874. A week later she came back to tell me that my father was all upset by my project—I could have expected nothing else from him—and was losing sleep over it. But I had also foreseen that there would be no absolute veto. The matter was never discussed between us. My people did not care to risk going contrary to my wishes, and they believed, not without appearance of reason, that since my health seriously limited my chances for the future, the wisest course was to let me do as I chose. They did, however, consult the head of the school, the excellent Abbé Guillaumet, who opined that there was no hurry, since I was barely seventeen, and that I would do better to remain in the school to prepare for the baccalaureate in arts and also that in science, since these diplomas would not fail to be of use to me, even in an ecclesiastical career. These were sensible suggestions, and they would so have impressed my parents if the head-master had insisted; but he did not, and I was left free to follow my own bent.

Thus it happened that I entered the diocesan seminary at Châlons-sur-Marne in the first week of October, 1874. My father himself conducted me thither, deeply chagrined, but saying not a word to make it harder for me. I arrived in my ordinary clothes, and was obliged to assume the cassock upon entrance. I donned the ecclesiastical garments with less satisfaction than I had anticipated, and accompanied my father back to the railroad station. Our parting was not a cheerful one. On my way back, at a dignified pace, towards the seminary—an object of interest to people who perhaps asked themselves if they had ever before seen a theological student of such juvenile appearance—in passing by the Saint Alpin church I met an intelligent looking man who uttered a cry of outraged horror. I did not catch all that he said, but heard enough to gather a castigation for myself and especially a vehement imprecation against the Church—that baby-snatcher!—that abuser of parental confidence! The author of this violent outburst was doubtless moved by good intentions, and had not enough considered what effect his language might have upon a youthful spirit not wanting in resolution. I crossed the threshold of the church and knelt within for a few moments. Coming out, I was prepared to face without flinching all the sarcasms and blasphemies of infidelity. I re-entered the seminary in complete repose of mind. Not knowing a soul within except the Superior, to whom my father had presented me, I went upstairs to the room that had been assigned me and arranged my few belongings while waiting for the evening service.

III

The diocesan seminary at Châlons was at that time installed in an old convent, threatened with ruin, next door to the prefecture. It was under the management of priests of the diocese. Some years before, the bishop, Monsignor Meignan, who had formerly been professor of Holy Scripture at the Sorbonne when a Catholic faculty of theology was in existence there, and who prided himself on his zeal for high standards of scholarship, had dismissed the priests of the Lazarist Mission, who had been in control, and replaced them with priests chosen from among his own clergy. The event had not justified his hopes, and now the prelate was solicitous only for his personal reputation as a scholar, no longer pretending to make of his school of clerical learning a centre of light and leading for the Church in France.

A venerable ecclesiastic, Abbé Roussel, who had grown old in the parochial ministry, was at the head of the establishment. He was no scholar, but had a vast experience of life and of men—even of bishops! I doubt much whether he greatly admired Bishop Meignan's learning, or thought it particularly solid. There were few profundities in his own theology. His conception of the clerical life was of the simplest —namely, what he had himself exemplified: an austere morality plus devotion to the souls of his flock. In his confidential moments he would poke fun at the theology and apologetic, in the grand style, of florid oratory and full orchestration, which Lacordaire had popularized, and which at that time still retained its prestige. The Superior was a man at heart all kindness, but in manner severe and almost harsh. His voice, given a staccato quality by asthma, seemed to have no other tone than one of command. He did not attract me, and it took me several years to discover that he was following me with a fatherly interest. It was not he whom I chose to be the director of my conscience.

Besides the Superior, there was the Bursar, a good old priest who taught us sacred eloquence with as much conviction as if he had himself possessed its secret; the professor of moral theology, a great reader of the *Univers,* pluming himself on his orthodoxy, not without originality, but almost totally lacking in culture; the professor of dogma and canon law, returned from Rome with an abundance of degrees, but more at home in certain drawing-rooms of the town than in his chair, where he was visibly bored, —a doctor but poorly furnished in his subject who, on the days when he really exerted himself, dictated to his hearers extracts from courses published by his former master in the Roman College, Cardinal Franzelin; finally, the professor of Holy Scripture and of church history, a devoted soul as innocent as possible of the principles of criticism, who had us recite from the most puerile textbooks, and who was capable on occasion of pointing out to us how St. John, the apostle, in his *Apocalypse,* had predicted,—in rather obscure terms, to be sure,—the Vatican Council! Bishop Meignan did not rate any too highly this teaching staff, of his own choosing. In 1882, when, having wished me to join it, he authorized me to remain at the Catholic Institute in Paris, he said to me: "What would you have done with this one or that one?"—laughing heartily the while.

The professor of philosophy was of a wholly different type. He sprang, like myself, from a family of tillers of the soil, and from the same region of Champagne. An uncle in the sacred ministry had inclined him toward the priestly office. He had been teaching only two years, having been made professor just after his ordination, without further preparation; but he had a keen mind and no end of good sense, he read largely in modern philosophy, and he commented sagely on our old philosophical manual of Sulpician origin, today much out of favor, which Renan has celebrated in his *Souvenirs of Childhood and Youth*. Renan omitted to say that this philosophy of Abbé Monier, closely allied as it was to that taught in those days at the University of Paris, was at a considerable remove from mediæval Scholasticism. The Abbé Ludot was not a mystic by temperament. He never bothered himself with the subtleties of theological dogma. I do not think he was ever seriously troubled in his faith, perhaps because he avoided going to the bottom of things. It was he to whom I went in the first instance for my confession, only to learn later that he was the heretic of the establishment. He passed for a Liberal Catholic because, unperturbed amidst the uproar that the Vatican Council had provoked in the Châlons seminary, as elsewhere, he had abstained from taking part against his bishop, who was a member of the anti-infallibilist minority, and also spoke with evident sympathy of Lacordaire and Montalembert.

But for Abbé Ludot I should have left the seminary at the end of three months, to join a religious order. At first, the exercises of piety, the well-sung services, the impressive cathedral ceremonies, greatly affected me. The morning silent prayer exalted me to the skies; I abandoned myself to it with a naïve fervor; no shadow of a doubt had then arisen to cloud my relations with the world of divine realities. In the church, the chants threw me sometimes into a sort of tremulous ecstasy. The sentiment of haunting melancholy, induced in me by the hymn *Placare, Christe, servulis,* at the All Saints' Day vespers, remains still vivid in my memory. But the more I gave myself over to my spiritual and mystical ideal, the less adequately did it seem to me the life of the parochial clergy responded to it, and I came to feel that, to give one's self wholly to God, one must join a regular congregation. To be entirely candid, the seminarist habit of mind impressed me as a bit common, beneath our sublime calling. A fellow-student had lent me some Dominican books—the Life of Lacordaire, by Father Chocarne, the Letters of Lacordaire to Madame Swetchine, and his Lectures. In brief, my dream was to become a Dominican, and as I was incapable of enduring the austerities of the grand order of Friars Preachers, I wrote to the Prior of the Third (teaching) Order. My application was accepted; but Abbé Ludot, whom I was obliged to consult, put a stop to the business. He remonstrated that I was too young to make so grave a choice, but was tactful enough to lead me to renounce it of my own will and without imposing his point of view. He consulted my mother, who hurried to Châlons, much disturbed by the announcement of this newest departure. My fine scheme had to be indefinitely postponed, and in the sequel I was never seriously tempted to resume it.

The year went on more prosaically than it had begun. I grew accustomed to my surroundings, and came to do fuller justice to the good qualities of my fellows. Also, I enjoyed the regular life, in which the use of every hour was fixed, and where one had fully half of each day to himself. The study of philosophy began to grip me, and I supplemented the lectures by a course of reading indicated for me by Abbé Ludot. The later months were more disturbed. The professor of church history had been so imprudent as to have dissertations prepared by the students on modern topics, such as the Concordat of 1801, Lamennais and his School, Liberal Catholicism and the Vatican Council, and to encourage discussions on these themes that even got beyond his control. It was perceived, or supposed, that among the seminarists who had followed the courses of Abbé Ludot there were a number of "liberals." With the beginning of vacation he was made *curé* of a large village near Sainte Menehould, and with his dismissal the philosophy of Abbé Monier was no more heard of. The following year, the new professor, a devotee of Scholasticism, introduced a textbook exempt from all compromise with modern philosophy. From that time forward, unmitigated orthodoxy reigned in the Châlons seminary under the crafty eye of its bishop.

From this event a lesson emerged that I did not then appreciate. Bishop Meignan had sacrificed lightheartedly a man whom he esteemed and whose faith, as he very well knew, was much less undermined than his own. Abbé Ludot never complained. I went to visit him in his parish. He was desolate at having to abandon a work that he loved and pupils who were attached to him; but he added no repining to his regret. He imputed the responsibility for his disgrace to the Superior, not looking for its remoter causes. He made an excellent pastor, adored by his parishioners. But the successors of Bishop Meignan —who was soon to be made Bishop of Arras and then Archbishop of Tours—neglected to appoint him to important posts that he was amply worthy to fill. He died in 1905, too soon to witness the end of my laborious Odyssey, which he had in no way foreseen and on which he did not exert the slightest influence. It was owing to him that I remained in the seminary; but all the subsequent critical evolution of my thought has gone on independently both of his teaching and of his personal convictions. Many things in my published works, which he followed with interest, were beyond him. On reading *The Gospel and the Church,* he found in it one serious omission—the absence of a general philosophy of religion—and he urged me to write a doctrinal exposition and positive apology of the Catholic faith, that would make it acceptable to contemporary science. When he made the acquaintance of *Con-*

cerning a Little Book, the first letter of which was
addressed to himself, he merely wrote me a few words
dominated by disquiet: "Where is it all going to
end?" He was totally at a loss to explain why I
should expose myself to the major excommunication
by refusing to retract explicitly and without reserve
the contents of the five volumes condemned by the
Holy Office in December, 1903.

IV

On the resumption of work in the fall of 1875, I
entered definitely upon the study of theology. It
opened to me a new world, and one that had a singular reaction on my mind. Precisely as the mystical
contemplation of the supernatural objects of faith is
in general a solace to the soul, and even to the intellect when it allows itself to be controlled by the
emotions, so the attempt to arrive at a more or less
rational analysis of belief may easily become of all
undertakings the most unsettling. Although I was
even then completely immersed in piety, and foremost among the members of the seminary for my
fervor, the first contact of my thought with Catholic
doctrine—with what was offered me as an authentic
interpretation of divine revelation—was an excruci-
atingly harrowing experience, and all that followed
harmonized with this unlucky beginning. I can say,
without exaggeration, that the four consecutive
years which I was obliged to devote at this period to
the study of Christian doctrine were for me four
years of mental and moral torture. I even wonder
today how it was that my reason stood the strain,

or that my already frail health did not succumb under it.

The fault did not lie altogether in the poor quality of the teaching to which I was subjected. I have described above what our professor of dogmatic theology was like. His lectures might have been more nourishing and yet have induced on my part scarcely less anguishing perplexities. The grandiose assertions of Cardinal Franzelin no more satisfied me than the clear, well-ordered, scientifically unpretentious paragraphs of our classical authority, the *Theology* of Bishop Bouvier of Mans. This work on theology, like that of Abbé Manier in philosophy, was conceived in the French manner, perhaps slightly tinged with Gallicanism, and for that reason superficially more intelligible. Relatively independent as it was of the older Scholastic models, it had the merit of possessing a certain lucidity. But this, when it is a question of theology, is not altogether an advantage. Since the Middle Ages, Catholic doctrine has taken on the form of a logical system. It is a coherent structure, of mutually sustaining parts; a splendid cathedral whose essential weakness, as Renan declared, lies in the flimsiness of its foundations. But Renan was able to see this even from his seminary days. Assuming that I had possessed his penetration. I was laboring under conditions much less favorable for giving it free scope.

Although faith is not a matter for demonstration, and no religion rests its claims, in point of fact, on purely rational grounds, Catholic Christianity undertakes to impose itself upon humanity, not indeed as a doctrine inherently subject to rational demonstration, but as a revealed teaching, a divine institution whose supernatural character and indisputable authority arise from the very circumstances of its origin. God has spoken, and revealed Himself from the beginnings of the creation to the first parents of mankind, and later to the fathers of the people of Israel; He instituted on Mount Sinai the sacred law, by which the Jewish nation is still governed; He inspired the prophets and dictated the Sacred Scriptures, which contain the announcement of a larger and final revelation, that of the salvation which He is preparing to consummate in the incarnation of Himself in Jesus Christ; He appeared in the Christ, and thus founded the Church with its dogma, its hierarchy, its worship. The proof of all these assertions is in the miracles which were worked by Moses and by the prophets, above all by Jesus, both in his lifetime and after his death, since he rose again two days after expiring on the cross; faithful eye-witnesses have made themselves guarantors of all these marvels, and the two Testaments contain their deposit, valid for all posterity.

Such is the basis of Orthodox Christianity—that is to say, a basis entirely inadequate to sustain the conclusion sought in the process of demonstration. It is declared, in effect, that the Bible, from one end to the other, is a historical document, only offering in certain parts mere difficulties of interpretation; that the miraculous accounts of the Exodus of the children of Israel, with the plagues of Egypt and the crossing of the Red Sea, as well as the manifestation of God on Mount Sinai, suffice to authenticate the Mosaic revelation; that the prophets look forward to the Gospel, Christ and the Church; that the miracles and the resurrection of Jesus, testified to by his disciples, confirm the profession he himself made of his divinity; and that the Church, inheritor of his grace and truth, is therefore a divine institution. No link in this entire chain of reasoning will bear a critical examination. But these premises once assumed, theology proceeds to co-ordinate its inferences. The early Fathers speculated upon the elementary data of faith as upon ascertained realities, and thence the Catholic dogma took shape as a carefully equilibrated, logically concatenated, all-comprehending system, gradually brought to its perfection by the labors of generations of men of genius. This system has stamped itself powerfully upon our entire occidental mentality, which at bottom has worked itself free from it much less than is generally supposed. For those who lack the necessary preparation and training to enable them to subject its starting-point to the test of criticism, this theology has the appearance of being a species of transcendent knowledge, an outcome of the age-long travail of the human reason upon the materials furnished by God Himself in His primitive revelation.

As I had no critical background, any more than those by whom I was being taught; as I saw no one and read no books that could arouse in me doubts as to the foundations of the Catholic faith; as it happened that the sections on the true religion and the Church, in which the proofs of the truth of Chris-

tianity are given, were not reached in our plan of
instruction until my last year in the seminary, it was
not on questions of fact and problems of history that
my mind encountered its earlier difficulties. I was
instructed in the economy of the plan of salvation,
in the genesis of that act of faith which is a gift of
God, while yet implying the free co-operation of the
believer; the mystery of Jesus Christ, at once truly
God and truly man; in the background of this mystery, that of the Trinity, secret of the divine nature,
developed in three distinct persons who are, nevertheless, essentially one; the mystery of grace, co-
ordinate with that of original sin and that of
redemption through Christ, an arrangement by
means of which the divine mercy is able to rescue
the lost humanity that God Himself had consigned
to perdition; the sacraments, means of grace, the
supreme gift of Christ, and the Eucharist, in which
Jesus perpetuates his presence in his Church. Just
in the degree to which certain of these objects of
faith had impressed me when employed as sources
of religious emotion, to that same degree their
Scholastic exposition in terms of naked intellect
filled my mind with an ill-defined disquiet. Now
that I was required to think all these things rationally, and not merely to feel them, I was thrown into
a state of prolonged disturbance. For my intelligence could find no satisfaction, and with my whole
timid, immature consciousness I trembled before the
query that oppressed, in spite of myself, every hour
of the day: Is there any reality which corresponds
to these doctrines?

The situation was one that cannot easily be made intelligible to those who have never experienced anything like it. I had not brought to the seminary the shadow of a thought contrary to the teaching of the Church, nor the least tinge of feeling out of accord with the vocation that I expected was to be mine; I offered myself to God ardently and in entire simplicity of heart, and I approached with unsuspecting mind the instruction to which I was being subjected. Yet it was that teaching, accepted in advance as the very truth, which now tormented me. As was natural, I confided my inner state to ·my· spiritual director who, after the departure of Abbé Ludot, was the Bursar of the institution. That excellent man, who had never known the shadow of a doubt, replied that I had fallen a victim to excessive scruples, and that I should not reproach myself with thoughts contrary to the faith which might force themselves on me involuntarily, but simply turn my attention to other things and forget these disturbing fancies. To a considerable extent he was right, and a physician would assuredly have proffered me the same advice. In view of my excessive sensitiveness of disposition, this inner anxiety had quickly taken on the character of a haunting obsession. It had not yet become a fixed idea; but this is the way, one presumes, that such ideas find entrance into our poor human reason and derange it. At bottom, my spiritual director was vastly mistaken in assuming in my case nothing beyond a temporary disquietude, due to over-subtlety of mind. What I was suffering from, without being able to divine the real cause of my ailment, was the false intellectual discipline to which I was being submitted. Studies dealing with matters of fact, duly systematized, where the conclusions emerge as results of direct observation, would not have produced any such morbid effect. When I finally came to apply myself to such studies some years later, in the same condition of health and in a like moral situation, I regained almost instantly the serenity of mind of which theology had deprived me.

My doubts concerning the faith, not having arisen from any discovery that I was capable of making of one or more particular errors in the Church's teaching, did not acquire in my mind the consistency requisite to influence the resolve that had led me to the seminary. The idea of going back to secular life, while I still enjoyed the freedom to do so, never entered my head. My will to serve God and his Church in the priesthood remained unshaken. I looked upon my involuntary doubts as one of those trials spoken of by mystical writers, and resolved to wait until it should please God that they should be dispersed. In the naïveté of my mind, I thought that serious unbelief was only found among people who were affronted by the moral standards of Christianity, and who felt a personal interest in the nonexistence of a God and of a place of eternal punishment. My good director of conscience took pains to commend intellectual humility; urging that a religion which had satisfied geniuses like Saint Augustine, Saint Thomas Aquinas, Pascal, Bossuet and Fénelon was surely not unworthy of our adherence. I did not then dream of answering him that these men had not lived in the Nineteenth Century, and that no one could tell what might have been the turn of mind of a Blaise Pascal who had been born a contemporary of Ernest Renan.

That which predisposed me to have confidence in the judgment of my director was the fact that ·the same effect was produced on my conscience by the teaching of Catholic morality as on my reason by the instruction in dogma. Morality, in the program of clerical studies, is properly casuistry—the science of the confessor, who has to judge when, how, and to what degree the Christian and ecclesiastical law is binding on the individual penitent. It is much less the general science of morals, the reasoned conception of duty, than the specific spiritual direction suited to the confessional. To an unsophisticated student, like myself, this knowledge I was acquiring of practical morality presented itself as the art of skilfully avoiding sin, while following a path on which one was bound to encounter simply endless possibilities of transgressing. That manner of interpreting duty filled me with confusion as completely as the Catholic fashion of understanding truth. Was I able to justify myself in face of so complicated a set of rules? Was I sure of not having failed to keep some of them? Should I be able to conform to them all in every respect? Assuredly my past was free enough from evil conduct, and in the present I was conscious only of a sincere and deep desire for the good; I felt no temptation to low standards, and especially no protest in my nature against the requirements of the sacred calling in which I was about to engage. I could, then, be quite tranquil, and yield myself to the grace of God.

However, I was anything but tranquil. I was even disturbed on one point which, in common sense, should have given me no anxiety. Nothing could have been more innocent than my habitual thoughts, feelings and conduct. My lonely childhood had been pure; the high school at St. Dizier had exposed me to no evil suggestions; the awakening of the sex-consciousness was retarded in my case by the delicacy of my physical endowment; and the prospect of ecclesiastical celibacy held no terrors for me. In fact, it repelled me not at all, for the good reason that I was not then able to measure the full scope and weight of this grave obligation. Its significance did not dawn upon me until later, when I was already a priest. No actual temptation coming to trouble me, I was fretted by mere phantoms of alluring thoughts. I dreaded yielding even to the imagination of that which was forbidden me. Yet, like all mankind, inevitably the idea forced itself upon me, since there is no escaping it. I met it perhaps more frequently than some, because my books of theology were obsessed by it. The matter is a most delicate one to discuss. The least unchaste of minds naturally responds to certain suggestions; the angels alone, if angels there be, can flatter themselves that they never once held a dubious thought for even an instant's involuntary pleasure in it. I should have wished to escape entirely; in point of fact, I came so near doing so that it is not worth dwelling upon.

On this score my director could hardly suppress a smile, as though my scruples witnessed to an excess of virtue.

They bore witness nevertheless against a moral discipline as false as was the intellectual discipline I had encountered in the study of theology. The essential principle of morality—a generous aspiration toward the good, not the meticulous obedience to a set of rules drawn up by experts—must be found in conscience, not outside of it. The unrest that I have described took flight when I came later to grasp what the profession of celibacy, strictly observed, demanded. Having always been loyal to this obligation of my office, I can now discuss it with no other concern than that of truth. In a sense, the scruples of my student years were empty; in part, no doubt, they betokened a degree of nervous depression and mental fatigue. None the less, they were in the main justified. The Catholic Church requires her priests to be something less than men. The true chastity is not what she teaches to be such. The false ideal which she upholds leads to the opposite of purity. Not that the rule of celibacy is very often violated. It is not possible to register a definitive judgment on the subject, for want of exhaustive data; but I am inclined to think that, among the French Catholic clergy, the rule is disobeyed more often than a majority of the laity suppose, though less constantly than is imagined by harsh opponents of the Church. My opinion is that an abnormal life, so far from leading to true chastity, opens the way to a perpetual ferment of impurity. It may be granted that the

senses and the imagination of those who preserve
their continence are in general under better control
than in the married state. I did not bring about my
exclusion from the Church in order to take to myself
a wife; but I do not pretend to any excess of merit
on this account over those who have themselves
defrocked so that they may be free to marry. If
they consider that the Catholic Church has no more
reason or justification for imposing celibacy upon its
priests, given the conditions under which they are
led to promise and required to observe it, than Cybele
and Attis had a legitimate reason for requiring of
their hierophants the well-known mutilation of their
manhood, they are perfectly right.

V

I sought a remedy for my inward distresses in exercises of devotion, hoping that in the end God might
grant me deliverance. I continued to pray with
fervor, and found my associates among the most
exemplary of my fellow-seminarians. There was in
the institution a chapter of the Third Order of Saint
Francis of Assisi; this I joined, and wore for several
years, under the dress of the secular clergy, the
Franciscan scapulary with the cord about the waist
—a small cord of symbolic meaning, tied in three
knots, as I remember it. I still feel the most cordial
regard for my classmates; they occupy at the present
time the best parishes in the diocese, and one is canon
of the cathedral.

As our regular courses were far from occupying
the whole of our time, I undertook in addition cer-

tain private studies. Abbé Ludot had done nothing
to prejudice us against the Scholastic theology, and
as St. Thomas Aquinas was held in high regard, I
procured his *Summa Theologica* and his *Summa
contra Gentiles.* After reading various treatises on
the Scholastic philosophy, I plunged boldly into the
study' of Aquinas, analyzing the first part of the
Summa Theologica, article by article, and meditating long on the ideas of the Angelic Doctor concerning the Trinity. It may naturally be judged that,
without a guide, I could not derive much profit from
such researches, and this was the case. Nevertheless,
these exercises in logical subtlety quickened my
reasoning powers, though the final outcome was not
a fortunate one. I dared not at that time avow it
frankly, even to myself, but the speculations of Saint
Thomas on the Trinity—the mystery of a God who
united three persons in one essence, the whole deduced from two definitions, that of essence and that
of person, conceived so as to fit the case and adapted
arbitrarily to the traditional dogma—had upon me
the effect of a huge logomachy. In place of enrich-
ing my mind, these speculations left, as it were, a
void, and their total effect was only to add to my
inner confusion and distress concerning the invisible
Object of faith.

However, a degree of solace now came to me. Our
professor of Holy Scripture had commended to us
the study of the Bible, and had suggested that a
knowledge of Hebrew would be useful in its pursuit.
Some time before, a priest who had been sent to
Germany by Bishop Meignan, but not retained in

the seminary, had inaugurated a course in Hebrew. One of his pupils had communicated a reading knowledge of the language to one of the upper classmen of my day. I went to school to this fellow-student, procuring a Hebrew Bible, and an elementary grammar and lexicon; then, having very soon reached the end of my companion's acquirements, I went on with the work alone. At once I had a sense of accomplishing something. As the Greek Bible is a text in favor with the Church, I acquired at the same time the Sistine edition of the Septuagint. Thus I puzzled out the Hebrew of Genesis, comparing it with the Greek of the Septuagint and the Latin of the Vulgate. Having no critical commentary to work with, I could make no troublesome discoveries, but the comparison of the three versions interested me exceedingly. I supposed, in all good faith, that it would aid me to a better comprehension of the inspired volume, and I was far from suspecting that this same process, applied with a more exact method than I was then able to improvise, would lead me ultimately to a different conception of Biblical inspiration from that of the official Church.

Three years passed by, at the end of which I was to be ordained to the sub-diaconate, a step implying the vow of perpetual celibacy. For a long time I had looked forward to taking that vow, and yet I questioned, in spite of myself, whether my life would not thereby be thrown away. Even at this critical moment, I did not dream of doing the obvious thing and returning to a secular vocation. I believed, and willed to believe, that Catholicism was the absolute truth. My director showed not the slightest hesitation in advising me to take the decisive step. That, however, did not prevent me from passing the night of the 29th to the 30th of June, 1878, the night before my ordination, without a wink of sleep. Stretched on my cot, in my poor, bare room, I went over all the arguments that I knew for the truth of Christianity. As ever, the demonstration seemed to elude me, the more closely I pursued it. I could not detect the flaw in the argument; still I suspected that it lay somewhere in the premises. When morning broke, I was in a state of exhaustion. I could think no more; but my will remained inflexible. I was resolved to belong to God, to Christ, to the Church. When the Bishop addressed to the subjects for ordination the liturgical admonition: "While it is still time, reflect; until now, you are free; . . . if you persist in your holy purpose, in the name of Our Lord, approach!"—I went forward without a tremor. We bent low before the altar, and litanies of the saints were recited over us. The tragic error of my life was consummated!

In the September following, I was designated by Bishop Meignan, on presentation by Abbé Roussel, to pursue further studies under the newly established faculty of theology at the Catholic Institute in Paris. I had not expected anything of the kind, and left the Châlons seminary regretfully. For one thing, I was in a condition of extreme nervous debility. At first blush, the Catholic Institute did not greatly appeal to me. A Jesuit, Father Jovene, taught there a fairly abstruse Scholasticism; Abbé Paulin Martin, a learned Syriac scholar, was beginning his work as professor of Holy Scripture, and found nothing more to his purpose than a reiteration of the theories of Cardinal Franzelin on the formation of the Biblical canon; Abbé Duchesne taught the history of Christian origins. Still young, he had not yet fully assimilated his learning, already vast; behind me at his lectures daring spirits murmured that he knew too much. I was overwhelmed by this first shock of real erudition. Returning to Ambrières for the New Year's recess at the beginning of 1879, I was obliged to consult the doctor who had watched over me from infancy. He ordered me to take a month's complete rest, and forbade my return to Paris for the present.

I went back instead for some weeks to the seminary at Châlons, and was there ordained deacon on March 29th. The Bishop decided in June that I must become a priest, and be inducted into the parochial ministry, since I had not justified the plan formed for me of going on with higher studies. I was twenty-two years and four months old when he ordained me on June 29th, with a Papal dispensation on account of falling short of the canonical age. Eight days later he preferred me to the pastorate of Broussy-le-Grand, a God-forsaken hamlet between Fère-Champenoise and Sézanne. The parish was one of the least desirable in the diocese, the practice of religion being almost extinct there. In all probability the officials wished me to realize that it did not pay to fall ill in disarrangement of their purposes.

In my retirement, I began to build up. My mind could not yet recover its calm, but I improved physically. During the terrible winter of 1879-80, the church was often extremely cold, but I stood it well. I saw but little of the other pastors of the region. My parishioners were not a little proud of having the youngest priest in France, but they did not show it by coming to church, except at All Saints. The village teacher who led the music, a pious school-mistress who brought her young pupils with her, and a few old women, made up the congregation to which my Sunday homilies were addressed. These discourses were none the less appreciated because of their extreme brevity. I pursued, meanwhile, my former studies under better conditions of health. At the end of six months, Abbé Roussel, who felt pity for my isolation, arranged a transfer to the parish of Landricourt, near Ambrières, where I was installed on February 2, 1880.

My health continued to improve, and I began to consider what future might be awaiting me. Abbé Roussel died not long after my arrival at Landricourt. In my last year at the seminary, he had given me every token of confidence and sympathy. His purpose, I have no doubt, was, after a certain experience of the parochial ministry, to recall me to his side as a professor. I could have liked nothing better, but his death put an end to such hopes. The life of a country parson did not suit me. My tastes inclined toward religious studies, which I pursued as I was able, not solely in view of an eventual professorship but because even then, in my naïveté, I was meditating the composition of a large work in which I proposed to demonstrate, from history and from philosophy, the truth of Catholicism. In other words, this meant that I was forever preoccupied with trying to prove this truth to myself!

It appeared to me then that my only chance of a future lay in the resumption of the project which had been abandoned at the end of 1878, that is, to return to the Catholic Institute in Paris and take the necessary theological degrees whereby I might give satisfaction to Bishop Meignan and thus impose myself upon his choice. To obtain the required authorization took a certain amount of diplomacy. Before soliciting an audience with the Bishop, I besought Abbé Monier, Superior of the seminary at the Catholic Institute, and Abbé Duchesne, with whom I had kept up relations, to write to him in my favor. Then I presented myself at the episcopal residence and asked permission to return to the Catholic Institute without cost to the diocese. Bishop Meignan received me kindly, and some days after, on May 10, 1881, he gave the leave which I had sought. Two days later I was in Paris.

I have since learned what sort of idea the Bishop then had of me. A year from that time, when the Rector of the Catholic Institute wished to attach me to his establishment, the Bishop of Châlons readily consented. However, encountering Abbé Duchesne, he could not conceal his astonishment. "You wanted a priest who came from my seminary; he must have a terribly limited intelligence." "Oh, not in the least," replied Duchesne, "no more limited than my own!" [1]

[1] See Appendix I.

CHAPTER II

AT THE CATHOLIC INSTITUTE IN PARIS

I

A S was natural, it was to Abbé Duchesne that I
turned for guidance in my course of study. It
is needless to add that he did not incline me toward
the Scholastic theology, which, for that matter, was
no longer taught at the Catholic Institute in Paris.
Father Jovene, forced by Duchesne's laurels to
bestir himself, had taken up the study of the Church
Fathers, and flattered himself that he was construct-
ing his theology on a solid underpinning of patristic
tradition. What he taught us was not pure Scholasticism, strictly logical in doctrine and deduction;
nor was it what is called "positive" theology, an
analysis and co-ordination of the patristic testimony,
applied to an exposition of the Christian dogmas;
still less was it the history of those dogmas. It was
a richly documented theology, distinctly original in
form, but not enough so in substance to make it
heterodox. The good Father had entitled his treatise
on grace: *De vita deiformi,* "Concerning the deiform
life," and he developed this theme before us in-
terminably. I was already past finding nutriment
in this sort of thing. Abbé Martin was engaged in
the futility of demonstrating the Mosaic authorship
of the Pentateuch, preliminary to losing himself in

the maze of New Testament textual criticism, where he was nevertheless acute enough to recognize the inauthenticity of the text of the so-called "three heavenly witnesses" in the First Epistle of John. That was his most daring stroke. I could not interest myself in a course so little enlightening. There was still Duchesne.

I saw him often and we soon became the best of friends. He was devoted to all his pupils, and especially attracted to me. He counselled me in my preparation for the baccalaureate in theology, which I achieved toward the end of June, 1881. Then, in order to conserve my time and strength, he persuaded the Rector, Monsignor d'Hulst, to allow my two months' attendance at the end of 1878 and the months of May and June, 1881, to be counted as a full year, so that I might be admitted in October to my first examination as licentiate, or candidate for the degree in theology, for which two years' attendance at lectures with examination at the end of each year were usually required. I prepared for this examination in the vacation, making use of note-books loaned by my fellow-students, and for the course in church history Abbé Duchesne allowed me the use of his own manuscript. The examination thus hurriedly prepared for had a totally unlooked-for outcome.

Abbé Martin had fallen ill, and was obliged to omit his courses during the year 1881-82. For the exposition of Scripture, his place was taken by Abbé Vigouroux, whose lectures we followed twice a week at the Seminary of Saint Sulpice. But a substitute must also be found for the course in Hebrew. Hebrew scholars, however, were not numerous in the diocese of Paris. Abbé Duchesne had a sudden inspiration, and reminded the Rector that I had shown exceptional command of Hebrew in my October examination. Monsignor d'Hulst took the hint, and it was decided that I should conduct that year's course in Hebrew for my fellow-students, with the grade of Instructor. Also, there was a private understanding between us that this course should remain in my hands after Abbé Martin resumed his teaching. So it was that Paris began to draw me away from Châlons. I was not disinclined to the change. However, Bishop Meignan would have to be consulted before anything could be finally settled. The life tenure of the Catholic Institute seemed to me far from assured, and the stir that was already being made regarding Duchesne was a warning to me that the situation had its perils. I had kept my old love for the seminary at Châlons, and intuitively felt that there my lot would be more untroubled.

In the lectures of Abbé Vigouroux I experienced a severe disappointment, of which Duchesne was the unsuspecting cause. When we parted for the vacation in the summer of 1881, he put into my hands the volume of Tischendorf's classical edition of the New Testament containing the Gospels, that I might gain some idea of the processes of textual criticism. But I went beyond his intention, not satisfying myself with observing the various readings of the manuscripts, but comparing the Gospel narratives with one another. I was astounded, the farther I progressed, never to have noticed the contradictions before. It became clearly apparent to me, as it must to every one who does not wilfully blind himself to the evidence, that these writings require to be as freely interpreted as they were freely composed. It is vain to treat, as rigorously historical, texts that are obviously not so in the least. My temerity, if such it was, did not yet reach the point of contesting the substantial accuracy of the facts, especially of those that have a place in the creeds of the Church. For instance, I saw clearly that the narratives of the birth of Christ in Matthew and Luke must have arisen from distinct sources, and are not capable of being reconciled so as to make consistent history. But I did not venture at this time to deny what, in these accounts, constitutes the substance of the Catholic faith, i.e., the virgin birth of the Savior. The same held good of the narratives of the resurrection; the gospel accounts are not reliable, yet I continued to admit that Jesus rose again after his death. It was an insecure position, but I was not, and could not then be, aware of it. What fell away from me at this juncture was the theological interpretation of Scriptural inspiration. I perceived that the sacred books were written as all books are written, only with less exactness and care than many. If the Holy Spirit had entered in, it could not be to transform them into historical sources of the first rank. This discovery was in no way disconcerting to me; on the contrary, my uneasiness of mind vanished in proportion as I advanced to a firm footing of critical certitude.

The instruction of Abbé Vigouroux ran counter to these elementary discoveries. That year the learned Sulpician was expounding the history of Biblical rationalism—i.e., of critical exegesis—to the sole end of demonstrating its aberrations and its criminal revolt against tradition. The lecturer was, and is yet, the leading French Catholic apologist for the Bible, but I must say that his instruction and his writings did more to turn me away from orthodox opinions in this regard than all the rationalists put together, Renan included.

It may be doubted, for that matter, whether he has rendered any lasting service to the cause he has undertaken to defend. In refuting the positions of criticism, it is inevitable that those positions shall first be made known; and, as this popular writer has very inadequately refuted them, notwithstanding his good will to do so—because criticism is not so easily refuted!—he has simply paraded before many minds the weaknesses of the Catholic position. The development of Biblical criticism from the days of Richard Simon is something more than a congeries of errors. Criticism has indulged in mistaken conjectures and fallen into exaggerations. But it has succeeded, none the less, in finally discrediting the older type of theological interpretation, and in placing the Bible on a level with other ancient sources. It has fully demonstrated its human character and gained for it the standing of an ancient literature. No matter if the work of criticism still remains incomplete, and if it must continue to perfect itself, now and forever; the rout of tradition is none the less irremediable.

My full realization of this I owe to Abbé Vigouroux. What to him were infidel objections, deserve rather to be characterized in many cases as sober realities, in contradiction to the abstract theses of the theologians. His answer to the supposed objections was not invariably conclusive. One found it easy, for example, to abandon all belief in the flood of Genesis after hearing the professor explain gravely that the passages attributed to the Yahwist writer (after the source in which God is given the name Yahwe) are a description of what was going on in the Eternal mind, while the passages called Elohist (after the source which employs as the divine name the collective noun Elohim) have regard to the revelation of these thoughts to Noah, and their practical execution; that, the flood covering only the then inhabited portion of the earth, the ark was plenty large enough to contain all the animal species known to Noah; that a calculation had been made, and the ark shown to be capable of enclosing six thousand, six hundred and sixty-six species, allowing so much cubic space to each couple—and much more of the same sort! I could not endure this childishness. To swallow it, one must have made up his mind beforehand to accept any reasons, however puerile, to buttress a foregone conclusion. I did not then realize that faith protects itself by an unconscious partisanship. When the partisanship has become conscious, the faith is no longer entire.

Perhaps it was under the influence of Abbe Vigouroux's lectures that I wrote the following sentences which I find among my papers, dated March 8, 1882:

Line of conduct.—On the one hand, routine calling itself tradition; on the other, novelty calling itself truth. The former no more stands for faith than the latter authentically for science. These two attitudes are in conflict as to the Bible, and I wonder if anyone in the world is able to hold the scales even between faith and science. If so, he shall be my master.—Broad and fair-minded exposition of the decisions of the Church on the inspiration, the canon, and the interpretation of Scripture. Entire hospitality to philology, to the study of the sources, without prejudgment; frank and straightforward exegesis, having regard to the oriental genius and to the natural character and supernatural mission of the Hebrew people.—Equal danger of according, and of refusing, too much to rationalism. Either we cease to be Christians, or we deserve to be taken for dullards and men of bad faith. *Here I find no guide into that middle way;* at least, I feel so, and I do not think in this that I am reacting too much from the tendencies of so and so. I must simply fare on under the eye of Providence. O, my God, give me twenty years of health, of patience, of labor, with that spirit of discernment, of sincerity, of humility, which admits of Christian learning without peril to the scholar, to the edification of the Church and the discomfiture of her enemies!

Thus, in my very first year's sojourn in Paris, I had the presentiment of a place to be taken in Catholic scholarship, and of a great task to be accomplished. "But to hold that place, I must have the ability; and am I able?" I wrote in my journal. I found the mission full of peril for the missionary, not by reason of external difficulties, but because there is "a knowledge that diminishes and destroys faith." I asked myself if I had not better go back into the country. "Perhaps," I said to myself, "it would be a good thing for a few years to get away from this Babylon where one's head is so easily turned." But, the Bishop of Châlons having indicated during May his intention of giving me charge of a general course in theology at the reopening in October, Monsignor d'Hulst wrote to him, requesting that I might remain permanently at the Catholic Institute. Bishop Meignan consented, all the more readily as the mere announcement of his project had stirred up opposition among the professors of his seminary, some of whom had scented in me the beginnings of heresy.

If I was already liberal, I was hardly as yet revolutionary. For, on the first of July, having returned to Ambrières for the vacation, I wrote in my journal, after making some reflections on the hostile attitude of the Church toward science: "As to reforming the present state of things, if nothing is more needed, nothing requires more prudence, more sustained endeavor, more kindly and persuasive earnestness. No satire; our enemies will only repay in kind. No equivocal insinuations; for these disturb the security of faith. No unworthy recriminations. Responsibility for the situation does not rest with any one in particular, and it would be foolish to offend in a body all those whom one desires to convert." The next day I was at Châlons, and there heard, without taking in its double meaning, this remark from Bishop Meignan: "If religion were not something divine, it would long since have been crushed under the weight of our ignorance." And the good Bishop insisted on the diplomacy that one had to use in dealing with a clergy so little enlightened; instancing Abbé Duchesne, and the extreme freedom of his language, more disquieting even than his free opinions. Against this comment, I did not see my way to protest.

II

At the opening of the academic year, 1882-83, I was excused from further studies in theology, but went on with my instructorship in Hebrew. Following the wishes of Monsignor d'Hulst, I entered the *École Pratique des Hautes Études* to take lectures in Assyriology and Egyptology. But I soon gave up the latter, as less closely related to Bible study. Arthur Amiaud, an admirable and devoted master, taught the former. I was alone in his class, and he gave me two hours weekly. This continued for several years, and was the means of enabling me to establish a lectureship in Assyriology in 1886 at the Catholic Institute.

As I had been plunged into the teaching of Hebrew with only an elementary knowledge of the language, I also followed regularly for three years Renan's course at the *Collège de France*. His method of teaching Hebrew in well known. He prepared for it little, if at all. At that time, he was expounding the text of the Psalms. He would take a verse, read it, translate it, read the Greek of the Septuagint for comparison, cite the conjectures of the Oratorian Houbigant or of some modern critic in emendation of the text, weighing every word, so to speak, and permitting himself all manner of digressions and repetitions. His opinion was that a professor of the *Collège de France* ought to work out his results before his hearers, and this he did before us, going but a little more slowly, I imagine, than in his own study. All told, his course made an extremely good introduction to the textual criticism of the Old Testament. He often digressed into related fields, as I have said, but mostly confined himself to that.

At this period, Renan, who cherished no enmity toward any living being, was still to me an enemy of the Church. I did not risk myself in his lecture-room without taking due precautions. My confessor, Abbé Monier, was consulted, and very sensibly urged that to take lectures for a time at the *Collège de France* was for me a patriotic duty. Abbé Duchesne accompanied me to the first lecture I attended. Priests were quite often to be seen there, but they went mostly from curiosity, sometimes camping at the door of the hall, and leaving when the professor said something that upset their pre-conceived ideas, which no doubt he occasionally did deliberately. I sat tranquilly in my corner, noting down what was pertinent to my use, and letting the rest go. What Renan had to say about the composition of the Biblical books contained few surprises for myself, and I laughed with the others when on one occasion a tall ecclesiastic, much per-turbed at hearing that Jeremiah might have had something to do with the composition of Deuteron-omy, suddenly fled, slamming the door behind him.

My ambition was some day to vanquish Renan with his own weapons,—using against him the very principles of criticism that I was learning there at his feet. I observe, in my notes of 1883, that I took great pains to forearm myself against all the influences, internal or external, that might tend to dull my love of truth or my reverence for religion. In my meditation on February 6th, I exhorted myself to sincerity and courage: "Confronted by new truth, do not search for expedients to be yourself persuaded, or to persuade others, that there is any necessary conflict with received ideas. Do not undertake, merely from dread of making a disturbance, to find the truth to be what is generally accepted as such." On the 10th, I counselled myself to moderation and sobriety: "attend in good faith, without distrust or levity. Voltaire could laugh at the Bible, or at the naïveté of its commentators; to us this is not permitted. The Bible is our book, and those in the past who interpreted it as best they could—no doubt at times awkwardly—are our fathers. The concerns of faith should not be treated lightly, any more than those of morals. There are topics in morality that cannot be joked about with impunity." To assure my independence of mind and character was one of my leading preoccupations. Abbé Duchesne would gladly have taken me into his house as a boarder; but I declined his kind offer. Notwithstanding such a brave show of independence, I felt myself totally incompetent for the undertaking that seemed to be thrust upon me. On March 9th, I wrote two lines: *"Tu quis es?*—A faint streak of courage against a background of disenchant-ment."

Each year, at the beginning of the long vacation, which I passed with my relatives, at Ambrières, I set apart several days for a sort of mental self-ex-amination, in which I undertook to strike a trial balance with respect to my thought, my faith, my studies and my religious experiences. It has already been made apparent that, since 1881, the traditional idea of an inspired Scripture had to be charged among the losses. In 1883, the entire system of the Church's doctrine and apologetic came up for assess-ment. "At the present hour, the Church is an obstacle to the intellectual development of human-ity," so I wrote at the beginning of my retreat, on July 6th. With this as a starting-point, I drew up a general critique of Catholic doctrine, in the form of a dialogue in which I voiced my objections and the Church responded. As was natural, I opposed the data of history to what the theologians teach re-garding the revealed character and the immutability of dogmas. I insisted that the beliefs of Catholicism had become an abstract system which no longer had any hold on intelligent minds, even among believers, and which were in defiance of what is most certainly known about the origins of the Bible and of the Jewish and Christian religions. The Church, as I conceived it ideally, replied, incidentally making im-portant concessions. This ideal Church said:

Perhaps my doctors in this present century have been inadequate to their task and have not appreciated that they were allowed to abandon the old formulas, that indeed they might almost forget them, in order to preserve to the world the truth of which I am the custodian. God will provide me, I hope, with men suited to this work and then you cannot longer accuse me of ignorance.

The rôle of these men—so I replied—will be more exacting than you seem to realize, O princess of an immutable verity. It is not your formulas that you must translate for us into a speech intelligible to the men of our age; it is rather your ideas themselves, your absolute affirmations, your theory of the universe, the conception you have of your own history, that you must renew, rectify and reconstruct.

But, as if I dreaded pressing the discussion too far in this direction, although my enumeration of the difficulties was almost exactly the same as I should make today, I excused the Church from further answers, and our colloquy drifted into an exchange of ideas touching the nature of God, in which we came to agreement on an idealistic theory of the universe that undoubtedly would be qualified by orthodoxy as evolutionary pantheism. My faith in the Church as the moral leader of mankind remained unshaken, and I was still too little convinced of my critical results to employ them as conclusive arguments against the substantial truth of her dogmas. Above all, I was so profoundly attached to the Church that it was repugnant to me to break with her way of thinking, and for the same reason I did not press my own to its logical conclusions.

There was here a latent contradiction, which the progress of my studies and of my relations with the existing Church—something different enough from my ideal—could not fail to make finally apparent.

In the course of the academic year 1883-84, I prepared, for the degree of Doctor of Theology, a thesis on the doctrine of inspiration according to the Bible, and to the ancient ecclesiastical writers from the Apostolic Fathers down to Tertullian. Monsignor d'Hulst had approved of my subject, and I had carefully conned my texts. In order that my Latin might not be too barbarous, I took the trouble to read Cicero's treatises, *De natura deorum* and *De divinatione*. The work finished, I carried it to the Rector, who wished to examine it before the professors of dogmatic theology had a chance to see it. He read it carefully, and handed back the manuscript, telling me not to show it to any one, and that its publication was impossible to contemplate. It was not that he considered my results fallacious; on the contrary, he affirmed that my idea of inspiration was in some ways the only tenable one. But it was important not to compromise the faculty of theology; the institution was closely watched by self-constituted inquisitors; there were already too many protests on the part of extremists against Abbé Duchesne; as I recall it, Monsignor d'Hulst had himself received an intimation from Leo XIII that the course in philosophy which he had inaugurated at the Catholic Institute must conform to the doctrine of St. Thomas Aquinas; in fine, my ideas might be admirable, but it would not do to divulge them— they would be only material for the Index.

What, then, was there in my Latin thesis so daring in its radicalism? A very simple, almost elementary, idea from which was drawn an eminently Catholic conclusion—at least from the point of view of an ideal Catholicism—and yet destructive of the real, Scholastic and Roman, Catholicism. In a few clear-cut phrases of the preface and the conclusion, I said that the inspiration of the Scriptures, having to do with existing writings, capable of analysis, was a belief to be controlled by the study of the books in question; that the psychology of the inspired authors was visibly the same as that of all men who write; that the element of the divine which might be added by inspiration changed not at all the nature of the writings to which it pertained, and, for example, did not transform a pseudonymous book, like the *Wisdom of Solomon,* into an authentic work of Solomon; that, if the revelation was contained in the Bible, and without error, as was declared by the Vatican Council, it must be under a relative form, proportioned to the time and the environment in which these books emerged, and to the general knowledge of that time and environment; that the insufficiency of the Scriptures as a rule of faith proceeded from their very nature, and that the magistracy of the Church had for its object the adaptation of ancient doctrine to ever new needs, by disengaging the substance of truth from its superannuated form; finally that authors like Irenæus and Tertullian had had a presentiment of this when they had opposed to the extravagant exegesis of the Gnostics, not the letter of the Bible rationally interpreted, but the ecclesiastical rule of faith, applied as a rule of interpretation to the Bible itself.

These were the ideas that, for the moment, had

attracted Monsignor d'Hulst, and had at the same time appalled him, because of the agitation that they must inevitably excite in the theological world. I do not mean to imply that he was prepared to accept them on his own part. He was not displeased to find me capable of framing such a theory, and was lavish in his congratulations. But he went no farther. I do not believe that he was then aware of a consequence of my premises which, for myself, I had quite fully recognized, namely: that the teaching of the Church, even in its most solemn utterances, was attended by the same relativity as that of Scripture—the word of Councils and of Popes not being above the word of God, but in point of fact manifesting itself under identical conditions. Monsignor d'Hulst came to perceive this later, and, in 1893, in the course of the theological tornado that raged over his article on "The Biblical Question," he remarked to me that my idea of "relativity" was calculated to bring the entire Scholastic and theological edifice down in ruins. He was right. That idea entirely undermined the absolute character of the Jewish and Christian revelation, of the ecclesiastical dogmas and of Papal infallibility. If Monsignor d'Hulst had been cognizant of all this in 1884, he could not have restrained himself from telling me so.

One morning in 1893, in the sacristy of the Church of the Carmelites, the excellent Abbé de Broglie asked me where I had acquired these notions, which had the same effect on his mind as on the Rector's. As the locality was not suited to an elaborate explanation, I could only reply by placing my finger on my forehead. The fact is that, while everything seemed to lead up to it, I had not really borrowed my conception anywhere. It need hardly be stated that Abbé Duchesne has never been guilty of speculations of this order and that, on this score, he is completely innocent of all my heresies. He has never made the least pretense of reforming theology, nor constituted himself the advocate of any such reform; and my theory, however little it might be worth, however dangerous it might prove to be, was distinctly theological and apologetic. It must have been original to some extent, for I had come upon it in none of my reading. My studies as a whole had led me to approximate to it, as well as the endeavor to adjust my critical conclusions to the faith which I was so anxious to conserve. Certain ideas of Renan's may probably have aided me to arrive at it, though they were scarcely more recognizable in the result than were the Catholic beliefs with which I started out. It was a result of subconscious gestation, not of conscious reflection to the end of building a system. The basic idea of my thesis on Biblical Inspiration flashed upon me suddenly in the middle of a night when I was sleeping poorly, in the early part of the year 1883. Anyone who chooses may believe, if he likes, that the source of the suggestion was diabolical!

My thesis having suffered sentence of death, I might have drawn the conclusion that my ideas were not workable. For that matter, it would have been little surprising if I had simply despaired of their future. But in the vacation of 1884 I felt exactly as in the previous year. It was otherwise in 1885, and especially in 1886. In these two years, I kept no record of my inner musings. I find, in a note dated November 15, 1886, the following:

For several months past, I have not been able to arouse in myself the slightest religious feeling. Since my second year in the seminary, habits of piety have been steadily counteracted in me by the dread of submitting to illusion. Perhaps that fear has been a weakness, but it no longer has a bearing, having totally lost its object.— I have hardly a thing to look forward to. I am determined to work and to serve the Church, which created, and to which pertains, the education of the human race. Without breaking with her tradition, and on condition of retaining its spirit in preference to its letter, she remains an essential institution, and the most divine upon earth. She has capitalized the subtilties of the theologians, but she has also gathered up principles of order, of devotion, of virtue, which guarantee the happiness of the family and the peace of society. To attempt today a reorganization of the moral life apart from Christ and his Church would be utopian. That much in the ecclesiastical discipline is superannuated; that the forms of our worship are not wholly in accord with the needs of the present; that the literal sense of the theological formulas becomes constantly less credible—all this I see more and more distinctly, as I come to know better the past of religion and of humanity. It may be that I deceive myself, and I remain entirely disposed, so far as concerns my own will, to admit the contrary of what I think, if that contrary can be shown to be true.—The interior conflict that I have undergone for ten years past, and which has only ceased in these recent months, has greatly exhausted me. I shall never recover my youthful resiliency of spirit. Well for me if only a little strength is left!—All the freedom I have to think my own thoughts does not compensate for the restraints on my freedom of action imposed by my position.

A sense of inner desolation speaks in these lines, a desolation unsuspected by any one, and one that was long enduring. I did not begin again to jot down my impressions until 1892. If I abstained from writing, it was because I found it too painful; and also because in certain hours of sadness my feelings were quite beyond expression. Nothing out of the ordinary occurred in 1885 and 1886. I forged ahead with my studies, almost without respite. I had made it a duty to read, in the course of each year, the whole Bible in the original tongues; in addition to which I devoted a great deal of time to Assyriology. I had transformed my second-year course in Hebrew into a course in exegesis, for which I made scrupulously thorough preparation, consulting Reuss's Bible Commentary and the best of the German writers on the texts that I had to explain; avoiding ready-made opinions and finished systems. It was not through having merely assimilated an alien body of doctrine that I gradually drew away from Catholic beliefs; rather because, little by little, without my own volition, my researches themselves detached me. Resolved to know whatever there was to be known, and unwilling deliberately to close my eyes to facts that were inconsistent with the received dogmas, I ended by admitting them to be facts. For a long while, I calculated that it was possible, notwithstanding the progressive abandonment of my former convictions, to remain in faithful communion with the Church. But it became in the end impossible to cherish this illusion any longer. What I was beginning to believe regarding the Bible, Jesus, the Christian principles and their origin, was the absolute negation of any supernatural character for religion whatsoever. Sooner or later I must come to the clear perception of this, and then I should be forced to admit to myself that the cause to which I had sacrificed my life was constituted, for the most part, of pure mirage.

The evidence came over me with overwhelming force on a certain day near the beginning of the session of 1885-86, when I had a long conversation, in my little apartment on the *Rue Littré,* with a friend who is now dead, on the legendary character of the Gospel narratives. This friend was the only person to whom I had ever opened myself freely on questions of this kind, for the reason that he was suffering, as I was, from discoveries that were thrust under his eyes. Neither Abbé Duchesne nor any of my comrades or connections knew anything of the drama that was going on within. I may have discussed, with one or another, problems of Biblical criticism or of theology; none, however, shared my intimate thoughts. Not that I had become either a resigned or a scoffing skeptic. That was never my tendency, although later, in connection with *The Gospel and the Church,* certain ecclesiastical personages whom I had not dreamed of honoring with my confidence took pains to attribute it to me. If in this they inferred, by way of conjecture, my feelings from their own, I regret very much for them that this circumstance should have lowered me in their esteem.

I was far from having lost all moral faith. What

had now departed was the ardor of enthusiasm that had supported me through a host of difficulties, which began the very first day I entered the seminary. That fine youthful confidence had succumbed with the idea that had originally inspired it. I had been able to blind myself, at least half-way, to my own state of mind, to the bearing of the essential conclusions of Biblical criticism, to the prospect of conciliating these with the traditional dogmas without abandoning the substance of the latter. Now I could not conceal from myself that the situation was other than I had imagined it; that I was out of sympathy with the trend of Catholic thought; that if one proposed to interpret the current dogmas in accordance with modern knowledge and the modern spirit, a more or less enlarged and renovated explanation would not suffice, dogmas like the virgin birth of Christ and his resurrection simply vanishing into thin air when once their objective certainty was gone; that a reshaping of the entire Catholic system was inevitable; and that, such a task being beyond human power, an insignificant professor of Hebrew and of Assyriology would be utterly out of his mind to undertake it! *No thoroughfare:* such was the painful *impasse* against which the dream of my youth had been rudely shattered; and some time was needed to enable me to regain the impulse to fruitful activity.

Those of a strictly logical cast of mind may naturally wonder why, not only the idea, but also the duty, of quitting the Church did not present itself to my thoughts. The idea could hardly help coming to me, but the obligation by which I felt myself held fast was that of staying in the Church. The real reason for this was that I still remained attached to it with the full force of my nature. Furthermore, I reminded myself that there can be no obligation to change the direction of one's entire existence at the bidding of speculative opinions which do not directly affect the conduct of life. One does not forsake an institution like the Catholic Church, I told myself, because it persists too obstinately in upholding the authenticity of a few books that are more or less apocryphal. No doubt other matters than literary problems were involved. The most essential beliefs were equally in question. But what are beliefs, even, if not symbols which derive their value from their moral efficacy? Was not this moral efficacy the one thing needful? Must one break with the Church because she was in arrears in relation to the scientific movement of the times? Or was science itself able to replace the Church in her moral mission? Certain men of light and leading might affirm it, but it had never been proved, and could it be? My own knowledge was still in the green stage and had no call to assume arrogant airs. The advance of my studies would certainly not lead me back to exactly the point from which I had started, but who could say whether they might not enable me to approximate it? I would settle down, then, a scholar in the service of the Church, sadly disabused of the great hope for an intellectual rebirth among the clergy that I had nursed for some years past, and that had been, moreover, almost officially, one of the reasons for founding the Catholic Institute; resolved to restrict myself to the domain of objective fact, as Abbé Duchesne held it was possible to do; giving myself unreservedly to the study of texts and to sacred philology, without preoccupation in behalf of theology or of apologetics.

If I did not succeed in keeping strictly within the limits of this well-meant and plausible program, it was, in the first place, because it proved to be impracticable in such a field as that of exegesis and Biblical criticism, where one encounters unavoidably, at every step, the theology and tradition of the Church; it was, indeed, because, under the pressure of circumstances, I allowed myself to be recaptured to some extent by my earlier ideal. Almost in spite of myself, I was led on to attempt the impossible, and it became necessary for the Church to impart to me, by a succession of violent censures, the knowledge that a priest has no right to be a Catholic merely in name; that his thought no more belongs to him than his volition; that Roman Catholicism proposes to dominate modern society and not to adapt itself to it; lastly, as Cardinal Merry del Val wrote to the Bishop of Langres in January, 1908, that my "continuance in the Church" was a "scandal" impossible to be endured.

III

Meanwhile, Abbé Martin's health grew steadily worse. In the autumn of 1889 he was granted leave of absence for a year, and went south to spend the winter, dying there in January, 1890. I substituted for him in the course in Holy Scripture (Biblical Introduction), and this course was permanently assigned to me, together with my former instruction in Hebrew and Assyrian. By a curious diplomatic arrangement, the secret of which Monsignor d'Hulst never confided to me, Abbé Vigouroux received the title of professor and head of the department, while I figured in the announcement of the faculty as his assistant. His share of the work consisted in giving one lecture a week during only part of the year, on subjects such as the influence on the inspired authors of their natural environment. The Rector saw fit to give the primacy to instruction of this sort, and to assign a secondary rank to my courses in the history of the canon of the Old and New Testaments. I presume that his reason for providing me with a merely ornamental superior was that mine was an unknown name, while that of Abbé Vigouroux figured prominently in Catholic Biblical science; also because his name, as a token of irreproachable orthodoxy, made a desirable addition to the Institute prospectus. Although in my instruction I was quite independent of my distinguished colleague, our proximity was not without its embarrassments. In 1893, when Monsignor d'Hulst relieved me of the course in Holy Scripture, Abbé Vigouroux was a party to the measure, and he it was who named my successor.

My new duties did not find me unprepared. I had worked out in advance a somewhat elementary plan of instruction which I felt was the only one, in view of the wretched state of Biblical studies in the Church of Rome, that seemed to afford hope of ultimate improvement. The following exposition of my scheme appeared in the fall of 1892 in the little periodical bearing the name of *Enseignement Biblique,* in which I proposed to publish a summary of my lectures:

We take our starting-point from the principle that it is indispensable to a knowledge of Holy Scripture to acquire a clear and comprehensive idea of the principal problems of Biblical Introduction, regarded from the historical point of view, and at the same time to acquire familiarity with the detailed interpretation of the sacred books by means of a critical study of the text. With this object in view, during the greater part of the academic year we treat the subject of Introduction, and for the last two or three months we study a single book or an important section of Scripture.

We connect this whole subject of Biblical Introduction with the definition of the Bible. For us Catholics, the Bible is that collection of books which the Church holds to be divinely inspired. A complete commentary on this definition would require some answer to the following questions:

1. What is an inspired book?
2. What books are to be regarded as inspired?
3. In what language were these books composed, and by what means and in what condition have they come down to us?
4. When, how, and by whom were they written?
5. What are their contents?
6. How have they been interpreted?

Our course not being exactly a course in theology or in apologetics, we do not proceed dogmatically, formulating theses to be proved and then confirming them by means of facts; but we proceed historically and critically, studying the facts themselves before arriving at our conclusions. The consequence is that, for us, Biblical Introduction becomes the general history of the Bible or, after the manner of Richard Simon, a critical history of both Testaments; and that our answer to the

questions proposed above consists in an exposition of
the following topics:

1. The history of the dogma of inspiration.
2. The history of the canon of Scripture.
3. The history of the text and versions of the Bible.
4. The history of the composition of the sacred books.
5. The history of the people of God, of Biblical theology, and of the religious institutions of Israel.
6. The history of Biblical exegesis.

We do not consider ourselves obliged to follow these
topics necessarily in their natural order. . . . We have
not yet undertaken to trace the history of the dogma
of inspiration, because of the special difficulties which
such a subject just now presents. . . . (In order to
treat it as it deserves) we must first examine the sacred
books themselves, and collect the data which they furnish to an attentive and sincere observer. Now the
critical investigation of the Bible is precisely the object of our Introduction in the five divisions which,
logically, follow that of the history of the dogma of
inspiration. Thus we have provisionally deferred our
treatment of that question, since in attempting it prematurely we should have risked provoking controversies
as irritating as unfruitful.

Hence the history of the canon of Scripture has been
assigned the foremost place, having been studied during
the last two years (1889-91). It is from Christian tradition that we learn with certainty which are the inspired
books. If the testimony of tradition had been perfectly
explicit from the beginning, and if its language had
never been hesitating or doubtful in relation to this or
that Biblical writing, there would be no history of the
canon. But the facts are otherwise. While the principal and essential portions of the sacred collection have
always enjoyed equal consideration throughout the
Church, certain more or less important books in both
Testaments have been, for various reasons, considered
doubtful. The history of these grounds for rejection
or for late admission, studied in their causes, their manifestations, and their mode of operation, joined to the
criticism of the available data concerning the forma-

tion of the Scripture collection, constitutes, properly speaking, the history of the canon. . . .

The history of the text and versions of the Bible is the subject that now occupies our attention. It is perhaps the driest part of our program of Introduction, yet it is none the less indispensable. Before forming an opinion regarding the origin and interpretation of the Biblical writings, it is requisite to know where to look for them, and in what degree the ancient manuscripts and modern editions represent the primitive condition, whether of the original texts or of the early versions of the Scriptures. The condition of the text and its critical value once determined, it is possible to discuss on a solid foundation the question of authenticity (history of the composition of the sacred books), and then to analyse their historical and doctrinal contents (history of Israel and of the founding of Christianity, history of Biblical theology). . . .

Finally, we come to the history of exegesis, to some extent a continuation of Biblical theology, and leading us back to the subject which we deferred in the beginning, namely, the history of the dogma of inspiration. In our studies, culminating at this point, we shall have been guided by the general principles contained in the decisions of the Church concerning the divine inspiration and the correct interpretation of Scripture. Having concluded our investigations, it will be requisite merely to gather up the results with which the critical history of the Bible in its different aspects as we have successively considered them will not fail to have furnished us, in order to treat with competence, if life is spared us, the problem of inspiration, and to determine with precision the principles of an exegesis at once orthodox and scientific.

The Introduction thus completed may serve as preface to a detailed critical commentary on the whole Bible. . . .

This is what it is our purpose to accomplish—what we should have been happy to find already accomplished by the Catholic scholars of France. The plan which has just been elaborated is far more extensive than we can personally hope to compass; we realize that it will not be given to ourselves to complete it. But we believe that, in one way or in another, it will be realized; that Biblical studies will be restored to their due place of honor among the French clergy, since nothing short of this is indispensable. We shall have contributed, or at least have labored, toward that essential goal. Others, coming after us, perhaps our disciples, will accomplish more than we can hope to do. *Exoriare aliquis nostris ex ossibus!* . . .

This program had about it an air of innocent candor which it was hoped might prevent too much attention being paid to the daring character of its innovations. It proposed nothing less than the rigorous and thoroughgoing application of the critical method to the study of the Bible; and the traditional doctrine of the Church figured in it only as matter of history, not of legislation governing doctrine. Only, the situation rested upon an enormous equivocation, since the Catholic beliefs which were the direct object of my researches had not ceased to be the official charter, recognized as such by myself, of my instruction. Nor could this equivocation be altogether evaded in my published language. Thus, when I declared that the definitions of the Church regarding the Bible would "guide" my studies, I meant this in an extremely latitudinarian sense, namely, in so far as these definitions pointed expressly to the beliefs I was about to investigate, that is to say, in so far as they were an indication for the historian, not a truth raised for the believer and the theologian quite above the plane of discussion.

I held to my course as here outlined for four years, and I could have continued in it indefinitely if I had sought, above all else, to keep up this patent equivocation, making a great parade of criticism in regions safe from any possible invasion of theology, and juggling with all the real difficulties I might encounter. It has been shown above that I understood well enough the technique of diplomatic postponement. When I was dismissed from my chair, the history of the Biblical text was to have occupied me for at least two years more; already I had appreciated the desirability, for the purpose of gaining time, of treating the history of exegesis before that of the composition of the Biblical writings, the history of Israel and that of Christian origins. I was persuaded, in truth, that time was working in my favor, and that certain results which for the moment would be sure to rouse astonishment and disquiet might, within ten or fifteen years, come to be accepted quietly, the ground being well prepared in the meantime. But it was impossible to get around every obstacle, nor did I dream of doing so, less than ever after I found myself able to deal with vital questions, my freedom of teaching then becoming something very precious to me. My pupils too became alive to these issues, and aroused in me not a little of the feeling which had inspired my early labors. They saw clearly that I toiled only for them, and lived only for them. Realizing that they were exposed, without suspecting it, to the painful crisis by which I had been overwhelmed, I was seized with a consuming pity. It was not in my power to spare them this trial, and I knew that it would not help them to avoid it if I were to dodge the difficulties. Hence the efforts that I made, from this time forward, to discover means of conciliation, at least provisionally, between the facts as they were critically established and the absolute dogmas of the Church.

IV

My hearers consisted of about two dozen young ecclesiastics, priests or seminarians, some of whom had been sent directly by their bishops to the seminary of the Catholic Institute, while others came from Saint Sulpice—either destined to return later to their respective dioceses, or to be received into the Sulpician Order, as teachers in its clerical seminaries. The majority belonged to Saint Sulpice, and the Catholic Institute had therefore to reckon with its head, Abbé Icard, a little, dried-up man, who for many years had heard catechisms in the parish (at that time administered by the Society), taught canon law, and acted as spiritual director for the Seminary, before being elected Superior-General.

Him the Duc de Saint Simon, who had no love for the Sulpicians, would have delighted to caricature. Saint Sulpice, molded upon the old Gallican tradition, had gradually turned in the course of the Nineteenth Century toward Ultramontanism, though without change in its essential spirit, and Abbé Icard had evolved with his seminary. He was incapable of the fanatical enthusiasm of a Louis Veuillot, but he had a firm belief in the Catholic doctrine in its entirety, and was capable of discussing it exhaustively, accurately and uninspiringly. On matters of doctrine he was inflexible, and this gave him such standing with Cardinal Richard, archbishop of Paris, that in any conflict between Saint Sulpice and the Catholic Institute he was certain to have the archbishopric on his side.

This had been apparent in the disputes which arose concerning the teaching of Abbé Duchesne. The latter had said too outspokenly that the Ante-Nicene Fathers had employed unorthodox language in the matter of the Trinity; he had demolished a mass of pious legends, especially those attributing an apostolic origin to many of the churches of France; moreover, he was in the habit of treating these questions in a tone strongly reminiscent of Voltaire. His opponents, however, were unsuccessful in expelling him from the Catholic Institute, and it is because of this that that establishment is proud today to count him among its honorary professors. But Abbé Icard was not much influenced by mere scientific prestige, and not apt to be impressed by the sort of immortality that academies have it in their power to confer. He forbade Abbé Duchesne's lectures to the students of Saint Sulpice, and his tenacity was so notorious that a wholly inoffensive course in church history, in charge of Father Largent of the Oratory, was specially instituted for their benefit.

In some mysterious fashion, the students from Saint Sulpice came into my courses forewarned against me. They seemed ready to believe in advance that my doctrine was uncertain and my knowledge unreliable. One day, when I was as yet teaching nothing but Hebrew, I had chanced to remark, without malice prepense, that the writings of Abbé Vigouroux were works of pious edification merely. This utterance had given great offense, and apparently Saint Sulpice never forgave me for it. Nevertheless, my students from that quarter invariably, after a few weeks or months, relaxed their suspicions, and the course proceeded without internal friction. The Society was even willing, on occasion, to profit by my abilities. In 1891-92, the Superior entrusted to me, for a third year of post-graduate Biblical study, a very promising young ecclesiastic who it was desired should perfect himself in the knowledge of the Semitic languages.

His attention, however, must have been early drawn to certain temerities in my teaching, though he was not a person to take a serious stand on mere vague rumors. At the closing public session of the courses of the theological faculty, on July 4, 1885, I had noticed the venerable Superior shaking his head in ominous fashion at that section of the report which dealt with my course of exegesis in the first chapters of Isaiah. This disquieting manifestation was explained to me a few days later by Abbé Monier. Interpreting the famous passage (Is. vii, 14), "Behold, a virgin shall conceive, and bear a son, and shall call his name Immanuel," I had ventured to assert that this, in its literal sense, did not refer either to Christ or to the Virgin Mary, and that the application of the text to Jesus, as made by the Gospel according to Matthew, appertained exclusively to its "spiritual" sense. This meant calling in question the literal accuracy of the prophecy, and Abbé Icard took pains to intimate, through the agency of Abbé Monier, that it would be well for me to use more caution in the future.

So long as I abstained from publication, no persecution for heresy could be instigated against me in the Catholic press. I was in no haste to make public the results of my exegesis, not merely from prudential considerations, but because I had no intention of declaring myself hastily on such delicate questions. Abbé Duchesne was unable to conceal his impatience; "When are you going to give birth to something?" he would say in his characteristically free language. Later on, he had reason, alas! to think me only too fertile.

His enemies were at a loss to conceive how this man, so outspoken on questions of church history, could be so circumspect on all those matters of exegesis where dogma is involved. In the first volume of his *History of the Early Church,* which has since been condemned, he skirts around rather than squarely faces every such question. He even has words of disapproval for those who dare to confront these matters more directly. It would be an utter misconception to suppose that he made common cause with me at the Catholic Institute when my teaching at length stirred up serious difficulties. The fact was quite otherwise. Duchesne, who considered his own temerities merely venial, has invariably found the condemnations visited on myself both natural and proper.

In 1892, when I began the regular publication of my lectures in *Enseignement Biblique,* he horrified

Monsignor d'Hulst by remonstrating with him as to the possible outcome of such an enterprise, since it was sure to arouse a protest from the Dominicans of the *Revue Biblique,* assisted by Abbé Vigouroux. This fear was the more exaggerated, as my little periodical was too insignificant to rival any other. At the same time, Monsignor d'Hulst, who in the beginning had greeted my project most cordially, said to me coldly as I handed him the first number, "I trust that this periodical will not prove dangerous to its editor." It is true that, two hours later, when he had read my leading article—containing the program already quoted from at length—he hurried to my room to bring me his warmest congratulations. Those of Abbé Duchesne were never proffered.

Dating from June, 1889, our personal relations were at an end, and we recognized each other only in our official capacity. My former master, Arthur Amiaud, had died on May 22, leaving vacant the chair in Assyriology at the *École Pratique des Hautes Études.* It was destined to remain vacant for several years, being assigned later to Father Scheil. Having seen how much it was to the advantage of Abbé Duchesne to hold a position of public instruction under the State, the idea had visited me of offering myself as a candidate for the vacancy. At this time, I was the only pupil of the School holding a degree in Assyriology,[1] and I have reason

[1] My thesis, a reconstructior of the Annals of Sargon, king of Assyria, was accepted but its printing had been delayed by reason of the considerable expense it would have occasioned. This is why I never received my diploma. Strictly speaking, I was not entitled to the degree, but this circumstance would not have stood in the way of my candidacy.

to believe that, if I had taken the steps required under the circumstances, I should have been given the appointment. This intention I expressed to Abbé Duchesne, who seemed to approve it. But he gave me no hint of the formalities that must be gone through with in order that my candidacy might be regularly presented and discussed at the meeting of the professors, set for June 10, 1889. I had taken for granted that he would propose my name; only later realizing that he had never agreed to do so, since he had omitted to inform me that a previous statement was required from the candidate. On the 11th of June, the Tuesday after Whitsunday, I called upon him to learn how things had gone at the meeting of the day before. He appeared somewhat surprised by my curiosity; then, almost offended, he told me that as a member of the Institute he deferred in matters of Assyriology to his colleague, Professor Oppert; that Professor Oppert was not acquainted with me; that, in fact, no one knew me; that he was prepared to support my candidacy if any one had proposed it, but that my name had not even been mentioned! A defeat would have been less painful to me than this mercurial fashion of treating the affair, which had, among other defects, that of arriving too late. I had not pushed my own project, having assumed that Abbé Duchesne, as a powerful friend, would do this more effectually. The respect that should always be shown for members of the Institute did not prevent me from telling him, in no uncertain terms, what I thought of this proceeding. Those were the last words he ever heard from me on his own premises.

I have related this incident, without significance in itself—and though it affords outstanding evidence of my evil disposition!—because it bears directly on the charge of Modernism that has lately been raised against Abbé Duchesne. Since the 11th of June, 1889, there has been no direct interchange of ideas between us. When I was expelled from the Catholic Institute in November, 1893, he did not come forward with any offer of sympathy, and I hasten to add that he was under no obligation to do so. When he was made director of the *École de Rome*, I sent him a note of congratulation. Some time after, he called on me at Neuilly, for the purpose of introducing his colleague of the Institute, Monsieur d'Arbois de Jubanville, who for some unknown reason wanted to see me. He came to visit me a second time in 1900 at Bellevue, knowing that I had barely escaped death the year before. "That event," he said, "would have brought sorrow to perhaps a dozen persons." Even if he were to be counted among these twelve eccentrics, it is very evident that Abbé Duchesne has not concerned himself with anything I have written for the past twenty-three years, that is to say, with anything that I have ever written.

It does not pertain to me to judge his writings from the point of view of their orthodoxy, and I have not the least inclination to pass a personal judgment on himself. I know that he has deserved all the successes of his brilliant career. But, before

Catholic opinion, his case should stand in an altogether different light from mine. Duchesne has always had a horror of what is called Modernism; he has always taught that the dogmas of the Church are unimpeachable and immutable; he has never written a line for the purpose of attacking or defending them, or to attenuate, correct or modify them by way of interpretation. In the recent letter, which he wrote to avert the condemnation of his *History of the Early Church*, he complains that his adversaries have resorted to the tactics of confounding his methods with mine. He is justified in so complaining. Our methods were always divergent, and there is every reason now to believe that they will remain divergent to the end.

V

The attacks upon my teaching began with the publication of my first book. It dealt with the *History of the Old Testament Canon*, which had been the subject of my lectures for the first half of the academic year, 1889-90. It was not my purpose in the first instance to print these lectures, since they contained little that was original; but Monsignor d'Hulst, who had caused Abbé Vigouroux to be named full professor on the strength merely of his popularity, was unwilling to name me such until I had attained the degree of Doctor of Theology. He had suggested my going to Rome in the Easter vacation of 1890, to acquire a degree which would only cost, he declared, the expense of my examination and the chancellor's fees. This easy prospect did not tempt me in the least, and I told the Rector that I preferred to receive my doctorate from our own faculty, according to the regular rules, which were rather more exigent than those governing the Roman doctorates. I offered to submit to an oral examination covering the whole of theology, and our professors of dogma made no difficulty about accepting the forty Latin theses, of which I offered a summary to serve as a basis for the usual scholastic disputation. For the written thesis, I offered my *History of the Old Testament Canon.* The book was submitted to the required censorship; a Jesuit professor of dogma, Father Baudier, scrutinized its doctrine, and Abbé Vigouroux passed upon its critical conclusions. Both rendered a favorable verdict upon the work, which was then put through the press. The disputation took place on the 7th of March, at the Catholic Institute, under the presidency of Bishop Lagrange of Chartres.

The theological examination had occurred some days before under less solemn auspices. Monsignor d'Hulst had cast toward me a look of anguish when I had replied to Father Auriault, a Jesuit, that the redactor of the first chapter of Genesis had not had the remotest suspicion of the doctrine of evolution, and had no more condemned it than he had approved it. The Rector led the discussion in a direction less compromising to the sacred authors, and my judges appeared in the end well pleased to discover that I was better instructed in theology than they had surmised.

The defense of my thesis on the Biblical canon

passed off without embarrassing incident. Abbé Vigouroux had the air of asserting that I had co-ordinated into a preconceived theory the testimonies of the Fathers hostile to those books of the Old Testament which had been regarded in the earlier Christian centuries as doubtful. I replied with some asperity that it was not my habit to torture my data in the direction of any particular conclusion, and that I had revised my results up to the last moment, in order to bring them into accord with the documents studied. "That is the way with these critics," said a venerable priest in the front row of the audience, in a loud whisper, "they are never sure of anything!"

In reality there lay concealed in the depths of the book an idea whose full bearing escaped my examiners, and yet it could not fail to cause them some passing disquiet. The original phase of my work consisted of an analysis of the deliberations that had preceded the definition of the canon of Scripture by the Council of Trent. The Tridentine fathers had been gravely embarrassed to bring the traditional witnesses into accord, and they had finally determined to sanction the collection that enjoyed the support of general usage, without pretending to resolve the difficulties which had divided the ancient doctors, especially Saint Jerome, who was hostile to the extra-canonical books of the Old Testament, and Saint Augustine, who accepted them. Assuredly, the fathers of Trent had had no suspicion of Biblical criticism, any more than had the ancient doctors; still, both seemed to admit vaguely that the canonicity of the Biblical books in no way implied their all possessing the same value. That was a truth of common sense, but the application of common sense to theological matters is always hazardous! My sage examiners had a presentiment that my remark, inoffensive as it was in appearance, might some day be turned to the disadvantage of the sacred writings; and, in fact, it was through this breach that I proposed to find a way of smuggling in the whole body of Biblical criticism, notwithstanding all that the Church officially teaches regarding the divinity, the authenticity, the veracity and the integrity of the Sacred Scriptures!

I was proclaimed Doctor of Theology and, as so high a title is not lightly to be acquired, the assembly adjourned to the Church of the Carmelites that I might make my confession of faith. Monsignor d'Hulst, seated before the altar, was the one delegated to receive it. Although the symbol employed in such cases had not then been amplified by the anti-modernist additions which it owes to the reigning Pope,[1] it was still long enough. Monsignor d'Hulst, seeing me overwhelmed with fatigue, encouraged my reading of it with his most compassionate expression. A slight movement of disquietude escaped him when I stopped short after the passage where the ritual made me promise that I would never interpret the Bible except in accordance with the unanimous consensus of the Fathers. Although I had long been familiar with the passage, the idea suddenly appeared to me so

[1] I.e., in 1913, Pius X.

extraordinary, and so out of accord with my inmost convictions, that I felt the need of taking a long breath before going on. The Rector's eye recalled me to the necessities of the situation, and I went on with the liturgy unfalteringly. Eighteen years later, to the very day, I found myself solemnly excommunicated by Pope Pius X because of my repeated refusal to assent to the acts by which he had sought to protect, against my too liberal interpretations, the symbol of Pius IV, augmented by Piux IX.

During the whole summer of 1890, a canon of Soissons named Magnier attacked my book in a series of articles printed in the *Univers*. These articles were extremely annoying and I abstained from reading them. Saint Sulpice meanwhile made no sign. Father Brucker, in the *Études*, gave me a not ill-natured review. The year following, my *History of the New Testament Canon* fared no worse with the reviewers. Canon Magnier was a voice crying in the wilderness, and all the more vainly because I made no reply. Toward the end of 1890, I had published in the *Revue des Religions*, edited by Abbé Peisson, vicar of the Church of St. Thomas Aquinas, a short study on the Proverbs commonly attributed to Solomon. My conclusion was that this collection bore no marks of authorship by a single individual, and that its final compilation must probably be dated after the Babylonian Captivity. The orthodox publications did not attack me for so slight a heresy, but I must have been denounced for it at Rome. For, in the summer of 1891, Abbé

Vigouroux, returning from a journey *ad limina,* came charitably to warn me that my opinions on Proverbs had been considered highly objectionable, and that if I persisted in such courses I could not escape condemnation by the Index.

At about the same time, I had begun in Abbé Peisson's *Revue* a series of studies of the Chaldaic-Assyrian religion. The two final articles, which appeared in November, 1891, and in March, 1892, concerned the Babylonian myths of the creation and the flood, as well as their connection with the narratives of Genesis. I had treated the subject in my course in exegesis in 1891, and had decided against the historicity of the Biblical accounts of the creation, permitting myself a little harmless diversion in relation to the harmonizing efforts which make out to discover the modern sciences of astronomy, geology and palæontology, all in the first chapter of Genesis.

Despite the horror that they are accustomed to profess for myths in general, I wrote, (the authors of these systems) do not hesitate to insert into the Biblical text a fully elaborated myth, though of a special kind—namely, a scientific myth, the like of which the ancients, to do them so much justice, could never have imagined. . . . All these contradictory, ephemeral, ill-defined and impossible systems of the artificial harmonizers leave not a shred of the Biblical data, unless it be that God is the creator of the world and of all that it contains. We arrive more directly at the same results by admitting that an old Chaldean legend, taken over into the service of the monotheistic idea, has furnished the framework destined to give an appropriate setting to the idea of God, the Creator.

My criticism of the accounts of the flood concluded with analogous reflections.

Should we not penetrate more deeply into the thought of the Bible itself by seeking in these grandiose histories rather for lofty religious and moral inspirations than for precise and particular facts, rigorously exact to the smallest detail? More than one orthodox critic must already have asked himself this question, and answered it perhaps by saying that the historical interpretation of these chapters offers to theologians the same kind of difficulties, and is the same stumbling-block, that the scientific account of the creation was to the judges of Galileo. The account of creation is true, although it is not historical, and though it is run in the mold of a cosmology no longer tenable. Who knows whether in the chapters that follow, there may not be narratives which are true also after their manner, although they do not contain all the elements of literally accurate history that we disturb ourselves to find in them?

To many readers, it will seem that these statements were well within the truth; but they were not in conformity with Abbé Vigouroux's system of apologetics, and great was the scandal at Saint Sulpice! It will some day be cause for astonishment, even in the Church of Rome—at least so I should hope—that a Catholic University professor should have been judged highly reprehensible for having said, in the year of grace 1892, that the narratives of the first chapter of Genesis are not to be taken as literal history, and that the alleged agreement of the Bible with natural science is a rather shabby subterfuge. But, in those years, to profess, even with the utmost circumspection, such opinions as those just referred to was an almost unheard-of perversity.

I was mistaken in believing that views so perfectly obvious, put forward cautiously, could not arouse against me men endowed with the least glimmer of intelligence. Abbé Icard, on his part, held firmly to the opinion that I was a propagator of heresy, and lacking in respect for the ecclesiastical tradition.

My articles were carried to him to read, and their bearing elucidated to him. He was told that my printed text did not include everything that my oral instructions conveyed to the minds of my hearers. To one who tried to get him to recognize the moderation of my language, the aged Superior replied that a smile could change the entire sense and purport of a phrase. Moreover, he said, he knew my smile was irreverent, and that students who entered my class room lost all their respect for Holy Scripture. I am convinced, that if my smile could have been printed at the same time with my text, it would be recognized today as much less directed at the Bible than at its interpreters, and that its irreverence was not for the Holy Spirit but for the Catholic apologists. However that may be, Abbé Icard decided to remove his pupils from this pernicious influence. At the opening of the academic year 1892-93, without giving previous notice either to the Rector or to myself, he forbade the students of Saint Sulpice to attend my lectures.

As has been stated above, the same prohibition had been issued some years earlier against Abbé Duchesne, without seriously compromising his position. For one thing, he was a great personage, crowned with the aureole of high prestige that sur-

rounds the members of the *Institut de France*. Then
it was known, or believed, that he had powerful
supporters among the laity; and it may even have
been that he was dreaded because of his caustic
manner of speech, rather intemperate than really
audacious. As for myself, from the day when Abbé
Icard pronounced me a dangerous influence, it was
taken for granted by all concerned that I was in far
greater peril than my eminent colleague had ever
been. Except among the clergy, I was practically
unknown, and even among them I stood very much
apart, not merely on account of my opinions, but
still more because of my manner of life. My
wretched health, my reserved disposition, and my
assiduous devotion to study had made a recluse of
me. Taking everything into consideration, I had
nothing to support me but the scientific value of my
writings—of no avail whatever once the question of
their orthodoxy had been raised—and the good-will
of the Rector, a resource that would be worth much
or little in proportion to his courage and his skill in
confronting the emergency.

At first, Monsignor d'Hulst was outraged by the
action of Abbé Icard. But the latter was a man
with whom even a Rector of the Catholic Institute,
a man of noble birth, and great-grandnephew of
popes and archbishops, did not venture openly to
quarrel. He grumbled in private at "Father" Icard;
and the death of Renan having furnished him with
the opportunity to write a long article on that former
pupil of Saint Sulpice in the *Correspondant* of Oc-

tober 25, 1892, he used the occasion to say that deficiencies in the instruction received at the seminary had very likely assisted the disciple of Abbé Le Hir in his loss of faith. "What would have happened," he inquired, "if, in (the domain) that historical scholarship opens up to the apologist charged with verifying the origins of Christianity, Renan could have received what our emancipated faculties of theology offer today to pupils whose minds are receptive toward science—a more assured initiation, less timid views, broader principles, and solutions better adapted to the new problems that have arisen?" This hypothesis, of questionable soundness in itself, was scarcely calculated to enlighten Abbé Icard, and it was sure to wound him the more deeply as an assault less on his person than on the Society of which he was the head. But Monsignor d'Hulst held that the moment had come for acting upon Catholic opinion. His wide reading and his extensive personal relations had led him to perceive, at least obscurely, that dogmatic theology was engaged in setting up, against the legitimate development of human knowledge in the field of history, a barrier of prejudices which sheltered themselves under the name of religion. The dream that had haunted my brain began to haunt his. He had caught sight of what he was soon to characterize as the Biblical Question, and he began to deem himself capable of solving it, for the greater good of the Church, and incidentally for the protection of his obscure professor of Holy Scripture.

VI

It was not of Monsignor d'Hulst that I had thought, as entitled to bring these grave matters to the attention of the Church, which to all appearance was innocent of their true importance. I had retained some connection with Monsignor Meignan, now become Archbishop of Tours and on the point of being made a cardinal. Early in October, 1892, I sent him a letter, in which I declared that he alone in all France could speak out with authority on matters of exegesis, explain the necessity of an evolution in the received teaching, give a sober estimate of the advance of Biblical criticism, and suggest the direction to follow in order to satisfy the demands of science without compromising the essential principles of faith. He himself would be the best judge as to the form to be given to this pronouncement. If he thought well to confine himself to a letter, written to me on the subject of my publications, I should be not only greatly honored but also immensely aided in the circumstances in which I found myself.

In place of replying in writing, the scholarly prelate, who was coming to Paris in connection with the affair of the cardinalate, made an appointment to meet me on the morning of October 24th at the *Hotel du Bon La Fontaine* in the *Rue de Grenelle*. In view of the capital importance of this encounter, I reproduce it here as it was noted down at the time, merely omitting repetitions and unessential details, of which naturally there were many in a two hours' interview. The Archbishop led the conversation throughout, smoking cigarettes as he talked, only pausing from time to time to ask me a question.

Meignan. I am at work on the second volume of my Prophets, and I shall find it necessary to consider the prophecies in general. The Book of Daniel gives me a lot of trouble. Don't you find that there are difficulties in Daniel, my dear friend?

Loisy. Truly, Monsignor.

M. Tell me what they are; or, rather, let me tell you. For one thing, the author, living, or being supposed to live, in the age of Cyrus, seems to know nothing of the history of his own times. On the other hand, he is well acquainted with the conditions under Antiochus Epiphanes. It is most singular! The prophecies are not usually as exact as that. But the prophets, after all, saw things in a vision. Ezekiel speaks of his visions of God.

L. No doubt. Yet that hardly accounts for Daniel's ignorance of his own times.

M. That is so. But, don't you see, we mustn't go too fast. The rationalists hold that Daniel was contemporary with Antiochus Epiphanes, which may possibly be. Tradition affirms that Daniel lived in the time of Cyrus, which is also possible. But, as priests, we are the advocates of the Church, advocates of tradition. The Church is founded on tradition; we cannot abandon tradition. The Protestants can say what they like about the Bible. They do not rest on tradition. . . . So you find that Daniel has its difficulties?

L. You have just mentioned the chief, Monsignor, the ignorance of the writer concerning the epoch in which he is said to have lived.

M. Good! That is a difficulty, indeed. Still, are we well informed as to what occurred?

L. We know that Cyrus did not take Babylon in the manner indicated by Daniel. The last king of Babylon was not named Balthasar, and it was not Darius the Mede, it was Cyrus, who succeeded him.

M. Are we sure of that? Perhaps this king of

Babylon had several names. Darius may have been a viceroy. These are possibilities, you understand! Tradition may be defended by means of possibilities. The Book of Daniel would seem to have been written in Babylon, since the author is well informed of things there.

L. Of some things, maybe, but not of the history. Babylon, with its temples and its worship, was still in existence at the time of Antiochus Epiphanes. Some sort of knowledge of Babylonian conditions does not prove the authenticity of the book.

M. That may possibly be. I believe that the book was composed at Babylon in the time of Cyrus, and that it may have been worked over and developed in the days of Antiochus Epiphanes. There you have another possibility, even a probability. But we are the advocates of tradition, and sincere, sincere advocates! . . .

Have you gone into the tradition relative to Daniel? Nothing can be more curious. Origen says in one passage that Daniel should not be cited because he is not a prophet. Saint Isidore of Seville—but he was not a very intelligent man, Saint Isidore of Seville—says that, according to certain doctors, the Book of Daniel may have been written in the reign of Antiochus Epiphanes. He does not condemn that opinion, nor do I; neither do I follow it. We are the advocates of tradition.

What do you think about the famous prophecy of the seventy weeks of years? [1]

L. It seems to be difficult to fix upon its point of departure and of arrival.

M. Oh! the point of arrival is the age of Antiochus Epiphanes. Have a care! This prophecy is looked upon as the most reliable of the Messianic prophecies; yet it is misleading! On the other hand, it was scarcely noticed until Bossuet; it was Bossuet who gave it stand-

[1] Daniel ix, 24. This passage is supposed to indicate the time comprised between the oracle of Jeremiah on the duration of the Babylonian Captivity and the advent of the Messianic Kingdom.

ing. The ancient interpreters are most uncertain on this subject. However, that is something it will not do to say out loud.

What do you think of the prophecies in general?

L. It seems to me, Monsignor, that the prophetical books of the Old Testament are a collection of sermons rather than of predictions.

M. That is certainly so. The prophecies cannot be taken literally in every detail. That has bothered me extremely as regards my book, but I have found a way to straighten it all out. Listen! The prophets see everything in a vision; God shows them things in that way; they see everything in the same plane; that is why it is all mixed up. And what is it they see?—the coming of the Kingdom of God. About that they say some extraordinary things; does not Isaiah [1] make lions eat straw? The Kingdom of God has never come; it will never come just as they depicted it—but it was a grand conception. There is no more than that in the prophets—they announced the Messianic Kingdom. That kingdom began to come with Jesus Christ, but for the most part it is still in the future. We do not know what may be. In any case, there you have the scheme for my treatment of the prophecies; they had this one great aim, the details must be grouped around that as one may. Let us be advocates of tradition!

In these matters it is not a good idea to rush ahead too fast. That excellent abbé of Saint Sulpice [2] who writes books on Assyriology is very cautious, and yet he renders good service, does he not?

L. Assuredly!

M. Nevertheless, his apologetic is extremely weak. For instance, if what he says of the Chaldean accounts of the creation and the flood is true—that these stories are older than our Bible narratives—there is no way of maintaining that the flood is a fact of history, or that the Biblical account of creation is in accord with science. He keeps on affirming it, when he ought to deny

[1] Isaiah ix, 7.
[2] Abbé Vigouroux.

it. Only, he can't deny it! Big books have been written to prove that it must have been so. We must respect tradition!

Don't overlook this, good friend, there never has been such a thing as criticism within the Church. How much did the Fathers comprehend of the Bible? Not a bit. And in the Middle Ages? And since? . . . Richard Simon was an intelligent man, and a great critic. But, mark this well, he was a failure. Bossuet put him down; Bossuet was in control. Rome has never had any understanding of these questions. The whole Catholic clergy is in a state of profound ignorance on the subject. To try to change all that is to run serious risks, for our theologians are ferocious; they will put us on the Index for simply nothing at all. Take my word for it, my young Loisy, one cannot be too careful. I had some part in starting you on a scientific career, and for this reason I have a right to say to you, Have a care! It is a father's advice. If you expose yourself to danger, those who think as you do will not come to your rescue.

The Jesuit fathers give us the measure of what it is possible to print on Biblical questions. They study them after their fashion. They have a lot of influence, the Jesuit fathers; one does not become a cardinal without their permission. It is best to keep on good terms with them.

Let us be advocates of tradition! It is true that no one knows where we are coming out. See what happened to the Eastern Church. The Catholic Church became petrified a few centuries later. The same destiny awaits her. But what are you going to do about it? No doubt, the divorce between faith and knowledge grows more and more accentuated. But this situation is not of our making; we have no responsibility for it. Bossuet, in putting down Richard Simon, suppressed for centuries all Biblical science within the Church. If you follow in the footsteps of Richard Simon, you will have no more chance than he; you will be condemned, just as he was.

Moreover, any concessions that we might make now

would amount to nothing. This is not the moment for encouraging rationalism, which is already very strong, and which we cannot flatter ourselves we shall be able to convert. The tradition of the Church is founded on miracles; we cannot deny the miraculous. But, if miracles are possible, my dear Loisy, everything is possible; we must believe it all.

Then let us be advocates of tradition, sincere advocates, always sincere!

The future of the Church in France is not brilliant. The suppression of the budget of worship is bound to come soon. Then, when the petty prestige of being a State functionary is lost to the Catholic priest, he will not have much left. I am convinced that our present social order cannot maintain itself without the Church, and yet I foresee that it is getting ready to dispense with her help. You are a thoughtful man; how does it all strike you?

L. I agree with you, Monsignor, that society needs the Church. I am also of the opinion that the Church might recover her influence over society. But the primary condition of that influence, as regards the enlightened classes, would seem to me to be a more or less complete revision of her religious teaching, beginning with her instruction about the Bible.

M. That is difficult; yes, it is quite impossible. You will only destroy yourself, and all for nothing. Once again, do take care! Some of the young men that I started toward Biblical studies have already come to grief.

See how I have conducted my life and my writings. They say I am on the way to be made a cardinal; and I believe the government has proposed my name to the Pope. The studies in which I have engaged have made my existence more bearable. The Bible, you know it well enough, is a very strange book. The truth is, we have to work in a room hermetically sealed. For my part, I have tried gently, very gently, to let in a little air; in all of my books I have insinuated something that might help. But what must be avoided above all things is compromising one's self. If my life has been fairly endurable, it is because I have always been most prudent.

I am delighted to have chatted with you about these Biblical questions, and I shall always be glad to hear from you.

I never saw Cardinal Meignan again, as he died in January, 1896. What impressed me most in our conversation was not the genuine goodness of the kind old man, who went so far in his confidences solely to spare me the consequences of what he foresaw was going to be a leap into the abyss. It was that he was far better acquainted than I, or than Monsignor d'Hulst, with the Catholic Church, and Rome, and the Vatican congregations. From the point of view of diplomacy, his counsels were wisdom personified. They seemed to me less praiseworthy from the point of view of truth and sincerity. The caution on which the venerable churchman piqued himself was, to my thinking, mere mundane adroitness. However, he wanted to give me the benefit of his experience. Even if he had been less ambitious for ecclesiastical preferment, he would have been no less circumspect in what he published. He was sincerely convinced that the teaching of the Catholic Church could never be dragged out of its traditional rut. For my part, I was in no way certain that he deceived himself here. But I believed it legitimate, indeed essential, to make the attempt, precisely in the Church's own best interest. Monsignor Meignan found himself at home in the old ways, since they had led him first to the bishop's mitre and next to the archbishop's purple. But I should be most uncomfortable in these, if they must mean a perpetual suppression of my most intimate and assured convictions, whatever might be my prospects of future advancement.

VII

The Archbishop of Tours having failed me, I did not seek another advocate. Nothing was farther from my thoughts than to induce Monsignor d'Hulst to write on matters of exegesis. I assumed that his position as Rector would make this unsuitable; he ought not to compromise himself by mingling in theological disputes; he could intervene in my favor with the bishops or with the Pope, only on the condition that his skirts were clear; finally, he had the best of reasons for not speaking out, namely, that despite his great general intelligence he was incompetent on questions of Biblical criticism. If he had suggested to me any intention of writing on the subject, I should have done my best to dissuade him. But he did not acquaint me beforehand with the resolution he had formed of discussing the "Biblical Question," and I first became aware of it when he sent me on January 20th a proof, marked "ready for the printer," of the article that he had prepared for the *Correspondant* of the 25th.

The success achieved in certain quarters by his article on Renan had undoubtedly encouraged him to go further. He proposed to himself nothing short of effecting a breach in the existing theological teaching. Such a breach he held to be a possibility in itself, and practicable for him to open up.

Also, I should then be free, because of this open door, whatever Abbé Icard might think of it, to pursue my researches. Here is the note that accompanied the proof of his article.

Friday.[1]

Dear Friend:

Before sending this corrected proof to the printer, I want you to see what I have written, asking you to notice that it is primarily a stroke of diplomacy, intended to gain a gradually enlarging measure of tolerance, then full freedom, by exhibiting to the inquisitors *rationes dubitandi* of which they are not aware.

This is why:

1. I have confined myself to the rôle of a mere reporter;

2. I have given prominence to the middle ground;

3. I have not mentioned you by name, though you have all along been foremost in my thoughts.

Yours most cordially,

MAURICE D'HULST.

The article of the Rector of the Catholic Institute was, then, written partly in my behalf. But the author not only proposed to safeguard me against possible heresy-hunters, and to save the reputation of his Institute; he also saw, in a not distant future, the whole range of sacred studies freed from theological embarrassments, and a multitude of souls who were now disturbed regarding the Bible re-established in their faith.

This is equivalent to saying that he was completely misled as to the effect which his article was destined to produce—first of all, because he failed to realize that no orthodox theologian could admit the

[1] Friday, January 20, 1893.

theory of inspiration that he sketched out under the caption of the "broad school" (*école large*). His initial error was in posing the Biblical Question on this dangerous ground of abstractions, where he immediately ran counter to the definitions of the Church and to the theology by which they are interpreted. For him, the great concern seemed to be the existence of errors in the Bible. Taken as a whole, Catholic tradition has never admitted error of any sort in the Scriptures, and, as is well known, it was for this reason that Galileo was condemned. Monsignor d'Hulst pictured in his article three schools of Catholic theology, of which two can be readily demonstrated never to have existed: the broad, the mediating, and the traditional schools, the last having the air of being esteemed the narrow school. He had himself invented out of whole cloth the system of the "broad school," and he unfolded it with visible self-complacency, all the while representing himself as a simple chronicler of current opinions, which he did not purport to make his own by expounding them. The system consisted in maintaining that the truth of the Bible was to be identified with the object of revelation itself, i.e., the doctrine of faith and morals, in such sort that all the rest—being merely matter of natural knowledge and of human history—need not be included among the objects of divine inspiration, and might therefore admit of error.

The elements of this theory were borrowed partly from a theologian of Lille, Abbé Didiot, and partly from François Lenormant, with a few ideas from my writings thrown in. Monsignor d'Hulst, however, jumped at conclusions. Evidently what he proposed was to expound my principles disguised as those of the "broad school"; yet not only had he forgotten my thesis on the inspiration of Scripture, which he had previously restrained me from publishing, but he had not even read the few pages in *Enseignement Biblique* where I had approached this question in the course of reviewing a German writer.[1] It has been seen above that my mode of accounting for the presence of errors in the Bible differed absolutely from that of the mythical "broad school." I continued to believe that the Bible, as a human creation, was subject to the inescapable relativity of all works by the hand of man, and so could not be wholly in accord, even in matters of faith and morals, with the truth of any other epoch than the one that fathered it. The "broad school" shocked the theologians by admitting errors in the Bible, and it flouted every jot of the evidence by asserting the doctrinal teaching of Scripture to be identical with that of the Church. But it is my opinion that Monsignor d'Hulst lacked the penetration to see this, and that, even if he had, he would not have ventured to admit the results of his premises.

We have seen, over his own signature, why the Rector chose to ally himself with the mediating school. It was for the purpose of emphasizing the fiction that he was a mere reporter, and in order not to assume personally the responsibility for the opinions which he attributed to the broad school;

[1] See *Études Bibliques,*[2] pp. 123-138.

not at all because he was especially favorable to the ideas, for instance, of the Abbé de Broglie, who as a matter of fact did constitute a mediating school all by himself. In the article, this second group, also mythical, freed its mind concerning the "broad school," in a two-page criticism of some severity, reproaching the latter for yielding too much to the spirit of rationalism, for having lost touch with tradition, and for not admitting a "reasonable" accord between Genesis and science. Truth to say, the mediating school was here struggling somewhat beyond its depth. The facile author must have smiled to himself as he wrote that its tendency was "probably the sanest and the most pregnant with promise."

I could not hope for the same good results from this article on the Biblical Question that the Rector evidently anticipated. It seemed to me that the real problems of exegesis were not even stated, since the true situation as regards the criticism of both the Old and the New Testaments was not so much as hinted at. But I did not foresee that the undertaking, instead of aiding me, was to do me more injury than my own productions. Yet that is what came of it. Nobody took any stock in the transparent device of the "broad school"; the persuasion being general that the opinions attributed to it were my own, and that the Rector had written solely in their defense. A violent polemic ensued. The orthodox papers and reviews vied with one another in refuting Monsignor d'Hulst, but without bringing me in any more than he had done. On his part, he uttered no word to disengage me from the "broad school." As for myself, I found no occasion to speak, not being directly attacked. It might have appeared that I was in no way involved in the controversy, and yet all who participated in it believed, and not without reason, that on it my fate depended.

At first the Rector stood his ground manfully, and held fast to his good intentions respecting myself. In the course of the last few years he had come to hold me in esteem, even in affection, and he would have nothing to do with my detractors. However, there was no intimacy between us. Although he was kindness itself, his rather lordly manner went against the grain. As was the case with all who knew him, I admired the abounding versatility of his mind, but that very versatility led easily into superficiality, since he took no time to go to the bottom of anything. His mind was wide open to all the new ideas, though from time to time his daring seemed to startle even himself, and then he would fall back on his inherited faith, and on the basic principles of theology that he had imbibed in the seminary. So far as I am able to recall, we never conversed for as much as two minutes together on any subject of theology or of criticism. The Abbé de Broglie, who knew him thoroughly, warned me not to count upon him too implicitly. But I did not need this counsel. The praises of myself in which Monsignor d'Hulst was wont to indulge, both in season and out of season, disturbed rather than reassured me. I can hear him yet, during one of the public examinations by our faculty, when I was questioning the candidates, pouring a veritable panegyric of my abilities into the ear of a Jesuit who disliked me. The features of the latter wore an obviously forced smile, which softened a little at the Rector's final words: "Unhappily, a breath would blow him away." That too exuberant enthusiasm might, I realized, some day or other be confronted by different sentiments. It was, indeed, destined to beat a retreat before one whose emergence on the field of battle Monsignor d'Hulst had never yet experienced—I mean, the sentiment of fear.

As the storm was growing more violent, and as the affair had been carried to Rome itself, the Rector thought it well to go there in the Easter vacation of 1893 to justify himself in person before the Pope and the Roman congregations. He was received with marked aloofness. From his article and the tumult it had excited, the opinion prevailed that the "broad school" was in control of the exegesis taught at the Catholic Institute, and that this was not to be tolerated. I do not know how Monsignor d'Hulst justified himself. In any case, he did not find it in his heart to say that the "broad school" was purely a diplomatic fiction; or that this school was in no wise to be identified with myself, in fact that the ideas he had conjured up under this name in no respect corresponded either to my opinions or to my instruction. He was a prisoner to the artifice which he had contrived for his own protection; but another was to be its victim. In allowing it to be understood that the "broad school" meant Alfred Loisy, and that he had been simply a chronicler of my opinions, he escaped the condemnation that menaced his article, saving himself at my expense through placing me in a position where I was helpless to defend myself. Still, he did not give way all at once. Important personages besieged him, remonstrating that in continuing to uphold me he was hopelessly compromising both his establishment and himself; that the Vatican was on the eve of issuing a public censure and would insist upon measures guaranteeing the orthodoxy of the instruction given at the Catholic Institute; that it was impossible to save me, and he was running the risk of ruining himself and me at the same time. It was the reactionaries in France who were clamoring for what Rome was thought to desire. They ended by persuading Monsignor d'Hulst that the best interest of the faculty of theology, of the Catholic Institute, and his own best interest, which he was told was that of his establishment, required that I should be relieved at least of the instruction in Biblical Introduction and exegesis. To this he at length consented. At this price it was guaranteed him that no censure would be laid against his article, Pope Leo XIII proposing soon to set forth in an encyclical the regulative principles of Catholic exegesis and, without mentioning names, to reprove the errors of the "broad school."

Monsignor d'Hulst returned little pleased with his journey. He came to see me on the 18th of May for the purpose of acquainting me with the decision that had been arrived at regarding myself. But he did not confide to me the actual grounds of his determination,—purely reasons of policy. For the first time, he seemed to think that my opponents were not altogether in the wrong, and that there might be some foundation for the scruples even of Abbé Icard. He assured me very gravely that my lectures suggested to my hearers doubts concerning the faith, and cited the case of one, a student of rare ability, whom my comments on the Synoptic Gospels had troubled quite recently. To this unlooked-for reproach, I replied that the true source of these doubts was the lack of accord between the instruction resting on critical and historical principles and the traditional theological instruction; that anti-critical teaching, for instance that of Abbé Vigouroux, was quite as likely to prove disturbing to faith by its utter flouting of reason; that the distinguished student in question had expressed to me the year before, in connection with my course on the earlier chapters of Genesis, an appreciation which I had every reason to suppose genuine. But much all that had to do with the case! The Rector ended by informing me, not without evident embarrassment, that he was powerless to sustain me against the growing opposition to my teaching, and that he would be obliged to relieve me of the courses in Biblical history, allowing me to retain only the courses in ancient languages. Two weeks later he came again to announce that he had chosen for my successor in the course in exegesis a scholar of irreproachable conservatism, Abbé Fillion of Saint Sulpice, who would fit in nicely with Abbé Vigouroux! [1] Abbé Fillion was in the habit

[1] See Appendix II as showing how the arrangement was brought before the Board of Bishops having oversight of the Catholic Institute, in August, 1893.

of embroidering the margins of the Bible with pious commentaries, and from time to time he would compose refutations of "the Germans." "At least," said the Rector, "no one will accuse him of making a fetish of criticism."

It was understood that my little periodical should continue, so that I might remain free to print in behalf of my readers the instruction that I was no longer allowed to give orally to the students of the Catholic Institute; and that my scientific activities should be in no wise curtailed by the change in my situation as professor. This may be taken as an indication that the revolution in my affairs was not brought about by any published indiscretions of my own, but by the imbroglio provoked by the article which the Rector himself had printed on the Biblical Question. I accepted the compromise, though it appeared to me to have only a precarious and uncertain future.

VIII

In my closing lecture, near the middle of June, I delivered myself on the same subject that Monsignor d'Hulst had treated earlier, namely, "The Biblical Question and the Inspiration of the Scriptures." I felt that I was entitled to express my mind on this problem, among other reasons so as to dispose once for all of the spectre of the "broad school," with which it in no way suited me to be identified. My hearers appeared to think it wholly natural that I should seek to justify myself before abandoning my chair; for they all knew, or suspected, that this lecture was to be the last they would hear from me. My discourse, simple and direct in form, was apparently well received, and I have no reason to believe that any of those who heard it were scandalized. Monsignor d'Hulst, who was kept informed of what went on in my class room, must have known in a general way what I had said. It was my intention to publish this lecture in my little periodical at the close of the year, as I had published my inaugural lecture at the beginning.

It never once entered my head that these inoffensive pages would simply horrify Monsignor d'Hulst, and be the occasion of my definitive expulsion from the Catholic Institute. I foresaw, indeed, a possible danger, but nothing definite. I preferred throughout to rely on the pure reasonableness of my principal statements and to take refuge only in my sincerity; as if it were not even conceivable that I could be condemned without being read, and as if my candor were not to seem, in the eyes of the high ecclesiastics who directed the Catholic Institute, a fault worse than my "errors" themselves. "That man has a conscience absolutely perpendicular," said Monsignor d'Hulst concerning me somewhat later.

My article appeared about the 10th of November, the academic year 1893-94 having already begun. It was only a few days before the annual meeting of the Board of Bishops having oversight over the Catholic Institute.[1] In it, after recalling the article

---

[1] It will be found reproduced in *Études Bibliques*,³ pp. 138-169. Cf. the inaugural lecture, on "Biblical Criticism," *ib.*, pp. 97-122.

by Monsignor d'Hulst and the polemics it had excited, I alluded to the fact that the Biblical Question had been treated by this writer in relation to the dogma of inspiration. Now this was not the most significant angle of vision from which to approach it. "On this account, after analyzing briefly the latest controversies," I proposed "to describe what the Biblical Question actually is, what means we have at hand for solving it, and finally how it is possible to get over the difficulties that arise from the point of view of theology."

It was matter for dispute "whether the dogma of inspiration does or does not admit of the belief that there are errors in the Bible"; those on the affirmative putting themselves in contradiction with the theological tradition, and those on the negative putting the dogma in contradiction with the facts. But the Biblical Question, rightly viewed, is a question of history; "we need no longer inquire whether there are errors in the Bible, but rather seek to know what the Bible contains of truth." This principle stated, I formulated "a certain number of conclusions which criticism outside the Catholic Church regards as final, since there are substantial reasons for accepting them as permanent acquisitions of knowledge."

The Pentateuch, in its present form, cannot be the work of Moses.

The first chapters of Genesis do not contain an exact and reliable account of the beginnings of mankind.

All the books of the Old Testament, and the different parts of each several book, do not possess equal historical value. All the historical books of the Bible, including those of the New Testament, were composed in a looser manner than modern historical writing, and a certain freedom of interpretation follows legitimately from this freedom in their composition.

We have to concede a real development in the religious doctrine contained in Scripture, in all its constituent elements: the doctrine of God, of human destiny, of moral obligation.

It is needless to add that, for an independent exegesis, the sacred writings, so far as concerns the knowledge of nature, do not advance beyond the notions common to the ancient world, and that these notions are clearly discernible in the opinions of their authors.

All these conclusions rest upon general observations as to matters of fact, which it is impossible absolutely to deny. What the situation calls for is rather an examination into their meaning and a thorough analysis of their details, as preliminary to a precise and accurate reconstruction of the history of the composition of the sacred writings, the history of the people of God, and the history of the Law and the Gospel.

From this preliminary work of criticism must emerge our solution of the Biblical questions, which are questions of history, to be dealt with after the historical method. As to the "inerrancy" of the Bible, it has to be taken in a sense entirely relative. "The Bible is an ancient book, a book written by men and for men, in a time and an environment remote from what we call modern science. The errors of the Bible are nothing other than the relative and imperfect aspect of a book which, precisely in being a book at all, was bound to have its relative and imperfect side." It might even be said, in a sense, that "these blemishes contribute to make the Bible true for the age that gave it birth."

In conclusion, I suggested, and not without reason, that the absolute notion of Biblical inspiration pertained rather to orthodox Protestantism, and that it was in practical contradiction with the fundamental principle of Catholicism. "A book, however true it may be, cannot be self-interpreting, cannot adjust itself to the intellectual, moral and social conditions of ages for which it was never written. This is the reason why the Church must continually add new explanations, while the Bible must remain what it is. . . . Whatever the advance of Biblical science appears to subtract from the prestige of Scripture only exhibits the more clearly the indispensableness of the Church's magistracy. Criticism thus serves as an apologist for the Church as against those sects which are based exclusively on the authority of the Bible."

And I took leave of my readers with the following words, expressive neither of false modesty nor of bravado, but of satisfaction in a duty done and of an assured trust in the equity of my eventual judges: "These opinions contain, at bottom, nothing novel. At the present time, they are held substantially as here described by many who, however, prefer, to leave the risk of expressing them publicly to someone else. But a word of sincerity and of reconciliation is always in place; if true, it can only benefit all alike, while it is easy to correct whatever in it may be misleading."

There was more of novelty in my article than I admitted or quite imagined; but, even so, it was far from revolutionary. It stated in candid terms the position that I proposed to take on Biblical questions, and it dissipated the equivocation in which

Monsignor d'Hulst had enveloped me with his diplomatic fiction of the "broad school." My intention went no farther than this. My language was not offensive toward any one. For that matter, this article has been thrice printed in the successive editions of my *Études Bibliques,* and has seldom been attacked in the Catholic press. Nor has it ever been condemned by the Church. Perhaps, after all, it contained more embarrassing truths than palpable errors.

Scarcely had Monsignor d'Hulst received the number of *Enseignement Biblique* containing my article, and taken cognizance of it, than he hurried to my room. At that time I was living close by the Catholic Institute, in the house where Littré died, at No. 44, *Rue d'Assas.* The Rector was in a state of veritable consternation. "What have you done?" he cried out at me, "I was trying to protect you by obtaining the bishops' consent to your keeping the instruction in languages; but this article spoils everything. If it is denounced to Cardinal Richard before the meeting of the bishops on the 15th of this month, you are lost. Don't you know that we are threatened with an encyclical on Holy Scripture, which is expected momentarily? The bishops are sure to condemn you without even waiting for the encyclical. If only you had postponed issuing your number until after the assembly of the bishops!" I replied that the idea of this piece of minor tactics had indeed visited my mind, but that I had shrunk from having recourse to it in accomplishing an act of sincerity concerning which no one in the world had the slightest reason for wishing me harm. Monsignor d'Hulst seemed recalled for a moment to the sympathy that he had formerly felt for me; his fears seemed to vanish, and he said on leaving me: "Well, let come what may, I at least will not carry your case to the Cardinal!"

Yet he himself took my article to Cardinal Richard, knowing full well what must be the consequences. He was not drawn into this inconsistency by his own spontaneous purpose. Certain of his associates, having regard chiefly to his interests, but probably also inspired by bad blood toward myself, as well as by a wish to safeguard the orthodoxy of the Catholic Institute, remonstrated with him that his position would be seriously compromised if some zealot or other should carry my article to the authorities; that he was in danger of injuring himself without the least prospect of saving me; that my ideas were more deserving of condemnation than those even of his "broad school"; that he was in no sense responsible for my imprudence in making them public; that his whole duty had been fulfilled in rescuing me once at his own grave peril; that my manifesto was a sort of infraction of the engagement made with the bishops at the time when I was relieved from my instruction in exegesis; finally, that the Catholic Institute could not retain me longer without great risk to its reputation and to the recruiting to it of students of theology.

In his consuming anxiety of the moment, the harassed Rector did not stop to discriminate clearly between the truth and the exaggeration contained in these assertions. Without saying a word to me about it, in a circular letter addressed to the bishops in August, 1893, he had promised them in my name that I would not trench on Biblical questions in my language courses. But even he did not dream of forbidding me to treat them in my periodical, which existed for this express purpose. I have asked myself since whether he may not have been piqued by my demolition of his fiction of the "broad school," and have wanted me to realize that his approval was my only resource. But I cannot believe that he would have acted under the impulsion of any such feeling. He was overwhelmed by the responsibility of his official position; having been persuaded that my own indiscretion in publishing my views had ruined me, and that in denouncing what I had done, my ruin could not be laid to his charge. Nevertheless, what he did pained him not a little. He held himself to be, and made himself, a slave to his office. It was repugnant to him personally to be my executioner. To his dying day he felt the need of explaining his conduct on this occasion. He could not have acted otherwise, he would say. No doubt he would have been glad to be more assured of this than he actually was.

Cardinal Richard had never read anything to compare with my article. To him, the five propositions in which I had summed up the assured results of Biblical criticism appeared of an unheard-of radicalism. He himself introduced my case before the assembly of bishops on the 15th of November.

These prelates at once judged that the presence of a man with ideas so extraordinary was compromising to the Catholic Institute, and they resolved without further ado to dismiss me by asking for my resignation.[1] "You threw yourself before a moving locomotive," said Monsignor d'Hulst to me a few days after this decision that I was to be suppressed. That locomotive was the assembly of bishops and the forthcoming encyclical of Leo XIII, both of which must be bowed down to in anticipation. Still, I could have told the Rector truthfully that it was he alone who threw me under the wheels.

[1] See Appendix III.

CHAPTER III

AT THE CONVENT IN NEUILLY

I

ON Friday, November 17, 1893, after his daily mass, Monsignor d'Hulst invited me home with him and there told me of the decision adverse to myself taken by the Board of Bishops entrusted with oversight of the Catholic Institute. He was brief and to the point. "Let's waste no time sentimentalizing over it," he said, by way of preamble. He seemed to me distraught by two conflicting emotions. For one thing, it must have been clear to him that my expulsion, occurring in the way it had, was far from reflecting credit on the institution under his charge, and further, if I were henceforth to live a broken life, that he could not entirely dissimulate to himself his own share of responsibility for this. On the other hand, he showed a very evident sense of relief at being finally rid of that troublesome Biblical Question, which had so nearly brought him to ruin on my behalf. He confined himself to telling me what the bishops had resolved, merely adding that Cardinal Richard had engaged to procure me a chaplaincy, and that His Eminence would grant me an interview on the morrow. For the moment it was evident he had no thought for the years that

155

were gone, the work I had done, or the devotion of which I had given proof, as none knew better than he. We parted coldly.

To myself, in view of this total ruin of all my prospects, it was clear that the past which Monsignor d'Hulst seemed to hold so cheap was gone, beyond recovery; that I was destined never again to enter the establishment to which I had consecrated the best of my energies and my affections; and that, if the aim of the bishops had been to show me to the door of the Catholic Institute, in reality they had brought me to the very frontier of the Church itself. It was repugnant to me then to pass that frontier, and it remained so for many years to come; yet I saw how easily one might be pushed across. On the morrow, I saw this even more clearly.

Among the moments of my existence that have most severely tried my soul, I doubt if any have been more painful to me than the few in which I have had the honor to converse with the late Archbishop of Paris. He was a man of a bygone age, using a dialect that conveyed nothing intelligible to me, and incapable of interpreting the one that I was accustomed to use. He had little cultivation, though his mind was not as narrow as his clergy were accustomed to say among themselves. He had brought from his native Brittany a faith of the consistency of granite, on which doubt had never left the faintest mark. He meant to be just, and he was truly good-hearted. From some of his associates I have heard that he was very charitable. But when it came to the Biblical Question, or, one may add, to any contemporary problem, he was quickly beyond his depth. He held firmly to the theological tradition of the Church, conforming with complete docility and scrupulously avoiding any personal opinion whatsoever. In his eyes there was something positively mystifying—beyond which some secret perversity must lurk—in others', and above all in priests', finding the remotest difficulty in making the same sacrifice of their intelligence. To cling obstinately to a belief of one's own, not in conformity with the corporate judgment of the Church, betokened a mind drunk with self-pride and delivered over to the power of Satan. As to just what was this judgment of the Church, the venerable Cardinal scarcely had the time to inquire, from books, or from a first-hand study of the relevant documents, ancient or modern. Rather, he depended on trusted theologians, belonging to the religious orders, to aid him in discerning it. To all the above, add a conscience meticulous in its devotion to the responsibilities of his charge, and anxiously watchful as to the purity of doctrine and the obedience to discipline of the clergy and Catholic institutions in his diocese, and a fairly adequate notion will be had of the remarkable personage before whom I was required to present myself.

The part he was destined to play in the successive crises of my ecclesiastical career may readily be conjectured. His voice was invariably for condemnation. Being informed that I was not personally unworthy as a priest, he usually addressed me in a tone of friendliness. At this first encounter, he told me, as though nothing else were to be expected, that the bishops had deprived me of my position at the Catholic Institute because they could not sanction the opinions I had put forth in my articles on the Biblical Question. The fact was that the bishops had passed no judgment on my opinions, but were fearful of giving the Catholic Institute a bad name, especially with the Vatican, by retaining me. The matter of my orthodoxy had influenced the Cardinal and certain others, but the majority had acted entirely from policy. Four bishops, so I learned afterward, without asking to have me retained at the Catholic Institute, had testified in my favor— Bishop Pagis of Verdun and Bishop Hugoin of Bayeux, both subscribers to *Enseignement Biblique,* Bishop Lagrange of Chartres, and a fourth who is still living so that I refrain from naming him. The Cardinal told me, in all good faith, that my errors were evidence of my having "read the Germans," and I avow that it was impossible to get him to understand that my opinions arose purely from the fact of my having read the Bible. He was unprepared to discuss the question on its merits; but on principle he saw no occasion for any debate. In his own eyes he was a judge, and a judge who was bound to keep the reasons for his verdicts to himself. "I am afraid that you have fallen into error," he said, in summing up our interview. Having been so ill-advised as to mention to him expressions of approval that had come to me from several ecclesiastical personages, notably from a foreign prelate who was at that time accounted very liberal, he hastened to reply: "I do not approve of everything that the Archbishop of X— does and says. The praise that he accords to your works is injurious to the Catholic tradition."

A fortnight later appeared the encyclical *Providentissimus Deus,* on the study of Holy Scripture, the mere anticipation of which had terrorized Monsignor d'Hulst, and decided the bishops to deal summarily with my case. At Rome it was not intended to be so sweeping in its effect as all that, and individuals close to Leo XIII and Cardinal Rampolla have since confided to me that the Vatican thought the bishops over-prompt in getting rid of me. Since I had already been restricted to teaching Hebrew and Assyrian, after my article on the Biblical Question a simple admonition would have met the needs of the situation, or else a temporary retirement such as had formerly been decreed in the case of Abbé Duchesne. But what was done was done, and the Pope refrained from asking the bishops to reverse their action.

His encyclical, though not wanting in good intentions toward the furtherance of Bible study, did nothing to lighten the task of the exegete. It recalled the traditional belief of the Church in the inspiration of Scripture, and reaffirmed the obligation of its interpreters to conform to Catholic doctrine and the teaching of the Fathers. The idea of a truly critical and historical exegesis was not expressly condemned, for the sole reason that its very existence was not so much as suspected. Thanks to this circumstance, the encyclical did not affect my writings, or did not apparently have them in view;

all it condemned was the system attributed by Monsignor d'Hulst to the "broad school," in his article in the *Correspondant*.

Nevertheless, under existing circumstances, I was unwilling to continue with the publication of my little periodical, and made up my mind to suppress it. The announcement to my subscribers was already prepared for mailing when I received a letter from the Cardinal, who felt himself authorized under the encyclical to order me to "suspend" my publication.[1] I affected to treat the order as merely advisory, and replied briefly that *Enseignement Biblique* no longer existed. From this time forward it was clear to me that the Archbishop of Paris cherished one fixed purpose toward me, and this was to prevent any teaching or writing whatsoever on my part. How this man, who had not read my books, and who indeed never read them, was brought to take such a resolve utterly passes my comprehension. Probably his opposition was fed by individuals in close relations with the Catholic Institute, but who were neither Monsignor d'Hulst nor the Rector who succeeded him. At one time this latter wanted to recall me to the chair of Hebrew and Assyriology, but met with a peremptory veto from the Cardinal.

On the advice of my friend, Abbé Alfred Joiniot, Vicar-General of Meaux, I determined to set myself right as regarded the encyclical *Providentissimus Deus* by sending a letter of submission to Leo XIII.[2] Nothing could have been easier, since there was not

[1] See Appendix IV.
[2] See Appendix V.

a word in the encyclical, apparently, that need cause me concern. However, to avoid all equivocation, I attached to my letter a memorial in which I explained to His Holiness, with an audacity only equalled by my candor, the manner in which I interpreted his instructions for furthering the historical and critical study of the Bible. My communication, forwarded by trusted and friendly hands, was not so ill received at the Vatican, but its effect was quite other than my friend Joiniot had anticipated.

The Pope read my letter; he even read my memorial with a degree of interest. But he also had it read by other high personages who, without finding in it any outstanding errors, judged it on the whole disquieting. Leo XIII did me the honor of sending a reply by the hand of Cardinal Rampolla, which was received early in January, 1894. His Holiness, said the Cardinal, had given his personal attention to the matters about which I had written him, and had been well pleased with my expressions of fidelity toward the Holy See; however, "by reason of circumstances and in my own interest," he would advise me to apply my talents to another line of studies. The use of a subterfuge of this sort to dispose of the Biblical Question was congenial to the mind of Leo XIII, but my friend was in consternation at having brought me to this *impasse*. After mature reflection, since it was a matter of advice merely and I alone could judge of my own affairs, knowing also that I could not hope fully to satisfy the theologians in any other line of study, I decided not to forget all that I had learned, but to continue my labors in the same direction. There was no necessity for showing to anyone the tactful letter from Rome, and I have no means of knowing whether or not Leo XIII and Cardinal Rampolla ever remembered afterwards the well-intentioned advice they had given me.

Cardinal Richard had pledged himself to the Board of Bishops to provide me with a situation in his diocese. All he felt obligated to by this was to take care that I did not die of starvation. On the other hand, his main concern was to see to it that I was not employed in any capacity where I could disseminate my erroneous ideas. His anxiety on this score was extreme. Having found Abbé Odelin, a member of the diocesan administration, kindly disposed toward me, I intimated to him that the most acceptable position to myself would be a chaplaincy in a *lycée*. But, such was the Cardinal's dread of introducing heresy into a State institution, he would hear nothing of it. Finally, in September, 1894, he appointed me chaplain of the convent of Dominican nuns at Neuilly.

Monsignor d'Hulst meanwhile made practically no effort to arrange matters so that my situation might be one more creditable to the Catholic Institute, or more favorable for the prosecution of my studies. Perhaps he felt that he was rather out of favor with Cardinal Richard, who accused him of having allowed himself to yield to the "seductions of science." To indifferent or hostile inquirers as to what was to become of me, he would say: "They will give him some petty chaplaincy;" while to friendly inquirers his reply was: "He will receive an honorable appointment." At the bottom, he was indifferent as to whether my situation was insignificant or not, for he regarded it as merely provisional. Abbé Icard had died on the 20th of November, 1893, and that meant a clearing of the horizon for the Catholic Institute. On January 28, 1894, the Rector wrote me of his purpose to "reopen for me the door of instruction on the side of Orientalism," and although I did not encourage this chimerical hope, I have reason to think that he persisted in it as long as he lived. I replied at once to his letter just cited:

I do not consider my return to the Catholic Institute either possible or desirable. With the conditions as you wish to have them, I cannot consent to go back. What I desire is the chair of Holy Scripture, in view of which you asked Bishop Meignan to release me to your faculty of theology. I have never wanted, and I do not now in the least want, the chair of Oriental languages. It is clear now that that might have been spared me; but, since I was dismissed from it, I do not feel the least inclination to resume it. All the ties being broken between the Catholic Institute and myself, and the manner of their rupture scarcely allowing their renewal under any circumstances, I have no other ambition than to work in peace, no matter where—in Paris if the authorities so decide, at home among my own people if Paris will set me free, somewhere else if opportunity offers. My life will not be long in any case, and I have a great deal to accomplish; so I must lose the least possible time. I like sometimes to fancy, in order to avoid holding any one individually responsible for it, that the Devil in his own proper person erased my name from the list of professors of the Catholic Institute, so that it can never be restored.

All relations between Monsignor d'Hulst and myself came to an end in January, 1895. I had sent him a simple card of New Year's greeting, to which he responded by letter, saying: "The silence that has fallen between us is very painful to me, and even more the resentment on your part which lies behind it. I have the consciousness, despite your conviction to the contrary, of never having betrayed by my actions the friendship which I have so many times manifested for you. . . . Nothing, or no one, not even yourself, can dissuade me from remaining very deeply attached by the double tie of esteem and of affection. I shall wait to hear from your own lips that you wish me to know that this will not be disagreeable to yourself." To which I answered that there was not much that looked like friendship in the happenings of two years before, and that, whether he willed it or not, the Rector of the Catholic Institute had had a responsibility for these occurrences which hardly left room for a friendly conversation. He did not further insist.

Less than two years later, on the 6th of November, 1896, he died, and I regretted having added a touch of bitterness to the sorrows of his closing years. I had been too hard on him, and had too severely judged his conduct. In truth, he was not to blame for the injustice committed toward myself. By nature he was loyal, brave and kind. If his acts did not always display these qualities, the fault was less his own than that of the institution which he served with a complete devotion, of the opportunist spirit of Rome and its bishops, and of the reign of terror which from that time forward weighed down the intellectual life of Catholicism. Monsignor d'Hulst, who had generously exposed himself for my sake, suffered more than I did, I verily believe, for what he felt compelled to do to my hurt. But it would have taken only a word from him of wholly spontaneous and trusting friendship to have made me forget all my resentment. That word he never brought himself to speak, and it cannot have been because he thought me unworthy to receive it or incapable of being touched by it. Perhaps there were matters which he did not care to trench upon, even in the most confidential relations, because he never permitted his own thoughts to dwell among them. He was too intelligent to have failed to perceive or to have divined my state of mind; nor did he dream of holding me in any way responsible for it. Yet he did not find it possible, either, to descend, even in the freedom of friendly intercourse, from the mystical region where he succeeded in keeping his own faith intact.

II

The convent of the Dominican nuns was located in a part of what had formerly been the park of Neuilly. The sisters belonged to the third (teaching) order of St. Dominic, and were members of a congregation having its headquarters at Nancy. They conducted a popular boarding school for girls. I was received by them very cordially, and never had reason to feel anything but complete satisfaction in my relations with the Mother Superior, a woman of fine intelligence and notable skill in the control of her establishment. These excellent women, sincerely devoted to their task, required of me only fidelity to my duties, and a tactful co-operation in the education of the young people committed to their charge. As for myself, I did my appointed work with the exactitude of a perfect time-piece. I felt that my ministry to the pupils should naturally be co-ordinated with, and even subordinated to, that of the sisters, women being endowed with special gifts for the education of their own sex. Thus it was that I had granted me five years of semi-solitude and of external peace at Neuilly. The Dominican fathers who frequented the institution, men of maturity and experience, showed me many kindnesses. Canon Pousset, senior priest of Notre Dame, who represented the diocesan authority in his capacity as superior to the sisterhood at Neuilly, was equally kind whenever the duties of his office brought him to the nunnery.

If Cardinal Richard, in transferring me from the teaching of Assyriology to hearing young girls say their catechism, had meant to get me out of harm's way, and dispose once for all of the embarrassing Biblical questions, he vastly deceived himself. For the catechism is also instruction of a sort, and the Cardinal, in placing me where I was obliged to deal directly with it, forced me to study and meditate upon it as otherwise I should never have done. My young pupils were divided, according to their ages, into three sections. My instruction to the oldest group took the form of lectures, and I was not slow in noticing that my young hearers gave me their close attention. While I was at the Catholic Institute I had been overburdened by the demands of my special subjects, and it was only in the vacations that I could spare time or energy for the consideration of the religious question in its wider bearings. Now my attention was concentrated on questions of belief every day and all the time. My exegetical work was not neglected, and moreover the studies that I now had in preparation dealt with the very problems that I found suggested by the catechism. It was during the years 1893-1900 that I constructed the first rough outlines of my volumes on the Gospels which were published in 1903 [1] and in 1908.[2]

After some hesitation I had abandoned the attempt to carry out the program planned for my former courses in exegesis, no longer having at hand the resources of an adequate library. The *Revue Critique*, of which I had been a collaborator since 1889, kept me supplied with Biblical commentaries in particular; and Abbé Chuquet, its editor, soon got into the habit of sending me all current books of value on the history and the philosophy of religion, church history, and the history of Christian doctrine. I began to develop an interest in the whole contemporary movement of religious thought; indeed, as a professor of religion, what better could I do? Nor was my reading confined to heterodox writers. My good friend, Baron Friedrich von Hügel, whom I came to know in 1893, sent me New-

[1] *Le Quatrième Évangile.*
[2] *Les Évangiles Synoptiques.*

man's works, and I studied them exhaustively. Newman's type of mind attracted me far more than did that of the Protestant theologians. I devoted myself assiduously to the study of his *Essay on the Development of Christian Doctrine* (1845). Thus it was that I prepared myself to teach the catechism.

How much better advised the bishops would have been to have confined me to Hebrew grammar and cuneiform texts! During the five years at Neuilly my mind was constantly absorbed in the endeavor to adapt Catholic doctrine to the exigencies of contemporary thought. It would be a serious error to imagine that this was an avocation for one's leisure moments, or a matter of merely speculative concern. On my own part, I never regained the simple faith of my childhood, nor could I accept literally a single article of the creed, unless it were that Jesus was "crucified under Pontius Pilate"; yet religion appeared to me more and more in the light of a tremendous force that had dominated, and still was dominant in, the whole of human history. All its manifestations had had their limitations, their faults, and their abuses; still they represented practically the summed-up moral endeavor of the human race. The Christian religion, a continuation of that of Israel, was distinguished among all others by the loftiness of its ideal. The Catholic Church was the spiritual mother of the European peoples, fallen indeed from her former estate, but still influential, and still potentially mistress of her future. If she could only learn to speak intelligibly to the modern peoples, no hostile power could prevail against her

To that Church, in spite of all that she had made me suffer, I remained sincerely attached. In May, 1893, Monsignor d'Hulst, citing Duchesne as an example for me to follow, had counselled me to try to gain entrance into the Academy of Inscriptions by means of my Assyriology. I answered: "Is it for the purpose of getting into the Institute that one consecrates himself to the priesthood?" Mere scientific honors which stimulate so many ambitions, even among ecclesiastics, were absolutely meaningless to me.

My present ministry offered occasion for many useful contacts with others. It was evident to me that the devotion of the holy women, whom I saw consecrating themselves utterly to the education of the young people confided to their care, had no relation to the abstract formulas of theology. They were sustained in it by the joy of self-sacrifice, of which they found their pattern-life in Jesus. Those nuns who take to meddling with matters of doctrine tend to fall a ready prey to heresy, and in this event to disbelieve obstinately; as witness Port-Royal. My good Dominicans could never have turned heretics—their thinking was not theological—and they helped me to understand that this is invariably the true way of thinking religiously. It was clearly apparent, as well, in my lessons on the catechism, that the properly theological parts of the doctrine passed entirely above the heads of the pupils and were never even noticed. The tawdry mysteries, over which the learned in ages past had sweat blood and water, did not arouse in those young minds the faintest interest. They were no more impressed by the mystery of one God in three persons than they would have been to learn that, in the arithmetic of Heaven, two and two make five. What counted, with them, was the direct appeal of goodness, of duty, and of Jesus as the model of utter devotion and the standard of moral perfection. But if mere dogmas are negligible, the Catholic practices retain their value as sources of elevating sentiment. The Christian ideal lives and operates in the ceremonies of Catholic worship.

Also the visits of priests and monks brought me enlightenment. At the Catholic Institute I had been in a position to study the Jesuits, and to see clearly that their purpose was not to conciliate the present age but, if possible, to dominate it. Also I had been brought in contact with the Sulpicians, kneeling piously before tradition, and indifferent to secular science and contemporary life. The Dominican monks whom I encountered at the convent in Neuilly seemed less desirous to dominate the world, and more disposed to come to an understanding with it. These Fathers never made me their confidant; no more than Monsignor d'Hulst did they share my professed opinions. Yet, unless I am greatly mistaken, not a few of them were agitating in their minds the problems of the present time, inclined to admit that something must be done to reconcile the Church and contemporary society, suffering within themselves from their inability even to avow their disquietude, and always anticipating, without too confidently expecting, the realization of the generous hopes that had led them into the order whose most illustrious figure was Lacordaire.

I derived a similar impression from my contact with the parochial clergy. A few of them, in truth, were of a total indifference, and this one could only deplore for the sake of the Church which they were called to serve. But many among them were preoccupied with present-day questions, with the ministry to the laboring masses, and with the instruction to be given to those of the populace who still remained loyal. These priests too felt that something would have to be done, and some of them openly said so; but what? Their life was constricted by its traditional molds, and their thought as well, which dared not emancipate itself. In this respect, nothing was more instructive than their clerical conferences. These I should have preferred to be excused from attending, but my request to this effect was not even replied to by the diocesan authorities. The curé of Neuilly, Abbé Tardif, was a man of excellent education, who had received me pleasantly as a member of his parish. At his request, not wishing to offend him by refusing, I acted as secretary to the conference, made up of the priests of Neuilly, Boulogne, Levallois-Perret and Clichy, and so felt obligated to be present at every session. The purpose was to discuss topics bearing on ecclesiastical science; but most of the time even those appointed to lead the discussions were visibly lacking in any genuine interest. They copied some well-known authority, and read what they had cribbed to the meeting. There was no real discussion, except on the part of one parish priest who piqued himself on his ability in theology. Abbé Tardif, who presided, was obviously in a hurry to get through, as if the time taken by the conference were wasted, as in fact it was. Even those who really had something to say were in no sense inspired to say it.

The Catholic Church, in France especially, was sick nearly unto death, and it was not alone in the sphere of Biblical studies that there was need for letting in a little light and air. Gradually, in the course of my investigations, of my observations, and of my reflections, the plan took shape in my mind of writing a book, in which I might deposit the whole fruitage of my limited wisdom. Not long before, Harnack had published his *History of Dogma*,[1] Wellhausen his *History of Israel and Judah*,[2] Auguste Sabatier his *Outlines of the Philosophy of Religion*,[3] H. J. Holtzmann his *New Testament Theology*,[4] Albert Réville his *Life of Jesus of Nazareth*,[5] and the memory of Renan was still very much alive. My notion was to elaborate, in contrast with these Protestant systems, a philosophical and historical interpretation of Catholicism, which should serve, at one and the same time, as its reasoned defense, and as a moderate statement of the internal reforms that must speedily be undertaken for the successful fulfillment of its mission to the world of today. The manuscript of this unpublished work, which I still have in my possession, written from notes jotted down from day to day for

[1] Vols. I and II, 1885; Vol. III, 1890.
[2] 1894.   [3] 1897.   [4] 1897.   [5] 1897.

several years previously, bears on its first page the date of July 30, 1898, and on its last that of May 4, 1899. It would make in print a bulky octavo volume, and from it I drew the material for several smaller books which made in their day a greater stir in the Church than I had dared to anticipate.

III

My treatise in apologetics consisted of twelve chapters.

The first served as a sort of general introduction, a criticism of the principal current theories of religion; first, of the popular Catholic notion as defined by the Vatican Council, and, lastly, of Newman's theory of the development of Christian doctrine, with Renan's and Sabatier's conceptions set in between. Two sections of this chapter appeared as separate articles in the *Revue du Clergé Français* for December 1, 1898, and January 1, 1899, signed A. Firmin—those, namely, which dealt with the theories of Newman and of Sabatier. The article on Newman led up to a plea for the extension of his idea of development by applying it not only to Christianity, but also and particularly to the Biblical revelation, which Newman seems to have entirely ignored. My criticism of Sabatier was in line with ideas that I have often used since as arguments against the primitive gospel of Liberal Protestantism —faith in God, the Father, who pardons sin—which is, as I maintain, neither the gospel as Jesus preached it, nor a true and fully articulated religion.

It would have been impossible to publish the two

opening sections, which like the closing ones were subordinate, though in more intimate connection with the main substance of the chapter. In the former, I set forth three postulates as forming the basis of the demonstration of Catholic truth—naming them respectively the theological, the Messianic, and the ecclesiastical. The theological postulate assumes that the fundamental religious ideas, beginning with the idea of God, have practically remained stationary, at least for a chosen remnant of mankind, from the creation of the world down to the present time. The Messianic postulate assumes that Jesus and the Christian Church were made the subject of formal and specific predictions in the Old Testament. The ecclesiastical postulate assumes that the Church, with the existing stages in its hierarchy, its fundamental dogmas, and its sacraments of worship, was directly instituted by Jesus himself. Now these three postulates, upon which rests the whole vast edifice of Catholic belief, are not only indemonstrable; they are positively shown by history to be fallacious. I suggested, indeed, a possible adaptation of each of these postulates to bring it into accord with the historical development—a potent process of growth, more intelligible and more satisfying, in a sense, even for faith itself, than any tissue of miracles. But it was not by means of such an introduction that I could hope to conciliate the orthodox theologians!

It was incumbent on me to recognize, at the beginning of the second section, that Renan, even while a student at Saint Sulpice, having expressly discerned the three postulates just described, and noted that they were put forward as certain and indubitable dogmas, had drawn the only legitimate inference, namely, that the Catholic religion cannot be true. I indulged the pleasing fancy of setting up a genealogical connection between the theology that Renan found himself thus forced to reject and his later profession of a religion of science. "It is not without interest," I wrote, "to observe that the spirit of the scholastic argumentation, after suggesting to him that religious belief is a matter of scientific certitude so far at least as concerns the so-called truths of natural religion and the claims of a primitive revelation, had first led him on into unbelief when he was able to demonstrate the absence of any such certitude, and had induced him later to search for a purely rational basis, on which to rest the further progress of mankind, in science. Nothing could be more instructive than this example to bring out the weaknesses of the so-called traditional apologetics."

The second chapter, entitled "Religion and Revelation," was also preliminary. It appeared, almost entire, in the *Revue du Clergé Français*, as three articles (June 1, 1899, Jan. 1, and Mar. 15, 1900): "The Definition of Religion," "The Idea of Revelation," and "The Proofs and the Economy of Revelation." The first of these continues the refutation of Sabatier. "Both reason and history," I declared, "require that its character as a social institution shall be expressed in any valid definition of religion." The second article would find itself today condemned by the decrees of Pius X, which require

Catholics to profess faith in the existence of an "external" revelation. I had no hesitation in denying that a revelation could involve "as it were, the violent and unaccountable insertion of ready-made ideas into a human intelligence and brain." The analysis which followed, of that operation of religious thought whose outcome we may call a revelation, implied the total absence of any supernatural machinery. This was reproduced in *Concerning a Little Book,* and it was condemned with that volume in December, 1903. In the third article, I formulated a definition of miracle which still seems to me true, though anything but orthodox. "Miracle, rightly considered, is the process of the universe and of life as it is contemplated by the inward eye of faith; . . . the same process of the universe and of life, regarded, in a fashion, externally by the understanding, is the order of nature—the domain of science and of philosophy." My manuscript contains, further, a summary treatment of the chief Biblical miracles, which was omitted from the published article. As to the prophecies, I went on to say that "the Scriptures are evidently a great repository of religious hopes and aspirations—assured hopes and infinite aspirations." This was going rather beyond the "great idea" about which Bishop Meignan had formerly discoursed to me; but of actual prediction not a shadow remained. I was in flat contradiction with the Vatican Council in what it decrees regarding the miracles and the prophecies as proofs of revelation.

In this article, I contented myself with explaining

that "the Scholastic notions of miracle and of prophecy, and the familiar arguments of the traditional apologetics, form the background of the definition of the Council, without being precisely its object"—a discreet, though inadequate, way of justifying the abandonment of these notions. In my manuscript, I recalled the three-fold postulate underlying the demonstration of Catholic truth, the ambush into which theology was betrayed by it, and the necessity for replacing the supernatural machinery by a vital development. That, however, had to be read between the lines of what I actually printed.

In order to avoid every excuse for easy and fatal misconceptions,—every pretext for those specious objections which disguise themselves under fine names like science and criticism,—it is requisite to perceive and to exhibit clearly what has been the age-long growth of religion and to reconstruct its successive stages, not with *a priori* reasonings or with poetic fancies, not even with the grandiose metaphors of antique symbolism or the abstract concepts of ancient philosophy, but by a reliance on the facts, the humble facts, which, however fragile or however fugitive they may be, are found today to resist all possible attack better than any syllogistic proof. . . . The religious life of humanity in all the ages, that of Christian and Catholic humanity pre-eminently, is a fact. A complete and exhaustive analysis of this great body of fact would be the positive and sufficient demonstration of the truth of Catholic Christianity.

After these introductory matters, there followed in the manuscript five historical chapters, bearing these titles: "The Religion of Israel," "Jesus Christ," "The Gospel and the Church," "The Gospel and Christian Dogma," and "The Gospel and Catholic Worship." The beginning of that on "The Religion of Israel" appeared as an article in the *Revue du Clergé Français* (Oct. 15, 1900), but an official intervention on the part of Cardinal Richard cut short its continuation. The four others, with some modifications, especially in the chapter on Jesus, were drawn upon for the substance of my two little books, *The Gospel and the Church,* in 1902, and *Concerning a Little Book,* in 1903. Except the last, all these chapters had been used in a simpler form as teaching material in my catechetical lectures at the convent of the Dominican nuns.

They set forth the historic advance of religion, and this advance was described as proof at the very least that religion is a great matter, and as certifying it to be such. But, after the historical exposition, one must confront directly the problems and the difficulties of the present. To this object were assigned three further chapters: "Dogma and Science," "Reason and Faith," and "Religion and Life." A chapter of much delicacy, entitled "The Intellectual Régime of the Catholic Church," served as a transition from the historical chapters to these later chapters of theoretical discussion, in which reformatory suggestions decidedly prevailed over considerations of apologetics. Except for a few pages inserted in *Concerning a Little Book,* nothing of the above has seen the light.

I regret today not having published my chapter on "The Intellectual Régime" in a small volume while I was still inside the Church. This criticism might at that time have been extremely useful. Now it would seem like an attack directed from the outside and so could serve no good purpose. The "régime" has been brought to such a state of perfection by Pius X that no least breath of discussion can even penetrate within it.

Nothing is easier than to point out its deficiencies. As a matter of fact, the Church has always recognized in principle, and the Vatican Council proclaimed openly, the autonomy of human science in its various orders, when restricted to their proper objects and methods. But in its own teaching, without seeming to be aware of it, the Catholic Church is still living on the science of antiquity, incorporated in its tradition. In its catechism and in its customary utterances from the pulpit particularly, it is in daily and hourly contradiction with the most elementary results of modern science, so that a crisis of faith is present, or at least is latent, from the primary school. Higher up on the scale of intellectual activity, and relatively to the freedom of the scientific movement, the freedom of Catholics is seriously limited; in the realm of the science of religion, it may be said to be practically non-existent.

It is impossible, I wrote, to formulate a new hypothesis or conclusion on any important point of natural science, rational philosophy, or historical criticism, without finding across one's path the barrier of a theological opinion. Present-day philosophy has no other aim than to attain, if possible, to a general conception of the universe and man, of their origin and of their end, that shall be in harmony with the scientific situation as it now exists. It is not, then, obliged to seek the law of its being from theology, which represents only the science

of the past, but from contemporary science, with which
theology too would do well to concern itself. Of late
there has been a great clashing of theological bucklers
against a young Catholic philosopher of the highest
ability, Maurice Blondel, who allowed himself to proclaim the autonomy of philosophy, affirming that there
is, properly speaking, no such thing as a Christian
philosophy, nor ever will be a philosophy that can be
considered ultimate. For having dared to utter these
elementary truths he was denounced at Rome, and doubtless owes it to being a layman that no condemnation
followed.—Put forth a theory on the nature of matter
and the composition of physical bodies, and you encounter the theologian brandishing as a formidable
weapon the definition of the Council of Trent on the
transsubstantiation of the bread and wine in the
Eucharist, and on the permanence of their "accidents"—
as if this definition, reflecting as it does the philosophical
conceptions of the Middle Ages, were in itself a standard
for the scientists of today, and as if they were to be
blamed for not finding their guidance there. Propose
a psychological analysis of personality, and the theologian advances armed with his theory of "hypostatic
union," and of the two natures, divine and human,
associated in the unique person of the Word, the Son
of God, he who in the flesh was known as Jesus Christ.
Publish a word in favor of the hypothesis of evolution,
and the theologian brings up against you the earlier
chapters of Genesis, whose authors assuredly had not
foreseen Darwin. Speak of the religions of antiquity,
of their origin and that of mythology, of the institution
of sacrifice and other religious usages, and the theologian
protests in the name of the literal truth of the sacred
histories. Mention the antiquity of the world and of
the human species according to geology, and archæology,
historic and prehistoric, and the theologian demands of
you whether you are not simply ignoring the Biblical
chronology, the universal deluge, and the inerrant witness
of Scripture. If science had waited to ask permission
of theology before going ahead, it would not have taken
a step beyond the Fifteenth Century; and if it should

choose today to show itself docile before the admonitions of the theologians, its development would be brought to a sudden standstill.

As to full freedom of criticism in scientific research into the subject of religion, the Church and the official theology have not the remotest conception of its possibility. "The scientific study of Scripture has never been conceived except as auxiliary to dogmatics. Even yet, no other significance than this is attached to it. The attitude of Bossuet toward Richard Simon typifies exactly that of theology toward criticism for the last three centuries. Criticism has no right to exist; there is no comprehension that it can exist; and all the roads by which it might seek to gain the light are deliberately blocked against it." On this point I was full of discourse, finding abundant illustration in the events of recent years: the encyclical *Providentissimus Deus*, the absurd decree of the Holy Office rendered on January 15, 1897, purporting to guarantee the authenticity of that most glaringly apocryphal passage in the whole Bible—the verse called that of the "three heavenly witnesses" in the First Epistle of John (I John, v, 7),—and the new Constitution of the Index, promulgated during the same year by Pope Leo XIII. "The ancient Scholastic theology, upheld, at least in appearance, by the pontifical authority and the ecclesiastical hierarchy, is making desperate efforts to control the scientific movement, which is invading the Church nevertheless. It is superfluous to point out the peril of such a situation."

It was, notwithstanding, a useful exercise to reflect upon the danger thus involved. The intellectual régime of Catholicism was having the effect of arousing the contempt or the open defiance of the entire learned world, of all enlightened spirits; within the Church it was resulting in a deliberate retardation of the general intelligence, with a mixture of all sorts of fanaticism and narrow conceit; it was encouraging on the part of Catholics in public life a conventional optimism and a perpetual want of sincerity; from a scientific point of view, the system of the *Imprimatur* and the dread of being placed upon the Index was resulting in a kind of permanent conspiracy against the truth.

But Catholicism is in reality not in the least this formidable spectre, made into a scarecrow by its adversaries, and into a fetish by some of its adherents. The abusive tendencies and the disastrous effects that have been signalized above are not the whole of Catholicism; not even, in reality, a constituent part of living Catholicism, but merely the débris of another age which hampers momentarily the life of today, as the dead branches of a tree in which, however, the sap is still rising.

The remedy could only be found in theology's coming to admit its limitations, and renouncing pretensions justified neither by its nature nor by its history.

IV

What I was able to write on the nature of dogmas will readily be divined. These I declared to be merely official formulations of Christian life and thought, in no sense adequate to their purpose, forever perfectible, in which it was foolishness to find absolute and immutable limits set to faith, and still more a rule whose restraint could be imposed on science. In order to exhibit the endless variation in even the most essential beliefs, I proceeded to sketch a history of the idea of God. "Religious feeling and the moral consciousness have created both the gods and God, but always with the concurrence of the reason, which has been able to conceive of the divine only in the same perspective in which it has viewed the universe as a whole. As human intelligence has ever made God in its own image, so the human conscience has ever formed Him in likeness to itself. The gods and God have never been more than the human ideal projected to the uttermost bounds of reality, where infinity begins." That which holds regarding our faith in God holds likewise of all our other beliefs. "The dogmatic formulas are invariably couched in terms of the knowledge of the age that gave them birth." Such being the case with all the formulations of theology, "theology and theologians have no choice but to allow science and scientists to cultivate in peace the domain that is indubitably theirs. God has delivered over the world to human reasonings. There is no way of recalling that concession, signed and sealed as it is in due and proper form."

It is a great lesson to learn, the lesson of inevitable self-limitation. Theology and science have both of them to take an essential step, which will consist in ascertaining how far their respective spheres extend. Both have made the mistake of thinking that their power was unlimited. Science has its limits, because it can only

apply to the knowable, and the knowable in experience
is determined, is relative. Theology has its limits because
it deals with the unknowable, which it must not reduce
to the proportions of the already known; it is inevitably
incomplete, symbolic. The Scholastic theology derives
directly from Greek rationalism; only it has introduced
a modification, in supposing that it was in virtue of the
Christian revelation that truth in its completeness
entered the mind of man, and further that the philosophical version of revelation, that is to say, theology
itself, was a precise rendering of divine and ultimate
truth. On the other hand, human reason, repulsed by
theology and divorced from faith, has never left off
believing in its power to solve all problems; it also, while
from time to time protesting its impotence, assumes the
right to judge dogmatically concerning matters beyond
its province. Nothing copies more slavishly the spirit
of certain Scholastic theologians today than the spirit
of the popular rationalism. Let science exert itself to
render mankind more and more intelligent, progressively
master in the world of matter—nothing is more essential.
But let it not make the pretense, on its own behalf and
by itself alone, that it can make men better—that will
end in rendering it ridiculous. Both theology and science
have the best of reasons for humility. Let them only
become sincerely humble, and they will no longer quarrel.

I expressed, further, the hope for a final reconciliation based on this change of spirit on the part of
both theology and science. I did not suppose myself
to be setting up a Utopia in assuming that the
ecclesiastical organization would end by comprehending its function as the educator of mankind, not a
power to dominate it. I flattered myself that dogmas, discarded or fallacious from a rational viewpoint, would permit of being interpreted in the light
of what moral significance they might contain. It
seems to me now that I was self-deceived. If the

moral ideal can no more be instituted by methods
congenial to experimental science than it can be fulfilled by a simple exertion of reason; if, consequently, positive science neither conceives nor constitutes by itself alone the life of the human spirit,
still it does not at all follow that our sole resource
must be in the evolution of Catholic theology, an
evolution accomplished by the theologians themselves and sanctioned by the ecclesiastical hierarchy.
So radical a change as would be indispensable to
produce this result surpasses the measure of human
probabilities, even of human possibilities.   The
evolution will take place, it is going on now, but
outside the Church and to its disadvantage; not
within the Church and with its aid, for to this the
Church would in no wise consent.

In the chapter on "Reason and Faith," dealing
with the inner life of the believer, I was too much
influenced by Newman in his theory of conversion,
with its three stages that marked the progressive
acquisition of religious faith: theism, individual-
istic Protestant Christianity, and Catholic Christianity.   These are artificial distinctions, since the
first stage does not represent a faith which has had
any definite place in history, and also because,
granting that Protestantism has certain disadvan-
tages, Roman Catholicism is not without others.   I
found no difficulty in reconciling the authority of
the Church with the relative autonomy of the individual conscience, by attributing to this authority
a merely pedagogical function.   But it is only too
evident that my signature alone did not suffice to

validate that kind of abdication, and that it would have required the assent of the Church itself, which is no more inclined to give it than to deny the absolutely binding character of its dogmatic formulas.

It was easy for me to conclude: "A recasting of the Christian teaching from top to bottom must be the essential prerequisite to a larger measure of success in the work of Christian education." Truth to say, I should myself have been gravely embarrassed if the Church, instead of condemning me after the publication of my historical chapters, had encouraged me to develop further my speculations on the dogmas and the faith, and had required me to set forth precisely what positive teaching I would suggest by way of substitution. While perceiving with perfect clearness the impossibility of retaining the traditional beliefs, I indulged the illusion that it was possible to continue the use of the ancient creedal forms, merely putting into them a more or less symbolical interpretation. But that meant running into the additional and dangerous complication of having a set of symbols suggestive of false ideas rather than of true ones. I should then have had to urge the Church to abandon preaching its God, creator of the world some thousands of years ago, its God-Man Christ, and its own infallibility, and to place the emphasis solely on the high ideal of justice and of goodness which is the true heart of its tradition. The Pope and the bishops would not have failed to respond: *Non possumus*. In fact, they could not.

Moreover, it is not in these terms that, in sober

reality, the question has to be posed. The Church might be powerless to alter its symbol; but no more did it fall to me to furnish another. To resolve the difficulty in practice, what was needed was not the formulation of a new set of speculative definitions calculated to replace the ancient dogmas; all that was required was to refrain from throwing these across the path of contemporary thought. The evolution of theology would follow by gradual degrees. The vital question, therefore, was whether it was possible to create within the Church a current of liberal opinion strong enough to give pause to theological absolutism, while at the same time safeguarding Catholic unity. The hypothesis remains far short of realization; yet from this practical standpoint which is the true one, my attempt at conciliation seems less illusory than the purely theoretical and impossible hypothesis that I brought forward in the first instance.

The chapter on "Religion and Life" envisaged the social function of the Church. I laid down the principle that there is "no veritable morality without a moral ideal; now the moral ideal is essentially religious; it implies a faith." Moral education was always a matter of tradition. The Church pretends to incarnate in that respect the tradition of mankind. She proposes herself as the universal educator—a sublime task, of which she must be credited with having created the very conception. She has carried it out, and she still carries it out in large degree; so much so that it does not readily appear by what other agency she can be replaced. But it is objected, not without appearance of reason, that the Catholic Church is a menace to the legitimate autonomy of the individual, of the family, and of society. I explained how this was not so at all, or rather how it need not be so, if the Church were to become what I desired that she might be made.

Autonomy, a relative autonomy of the intelligent individual, belongs to the logic of human progress. The Church will recognize this. She will not proclaim the infallibility of the individual, which would be an absurdity. She will not proclaim his absolute independence relative to all instruction, especially to the religious tradition of the Christian centuries, which would be an additional folly. She will not oblige all her children to criticize their own beliefs, since they have for the most part more pressing duties to perform. But she will encourage each of them to acquire and to conserve what one may call the personality of faith and of religious knowledge, the originality of an individual conviction within the unity of a common profession. She will not be surprised if the more enlightened among them are more individual and more original in their manner of interpreting for themselves the traditional beliefs. She will end by applauding the toils of the greater to the profit of the humbler, and her intellectual régime will grow more and more liberal without ceasing to be tutelary. For she will not forget, she cannot and must not forget, that liberty is but a means, not an end; and that the fullest measure of truth is realized, not through liberty alone, but through harmony between the authority which instructs and directs and the free activity which learns, which seeks, and which finds.

I understood the autonomy of conscience in the same relative sense.

We are good by ourselves and for ourselves. But we do not cease to live in part by others and for them. A constant influence from the moral atmosphere that is breathed in a religious environment is the normal pre-requisite of moral autonomy, of its preservation and its progress among individuals.   This vivifying atmosphere is found, as nowhere else, in the Catholic Church.

Continuing, I explained how the Church under-stands the direction of consciences, which is in no sense their subjection.   I even went so far as to justify the obedience of members of the religious orders, because in principle it is voluntary: "The superiors of these communities are only the higher servants of a rule and of a work which are accepted by all as their common law and mission.   It is the rule which commands, and not those who ad-minister it."

Being in such fine fettle, I went on to discuss in some detail the question of public education.

The spirit of the society in which the secularizing of all the schools has been undertaken was already an entirely secular spirit.   France was not deeply attached to that religious instruction which the State has now refused to sustain; she did not revolt against those who pledged themselves to supersede it. . . . So-called Catholic education is not a sacrament that automatically makes those who receive it religious; it has this effect only on a negligible minority.   So serious a defect as this must lie in the system employed.   It is a mistake to suppose that the education of young people, even of children, requires that the least credible of Bible stories should be presented to them as true to fact, or that they should be expected to yield implicit belief to formulas which they cannot later, or ever, hope to understand. All children who are told the story of Jonah and the whale do not ask whether or not it ever happened; but a great many instinctively suspect that it did not.   Their teachers profess amazement later that they should have lost their faith so easily; but they never had the kind

that was assumed to have been imparted to them. Their
minds quite naturally rebel, without any ill-will being
involved, against a conception of God, of the universe,
of man, which, no longer having reality for us, no longer
has reality enough for them. It is a self-deception, as
well, to imagine that children need only to be directed
and chastised, without knowing clearly the reason for
what is commanded and what is forbidden them. Very
quickly they discern that it is not God who teaches
them out of our mouth! Their moral consciousness takes
its character from the judgments which they frame for
themselves, and their strength of moral will from the
initiative which they display in doing what they deem
to be right.

From the practical viewpoint, I regretted that it
had become customary to oppose Catholic and lay
schools to each other, when the difference was one
rather of name than of fact. In secondary education,
high schools of mixed character like the former
Stanislas, or institutions like the Catholic public
lycées (the schools named for Bossuet, Fénelon and
Massilon in Paris) seemed to me greatly preferable
to either purely Catholic or purely secular institutions. I deplored the fact that Church and State
had not increased their number. As to the higher
education, if I recognized the importance of institutions for the advanced study of religion, I professed
my inability to comprehend the occasion for Catholic
universities. The condition of these appeared to me
extremely precarious and their future doubtful.

Placed under the immediate control of the bishops,
under petty surveillance by clerical opinion and the
clerical press, and under the oppressive and defiant
direction of Rome, these establishments find themselves
in the situation, compromising and perilous in the highest

degree, of being obliged at one and the same time to be modern and to be archaic—modern, because an education that has to rival that offered by the State cannot fall behind without loss of respect; archaic, because that education must be satisfactory to persons who cherish aims that have no connection with scientific progress. Catholics, organized as a political party, were ambitious to possess higher schools of their own, but they have not succeeded in making them work. That is what stands out most clearly in this matter, which is not a brilliant affair; indeed, far from it.

My reflections on Christian marriage and on ecclesiastical celibacy had nothing original about them. So far as celibacy was concerned, a reform seemed to me desirable, but impossible to realize at present. The relations between Church and State under the Third Republic suggested to me the following remarks:

The separation of Church and State remains perpetually in anticipation, but never perhaps have these two, who now threaten divorce, sustained more intimate relations. The government of the Republic, the most secular of all governments, is not content with choosing and naming the bishops, the official representatives of the Catholic religion; it negotiates with the Pope for his support in electoral contests, and the Pope lends his support to republican as against monarchist candidates. Never were the most Christian kings minded to invite the Popes thus to meddle in their statecraft. But our government receives from Rome a real service and gives nothing in exchange, unless it be the maintenance of the Concordat, that is to say, of a treaty which is, at bottom, onerous only to the Church. Leo XIII has not renounced a single pretension of his predecessors, but is holding himself in reserve for the right moment. While believing it to be imminent, he is doing his best to prevent that moment from ever arriving. In his negotiations with the secular powers, he tries to moderate and to delay ever so little the process of secularization, while at the same time he prepares for its inevitable success in the near future. If it were to happen that, within some twenty years, the public mind were not entirely at ease on the question of clericalism, and there should be a Catholic majority in the French chambers of parliament, still these well-disposed politicians could do nothing to modify the work of secularization. They might even suppress the Concordat, especially if the Church at that time should be ruled by a true pastor, and not by a diplomat, all having seen in the end that the Concordat is only a means for enslaving to the State, which ought not to enslave anyone, a Church whose influence can be healthful only on condition of its being free. Whatever surprise the future may hold for us, it is evident that all the parts of the old machinery which kept the Church and the State interlocked together are now racked apart and ready to fall to pieces. No power in the world is capable any longer of readjusting them with any promise of permanence. All the endeavors undertaken by the Church for the restoration of past conditions can end only in the more surely preparing for their disappearance.

This is not to say that the Catholic religion has become useless to present-day society; quite the contrary. But its influence must be exerted in other directions. For the last time I sketched the type of the representative Catholic believer of the older generation, with a view to showing that the mass of our contemporaries, and that modern man in general, could no longer conform to it.

The old-fashioned Catholic is, above all, a man who goes to confession, who goes often, all the more so in proportion as he indulges less frequently in actions that Catholic morality regards as sinful. He is a man who practices intellectual obedience, admitting implicitly

everything that is taught by the Church, and accepting
without question all that he can grasp of that teaching;
never discussing either the meaning or the logical outcome of what he believes; comporting himself in the
Church as a disciple, who accepts from her whatever he
is to think on all the great, vital matters of human life,
whatever he must do to be an honest man, and whatever
rites he must fulfill to be a loyal Catholic Christian.
He is thus a man all of whose activity finds itself regu-
lated by external authority, and who feels no concern
to do his own thinking—who, indeed, would regard himself as culpable to take such a liberty, since he esteems
intellectual timidity as a positive virtue. He avoids
thinking at all on religious questions, from fear of thinking wrong. He learns about religion in safe writings
recommended by his spiritual director, and his only ideas
are those guaranteed to him as perfectly orthodox and
perfectly reliable. This type of Catholic is still to be
found, it cannot be denied; but the type is not numerous,
at least in its perfection, in spite of all that is done to
multiply it. The reason is that it is attainable only at
the price of an unnatural abdication, which many resist
as if by instinct, and which others specifically repulse as
a violation of their personal integrity.

And, also for the last time, I developed the program of an ideal Catholicism, in which the individual
would be permitted to have faith, virtue and independence of initiative, in co-ordination with the
faith, the rule, and the action of all combined. I
did not then doubt that my ideal was capable of
realization in Roman Catholicism, and did not ask
myself whether, peradventure, it might not be
essentially incompatible with it.

A chapter entitled "Past and Future" contained a
brief summary of the results and anticipations of
the entire book. The Church has been always really,
profoundly, in process of change, while remaining

self-identical; why should she not continue to change, since new changes are indispensable to the continuance of her normal effectiveness?

How much one deceives himself in supposing that the Church would rather perish than continue to change! The present situation of Catholicism is the same as at all the critical epochs of its history: that is to say, the majority of the faithful, of the priests, of the theologians and of the bishops are living on what has been acquired, looking back and regretting the past, deploring the misfortunes of the present, and unable to conceive a remedy other than the exercise of a jealous watchfulness over the traditional deposit of doctrine, of moral discipline and of worship. What is understood as tradition is whatever has been inherited from the preceding generation. Any innovating idea, therefore, is found to savor of heresy. The more clear-sighted, if they are clever, are governed by their ambition for a career, and flatter the general opinion. The Church bears a strong resemblance to an old woman who insists on seeing the furniture of her room always in the same places, seeing the same ornaments on her mantel, the same flowers in her garden and the same dishes on her table. Who can break through this routine? Men comparable to those who formerly rebelled and rose superior to the traditional inertia; for so the Church has always been! If she has forever changed, one may say that, in a sense, she has changed in spite of herself, and especially while protesting that she had never changed at all. This is why the Church, if she is to survive, will go on changing to the end.

The illusion, I now believe, was on my part. The present situation of the Church is not what it was at the epoch of the great heresies, nor yet in the Middle Ages, nor even at the time of the Protestant Reformation. It resembles, rather, that of the decadent Paganism in the first centuries of our era, when it became evident to all the more enlightened spirits that the old national cults could maintain themselves only by means of new interpretations and a sort of fundamental transformation. The transformation was not successful, and the young and living Christianity took the place of those superannuated religions which proved impotent to renew themselves down to their very roots.

Judicious persons have often remarked to me that I wasted a great deal of time over this apology for Catholicism, which utterly failed to prove its thesis, and that I should have done far better to reserve all my energies for purely scientific productions for which the age might have given me recognition. But I did not have full freedom to devote myself to these purely scientific productions, since I was a teacher of religion, a professing Catholic, and in the exercise of Holy Orders. The truth is, I was engaged in elaborately proving to myself why and how I could, and indeed must, still remain in the Church.

Moreover, it would be a total misapprehension as to the significance of these studies to deem them an apology for the existing Catholicism. They should rather be taken as a criticism. In reality, my work was a historical and philosophical discussion of the Christian past, from which were deduced certain significant lessons for the present. It was in no sense a disadvantage to have meditated for several years on the fundamental problems of religion, from both the speculative and the practical points of view. At the present time a professor of the history of religions, I do not find that this preparation has been by any means wasted. Whole sections of my historical synthesis survive in my latest publications.

An advantage which appears to me conspicuous, though its nature is not such that it will be generally appreciated, is the intimate acquaintance and sympathy thus acquired with religious phenomena, especially with the spirit and operation of Christianity in the course of the centuries. My researches during the twelve years passed at the Catholic Institute, limited as they were to Biblical criticism, had taught me primarily what reasons might be found for not believing in the Christian revelation. Wider studies have enabled me to penetrate farther into the actual economy of religious faith, and have brought me to see in religion something quite other than a mental aberration. I venture even to say that, thanks to these later studies, my purely intellectual dissent from the Catholic Church has lost much of its significance in my own eyes. If I have never been able to take a hostile attitude toward either religion or the Church, it is because I am fairly well acquainted with both.

CHAPTER IV

AT THE ÉCOLE PRATIQUE DES HAUTES ÉTUDES

I

ON the 20th of September, 1899, towards four o'clock in the afternoon, my mother, with whom I had come to spend a month's vacation, heard the sound of an inert body falling heavily on the floor of my room. She ran up, and found me unconscious, lying in a pool of blood. During the day there had been slight vomitings of blood, of which I had not spoken, to avoid disquieting her. A more serious hemorrhage of the stomach had brought on a dead faint and made manifest the gravity of my condition. I went to bed, and on the 23rd a fresh hemorrhage brought me within a hand's breadth of death. For several days there seemed little hope, and it was certain that, even if I recovered, many months would be required for convalescence. So I dictated a letter to Cardinal Richard, resigning my chaplaincy. A few days later I learned from the Prioress of the Dominican nuns that the letter had reached its destination and that the Archbishop had at once named my successor.

By the beginning of November, I was able to take up my residence at Bellevue. Monsignor Mignot, then bishop of Fréjus, who had followed my work with interest for several years, was good enough to request for me from Rome an *indult* or exemption from the usual regulation, permitting me to say mass in my own room. This exemption was granted for seven years, and placed me in a somewhat unusual position from the canonical viewpoint. In principle, I still belonged to the diocese of Châlons, but I had been assigned to the Catholic Institute in Paris, and the bishopric of Châlons paid no further attention to me. At the Catholic Institute and at Neuilly, I was under the jurisdiction of Cardinal Richard, but I left it in quitting the diocese of Paris, and Meudon-Bellevue was in the diocese of Versailles. There I was only a stranger, provisionally in residence. The bishopric of Versailles countersigned my exemption, and refrained entirely from meddling in my affairs. Just because no bishop had, or claimed, jurisdiction over me, I enjoyed much fuller freedom than a priest in the ordinary exercise of the parochial or the teaching ministry. This was what I had wished, and I was fully resolved to take advantage of it.

My retreat to Neuilly had not cut me off from all connection with my former subscribers to *Enseignement Biblique*. In 1896, with the help of two friends, professors at the Catholic Institute, and of several laymen of intelligence and good-will, I established the *Revue d'Histoire et de Littérature Religieuses*, in which I continued to publish numerous articles, mostly exegetical. In order to avoid attracting too much attention, not all of these were signed with my own name, but a number of different pseudonyms were employed, which had the effect, for a considerable time, of throwing inquisitors off the scent. My chronicle of Biblical Books Received, in which I reviewed current works in exegesis, was signed "Jacques Simon." In 1897 a double of "Jacques Simon," "François Jacobé," was bold enough to maintain that, in the original redaction of the Third Gospel, the canticle, "My soul doth magnify the Lord," was attributed to Elizabeth, the mother of John the Baptist, instead of to Mary, the mother of Jesus. That opinion later figured in the catalogue of my heresies, whose condemnation Cardinal Richard was to seek at Rome. For the time being, no special notice was taken of it, because "Jacobé" put forth his conclusion very modestly; too modestly, indeed, for in 1900 Professor Harnack, without having seen my work, arrived at the same conclusion, supporting it by similar arguments, and is still regarded as its originator.

In the year 1896, there came a reawakening of the desire for a closer accord between the Church of England and the Church of Rome; a periodical, the *Anglo-Roman Review,* having been founded to further that rather chimerical expectation. The editor of the *Review* thought that I might be able to give his Anglican readers a helpful glimpse of the liberal spirit in which the Catholic clergy confronted questions of exegesis. Probably he somewhat overshot the mark, and the High Church theologians doubtless thought I went to extremes. My article was a criticism of Renan's *History of the People of Israel,* and in it I showed myself more daring than the author himself. But this bit of writing was scarcely read outside of England, where it is not the custom to denounce any one to the Congregation of the Index or to the Holy Office.

Meanwhile, on Sunday, September 27th, 1896, a member of the Society of Jesus who wished me well —he had formerly been a student in my language courses at the Catholic Institute—came to confide to me in the utmost secrecy the news that my condemnation was being sought at Rome. He had his information from a member of the Order who was on the spot and knew whereof he spoke. I do not in the least imagine that the denunciation had been preferred by other members of that Society. In any case, nothing came of it. Pope Leo XIII would not have countersigned an order putting my works on the Index unless it had been opportune, and it was not so just then. Perhaps his object was, like that of the good Fathers who gave me the hint, to intimate that I should be extremely careful.

I have already referred to the articles signed "Firmin," in the *Revue du Clergé Français,* edited by one of my former pupils, Abbé Bricout. These began in 1898 and were continued through 1899 and 1900. I published in the same review over my own name, in 1899, two long articles on "The Origins of the New Testament," which were primarily a discussion of the views put forth by Professor Harnack in the first volume of his *Chronology of Early Christian Literature.* No limit was imposed upon me in the criticism of Protestant exegetes, provided I refrained from expressing my personal convictions, which were even more radical. Other articles appeared over the name of "Isidore Desprès," who furnished, in February, 1899, a study, curious enough in certain of its aspects, entitled "Catholic Opinions on the Origin of the Pentateuch." [1]

Desprès was visibly amused by the quarrel that had arisen between Father Lagrange, a Dominican, and Father Méchineau, a Jesuit, relative to a study read by the former before the International Congress of Catholic Scholars at Freiburg in August, 1897. Father Lagrange had discussed "The reasons which have prevented Catholics from abandoning the Mosaic authorship of the Pentateuch." Baron von Hügel had read before the same Congress an admirable exposition of the results of the criticism of the Hexateuch (Pentateuch plus Joshua), but there had been no reference to it in the Catholic journals or reviews. The innocent Desprès pretended to be astonished at this oversight, and took pains to analyze elaborately a dissertation that could not fail to be extremely instructive to his readers. Then he turned his attention to Father Lagrange's paper and, with the same innocent air, exposed its true purpose: "Let us not be deceived," he wrote; "from critical analysis to refutation is but a single step; and what we have here is, in fact, a refutation of the traditional thesis." And Desprès went on to complete the arguments of Father Lagrange. But he devoted himself especially to refuting Father Méchineau, who had undertaken to defend "tradition" against the learned Dominican. After this, he allowed him-

[1] Reproduced in *Études Bibliques*,³ pp. 194-259.

self the mischievous pleasure of citing an English Jesuit (not Father Tyrrell) and a Catholic priest of the same nationality who had written on the same lines as Baron von Hügel.

The following year,[1] Després ventured to comment on that portion of the Papal encyclical of September 8th, 1899, which dealt with Biblical studies.[2] Baron von Hügel, who is goodness personified, has never forgiven me for that article, and it was solely to avoid wounding this dear friend that I abstained from reprinting it in the third edition of my *Études Bibliques,* where a place had been reserved for it. This time, indeed, Després coldly pushed home some cruel truths. He showed readily enough, on the basis of the new encyclical—in which the papers read at Freiburg as well as my own writings were referred to, without definite citation, as "dangerous imprudences," already reproved by the encyclical *Providentissimus Deus*—that the Pope, contrary to what we had imagined, had intended, in publishing this earlier warning, to condemn all criticism without exception.[3]

It is plain, so wrote Després,[4] that *the Holy Father does not appreciate the work of Catholic critics, either in itself or for its scientific value.* That work, we may say in passing, is not judged unfavorably by experts *outside the Church.* But the question is as to its relation to the Scholastic theology and the proof from Christian evidences which has been *traditional since Bossuet.* In the

---

[1] June 1, 1900.
[2] Letter to the French clergy, on ecclesiastical studies.
[3] See Appendix VII.
[4] The more daring parts are printed in italics, to obviate the need for further special allusion to them.

Scholastic conception, Biblical exegesis is merely an auxiliary science or, more accurately, a branch of theology. No other reason is perceived for its existence than that of sustaining dogmatic theses, or of furnishing arguments against heresy and incredulity. That Biblical science can enjoy a relatively independent existence, like every other branch of human knowledge, with its own object and method, both purely historical—*this is an idea absolutely new and almost revolutionary for Catholic theology.* . . . This is why Leo XIII condemns the new criticism as too advanced in theology and perilous in apologetics. *Envisaged from the viewpoint of Scholastic theology*, the opinions recently put forth by Catholic critics touching the origin of the Pentateuch appear indeed to destroy the whole structure of Christian evidences, and to compromise the authority of the Old Testament, as well as that of the Savior and of the ecclesiastical tradition. *It is beyond his comprehension how sensible persons can leave the firm standing-ground of received opinions to embark on an enterprise full of hazard and uncertainty. The exceptionally harsh language of the Sovereign Pontiff thus requires no explanation, and it would savor of impertinence to endeavor to justify the critics.*

Nevertheless the purpose of Catholic critics has not been to snatch by one bold stroke, from heterodox critics, the arms which the latter have employed against Catholic tradition. The scholars in question are neither theologians nor apologists by profession. Judges *of moderate penetration* have sometimes supposed them ignorant of theology because they did not speak its language. If they have endeavored to show how their opinions as scholars were not subversive of religion, and might even help towards an apologetic reared in sympathy with the spirit of the times, what they have done that shows initiative, *without perhaps being themselves entirely aware of it*,[1] has been to treat the Bible as we have explained, in beginning to erect Biblical science as an independent discipline, and not a mere appendix to theology. . . . Will exegetical science be able to establish

[1] Desprès does not here refer to Firmin.

itself among us in this wise on its own ground, by the same token as philosophy or ecclesiastical history? It is a question into which for the moment we are not required to go. It may be said, however, *that the pontifical documents actually decide it in the negative, without having posed and discussed it on its merits.*

No more has the tentative of the critics been inspired by a taste for mere innovation. They have become critics at their personal risk, and *they are not all so to the same extent,* or by mutual agreement. Circumstances, environment, professional duty, and their own researches have led them out of the beaten tracks. It has been their hope to demonstrate that Biblical criticism within the Church is not, as is generally believed, and as appears when it is looked at distantly from without, simply an engine of war directed against Christian and Catholic tradition. . . .

At the present hour, *they are not in a position to defend the tradition which Leo XIII reproaches them with having abandoned, or to uphold the validity of the proofs which they have already demonstrated to be weak.* The theologians who flatter themselves with never having surrendered anything to criticism have only to follow the progress of the latter, as the Sovereign Pontiff has recommended, while still sustaining the opinions *called traditional;* they have already lost too much time in combating, *often by way of misrepresentation,* the conclusions of Catholic critics. A more urgent task now devolves upon them—that of exposing *with entire sincerity* the present status of Biblical criticism among Protestants, and of demonstrating *by reliance on facts* that all the results of this criticism are arbitrary, and *that the science of the Bible is still comprised in its entirety in the theological commentary upon it.*

The irony of Desprès was not without a hint of bitterness. But he was comparatively immune, in that the accredited defenders of orthodoxy, although keenly irritated against him, did not undertake to secure his condemnation. They chose rather to

direct the blows of ecclesiastical authority upon
Firmin, who had published early in the year his
articles on revelation, and who was not likely to
abstain from providing their sequel by going on to
describe the history of that revelation in both Testaments.   Firmin, in fact, brought out on the 15th of
October, 1900, an introductory article on "The Religion of Israel."   In the number of November 1st,
at the head of the first page, appeared a letter from
Cardinal Richard, reproving the article already
printed, as contrary to the definitions of the Vatican
Council and of the encyclical *Providentissimus Deus,*
and forbidding the continuance of the series.   The
editor of the review bowed to the Cardinal's censure,
which prohibited him from receiving henceforth any
article whatever from me, no matter what its subject.   Thus ended my collaboration with the *Revue
du Clergé Français.*

From his letter it did not appear that Cardinal
Richard had had my article examined by any committee of theologians.   He had probably been induced to read its first page only, where I had para-
phrased in my own fashion a few lines from Bossuet.

The progress of the study of ancient history, wrote
Firmin cheerfully, has had the result that practically
nothing is now known touching the first five periods of
the *Discourse on Universal History,* "the earliest ages
of the world," which Bossuet supposed he knew so well:
Adam or the creation, Noah or the flood, Abraham or the
beginning of the covenant, Moses or the written law, and
the siege of Troy, "occurring about the year 308 after
the departure from Egypt and 1164 after the flood."
That great writer was able to mark the date of the creation, 4004 before Christ; why then should he not have

dated the siege of Troy? . . . The chronological data of
the Bible remind us at the present time of a slender
thread thrown in guise of a bridge across an abyss whose
other side is out of sight. To depict scientifically the
primitive history of humanity, as well as the ancient
history of Israel, we must admit the existence of profound obscurities. It may be affirmed at the very outset
that the history of Israel is relatively clear from Samuel
and Saul down. Farther back, remounting to Moses, a
few details are half seen against a cloudy background.
Beyond Moses, to Abraham, certain indefinite figures
may be vaguely discerned amid the shadows, but back
of Abraham the night closes down completely. The first
chapters of Genesis do not tell us, and do not undertake
to tell us, under what circumstances either man or religion
came into existence, or how they comported themselves
in the course of prehistoric ages.

All of which was indubitably true; but it was
equally indubitable that neither the Vatican Council
nor Pope Leo XIII, in the encyclical *Providentissimus Deus,* had had any prevision of novelties like
these. Could it be that the narratives of Genesis
were not transparently clear and exact? Might
not one read there that God had made Adam and
Eve with his own hands, that he had spoken with
them face to face, and likewise with Noah, Abraham
and Moses? How was it that Firmin found anything shadowy here? What he affirmed in the body
of the article, touching the origins of Israelitish
monotheism, the primitive character of Israel's God,
circumcision, the distinction between pure and im-
pure, the sacrifices, the feasts, and the ark of
Yahweh, were at bottom scarcely more orthodox, but
escaped the attention of Cardinal Richard and likewise that of his theological advisers.

I have never learned how the Archbishop of Paris was induced to condemn my article. The censure appeared to be hastily put together,[1] as if made to order. I have been told that several French ecclesiastics, who came together at the International Congress of Catholic Scholars at Munich, in the summer of 1900, had resolved among themselves to suppress at all costs the articles signed by Firmin. But I have some difficulty in believing that these men, zealous as they were, could have induced Cardinal Richard to act without an intervention from Rome. It has been deemed by some a merit on the part of Leo XIII that he never condemned me. The reason was that Leo XIII affected, as much as possible, to regard the disputation in which I had been concerned as a "French affair." He refrained from committing himself with regard to it, but he was entirely capable of suggesting privately to his bishops what measures they should take. It will appear a little later how this was managed in connection with *The Gospel and the Church.*

In any event, Cardinal Richard's letter created for me a new situation relative to the Church and its hierarchy. Until this moment, my person and my opinions had not been formally denounced as suspect, my expulsion from the Catholic Institute having been regarded, and very justly, as a measure of policy. Now began the process of making me almost a heretic, and it was not very difficult to foresee that soon enough I should be in danger of becoming a heresiarch. Under these conditions, I

[1] See Appendix VIII.

felt that I must most scrupulously safeguard my independence. When I had arrived at Bellevue, an influential layman had obtained for me, from the archbishopric of Paris, a modest pension, paid out of the diocesan fund for infirm priests. From the time when the editor of the *Revue du Clergé Français* communicated to me the Cardinal's letter, and even before it was published, I felt that it was incumbent on me to renounce this subvention, and I signified this resolve to Abbé Poudroux, chancellor of the archbishopric, in a letter dated October 26th.

It is not for me, I wrote, to discuss the judgment of His Eminence, which attacks a pseudonym, nor do I wish for the present to augment by a public defense the excitement that is likely to result from this judgment. The article in the *Revue du Clergé Français* was printed, for the most part, several years ago in the *Anglo-Roman Review*, without arousing the slightest protest, and the questions treated in it are not among those whose relations with theology are susceptible of facile handling. I am persuaded that His Eminence has consulted only the interests of truth, as his best judgment and conscience have shown them to him. But I consider that it is not permitted me to take further advantage of the liberality of His Eminence, and I am constrained to return to your hands the amount of the pension which the archbishopric of Paris has remitted to me during the present year.

II

Aid came to me at this juncture, for the first time, from the lay element in French society. For several years I had been acquainted with Monsieur Paul Desjardins. He arranged for me an interview at his house with his father-in-law, Monsieur Gaston Paris, administrator of the Collège de France. Monsieur Gaston Paris was kind enough to interest himself in my situation, and it was agreed between us that he should speak to Professor Albert Réville, to secure my admission as lecturer in the section of the science of religion at the *École Pratique des Hautes Études;* to the Minister of Public Instruction, who at that time was Monsieur Georges Leygues, for the purpose of obtaining an appropriation for the new lectureship; and to Monsieur Philippe Berger, of the Academy of Inscriptions, to request my appointment as assistant in the preparation of the *Corpus Inscriptionum Semiticarum.* All this was accomplished. Monsieur Paris brought these several negotiations rapidly to a successful conclusion, and on the 12th of December, before a numerous and sympathetic audience, which included a goodly sprinkling of the clergy, I began a course of lectures on "The Babylonian Myths and the First Chapters of Genesis."

This outcome of my condemnation had scarcely been foreseen by Cardinal Richard. His settled purpose had been that I should never again engage in public teaching in Paris. The change was accomplished before he could move to put any obstacle in the way, and even if he had seen fit to act, I should have overriden his opposition. He hesitated about protesting against an accomplished fact, but he wrote to me, on the 26th of December, that he would be "very happy" to see me. I went the next morning to his office, and we had another of those mortal encounters which I have mentioned above. The Cardinal, assisted perhaps by a report furnished him, so it was said, by the Jesuit, Father Brucker, touching the last article by Firmin, had prepared a little homily on the errors that I had ventilated and also on the danger I was now running in belonging to a teaching body that included several Protestants, notorious for their advanced ideas.

As the method pursued in condemning my articles had aroused my indignation, I did not allow the Archbishop to proceed with the tranquil development of his discourse.   At the outset I told him that, in civilized countries, persons were not condemned without a chance to defend themselves. "I acted after the manner of the Index," said he to me with all candor; "do you blame the Index?"   "Monsignor, I do not admire the Index."   And we continued this fencing of contrary opinions, the Cardinal invoking the Councils of Trent and of the Vatican, the encyclical *Providentissimus Deus,* the inspiration of the sacred authors which protects them from all error, and reasserting that I had fallen under "the influence of the Germans"; myself trying to make him understand that the Councils had nothing to do with the historical situation as it affected the Bible, that the apologetics of Abbé Vigouroux had done more to turn me away from so-called traditional opinions than all the "Germans" put together, and that the instruction at the *Hautes Études* was purely scientific and in no sense directed against the Church.   Some of the good Cardinal's utterances were truly diverting in their simplicity.   His attention had been called to my articles in the *Revue d'Histoire et de Littérature Religieuses* on the

Fourth Gospel, and he had probably glanced over some of them. "I am reading your commentary on St. John," he remarked, "and I do not altogether understand it. You consider the Fourth Gospel to be the expression of the author's own experience and reflection; what I do not see is, where the operation of the Holy Spirit can come in." It would have been next to impossible for me to have made the venerable prelate understand that, divorced from the thought of the writer, the operation of the Holy Spirit stood every chance of losing itself in the void!

Some remarks were interjected with the intention of dissuading me from attributing any importance to the encouragements that had been given me by this person or that. The Cardinal repeated, with perfect naïveté, a conversation which he had held years before with my predecessor at the Catholic Institute, Abbé Martin, in which these two saintly personages had together reached the conclusion that there was a striking resemblance between the spirit of Monsignor d'Hulst and that of Renan. An archbishop of the south of France, who wished me well, and who had recently published a letter on apologetics, was taxed with "subjectivism," a very weighty word, which the Cardinal never employed save on grand occasions. We parted little pleased with each other, and I did not again meet Cardinal Richard until the year 1904.

I remained at the *École Pratique des Hautes Études* without looking upon myself as a fixture. The death of Auguste Sabatier, in the spring of 1901, left vacant the chair of Early Christian Literature. I offered myself as a candidate for this chair, but the Section decided in favor of a rearrangement which had the advantage of introducing a new subject, the religion of the ancient European peoples. It is my opinion that I might have been elected if I had been willing to leave the Church. But, while I perfectly realize that as a matter of principle the instruction in Christian origins could not be assigned to a theologian who would have subordinated criticism to his individual prejudices, I considered that this objection did not apply to myself and that all persons of intelligence must fully realize this. Years before, Abbé Duchesne had been admitted without difficulty into the Section of philology and history. The Section of the science of religion had no occasion to be more exacting. It was excessively distasteful to me to have it apparently expected that I should abandon my ecclesiastical profession before I could become entirely acceptable. Possibly this was a pure misconception on my part, but such misconceptions have their consequences, and I considered my connection with the École des Hautes Études to be merely temporary. My intention was to remain there a few years only; so long as it afforded me a useful opportunity. For the present the prestige of a connection with the State system of education was an advantage, and my entrance to the École had disconcerted not only Cardinal Richard but my adversaries generally.

Beginning with the year 1901-02, I entered in my lectures upon the criticism of the Gospels, taking up first the parables. In 1902-03, I discussed the accounts of the Galilean ministry of Jesus, as given in the Synoptic Gospels; and in 1903-04, the accounts of the Jerusalem ministry. Thus slowly grew my commentary on the First Three Gospels, which was published in 1908. My difficulties with the Catholic authorities did not arise from these courses. My volume on *The Babylonian Myths and the First Chapters of Genesis* was in no sense more orthodox than the article by Firmin on the religion of Israel; yet it received no censure. Cardinal Richard kept himself informed as to my teaching, and a fairly complete and accurate summary of one of my lectures of 1904 was discovered among the Montagnini papers. But this uneasy solicitude was held in check by the official standing with which I was now invested. To censure instruction given at the Sorbonne appeared too daring a venture, and it was not dreamed of, at least under Leo XIII.

Not that no attempt had ensued to bring about some serious consequence of the condemnation of Firmin. In the spring of 1901 a denunciation had been brought against me before the Holy Office. It had its origin in France, and there is every reason for believing that its author was the Archbishop of Paris. An ecclesiastic of high standing who had learned of it wrote to Cardinal Mathieu, who had the goodness to speak a word in my favor to Father Lepidi, Master of the Sacred Palace. It goes without saying that Father Lepidi kept his own counsel as regarded anything that might have passed concerning me at the sessions of the Holy Office. But he thus expressed himself in a note addressed to Cardinal Mathieu: "It would be well if Abbé Loisy would be good enough to send me his writings, in which his system on the Bible may be found, marking for me the passages to which objection has been taken."

This language would seem to show that at that date (May 7, 1901), Father Lepidi was as little informed as possible of anything that concerned myself. I wrote to him, forwarding a copy of my *Religion of Israel.* All the articles being in print when Cardinal Richard had condemned the first one, I had had the printing completed and kept the copies in my possession. I related to Father Lepidi what had occurred in relation to these articles, adding that the Cardinal had no more required of me an explanation of my work than he had given me one of his condemnation of it.

I should be wholly unable, so I wrote, to point out to you the writings in which I set forth my system on the Bible, because I am not aware of having any system. I have no preconceived system of apologetics; I set forth the facts as I understand them and, without doing them violence, I attempt to gather up the testimony that they offer to faith. I have no express system as regards the inspiration and the interpretation of Scripture. I believe that the Bible is inspired in every part, and inspired that it may be true; on the other hand, I take its text as I find it, and confine myself to interpreting it in its historical sense, by replacing it in its original environment and seeking to enter into the spirit of those who composed its books. I have no recollection of having written on inspiration since 1893. If there is occasion for it, I can send you the two relatively brief articles which I then published on this subject. The discussions on inspiration have always seemed to me sterile; the Biblical question does not lie here. There exist an infinite number of Biblical questions, which are all of them problems of history.

The affair had no further consequences. Father Lepidi never replied to me. In September, 1901, I wrote to thank Cardinal Mathieu, sending him a presentation copy of my *Babylonian Myths*. Knowing him to be a man of parts, I said:

Well informed persons assure me that my errors are not, perhaps, very grave, but that I ought to write in Latin so as not to scandalize the laity by uncovering troublesome questions. Assuredly, the French public, in so far as it concerns itself with these matters, ceased to be troubled by them a long time ago. If Renan could have been persuaded to write in Latin, I should show a bad grace not to follow his example. Nowadays, all the Latin in the world would not avail to restore to ignorance those who have read his writings or who still read them. The only excuse for writing in Latin would be in case one proposed to instruct the theologians; and would it not savor of impiety to assume that they needed to learn anything?

Monsignor Mathieu kept within safe limits, replying in an earnest and friendly tone, and suggesting that I should come to Rome to talk over matters with Father Lepidi. The latter had probably surmised some personal animus in what I had written him concerning Cardinal Richard, for the letter from Cardinal Mathieu terminated with this paternal counsel: "Never give way to bad temper, be careful how you voice your discontent, and do not spoil by these imprudent utterances a destiny that may be glorious and useful for the Church." If I am forever lost, it will not be for want of good advice!

III

My friends were much more concerned than I was myself to protect me against condemnations by the ecclesiastical authorities. From 1900 to 1903, Cardinal Richard knew no rest until he could bring about my censure on the part of Rome, and the advent of Pius X gave him the chance for which he had waited. I was informed of his activities, and understood their motive. He was assured that the younger clergy were increasingly losing their respect for tradition and disdaining Scholasticism, and particularly the two great Councils which it had inspired—that of Trent and that of the Vatican. The Cardinal had come to look upon me as the principal actor, or malefactor, in this movement, and he proceeded against me on the basis of this conviction.

For my part, I was not unaware of the movement in question, which the force of circumstances and not my limited literary activity had unchained. To a certain extent I was its organ, my position giving me enough liberty so that I could speak out for all those who dared not say anything. I perfectly realized that there was still time for me to make a successful career in the Church, by following the line that Monsignor Meignan, with his magisterial grasp of the situation, had formerly indicated to me. But I was restrained from doing so by reason of all those whom I knew to be tormented under the yoke of the old theology, and who formed the habit of more and more counting on me to aid them to breathe more freely. Abbé Monier told me that some of those who pretended to be my disciples were much less reserved in their language than myself, and that Cardinal Richard had some justification for being alarmed. I myself perceived the intellectual anarchy which was beginning to invade the Catholic clergy, and no more than to him did this seem to me a gain. Only, I did not believe that it could be remedied by any such rigorous methods as had already been tried against myself. I was convinced that the Church could not prevent the infiltration of modern ideas, and that a régime of intellectual oppression, besides being a present torture, was preparing for the Church still worse catastrophes in the future. The movement did not need to be exterminated, but to be directed. It was on this account that I allowed myself to be proposed to the Holy See by His Highness Prince Albert for the Bishopric of Monaco, and at the same time (1902) I published a little book that has made something of a name in the theological world, *The Gospel and the Church.*

The least modicum of worldly wisdom would have led me to avoid this presentation and to postpone this publication. The presentation had no chance of being confirmed so soon after the condemnation and denunciation on the part of Cardinal Richard, of which I had been the object. It might, and doubtless would, have been agreed to a few years later, if I had meanwhile made myself a resolute "advocate of tradition." *The Gospel and the*

Church was in no sense the manifesto to be expected if I were to assume this attitude; the book was even exactly the contrary, namely, a kind of program for a progressive Catholicism, contrasted with the program of liberal Protestantism which had been formulated shortly before by Professor Harnack. The fact was that I felt impelled to serve the Church in the impending crisis, whose gravity I clearly recognized, but that I did not care for ecclesiastical dignities in themselves, and did not wish in any way to arrive at them to the detriment of what appeared to me to be the present interest of truth as well as of the Church.

I have never been able to ascertain how it was that the Prince of Monaco could have been induced to inscribe my name on the list of three candidates whom he was required to submit to the Pope's choice for his bishopric. He communicated this intention to me on the 26th of January, 1902, after which several months went by without a word on the subject reaching my ears. On the 4th of October, the Prince summoned me before him for an audience on the following day, at which time he told me that the presentation had occurred, but that Leo XIII had rejected all his candidates, none of whom, according to the Pontiff, had "the requisite qualifications for the episcopate." The Prince was determined to stand his ground. Now, during the summer, a Parisian priest who was a friend of mine, through the mediation of a member of the Combes cabinet, had had my name inscribed on the list of Monsieur Dumay, Director of Worship, among the eventual

candidates for French bishoprics. On October 21st,
I saw Monsieur Dumay, who received me pleasantly.
He was acquainted with the Monaco incident, and
thought the Pope would accept me more readily for
that see than for a bishopric in France. "If the
Pope accepts Prince Albert's proposal," he said to
me, "in a few years we will negotiate your translation to a French see; if he refuses, we will take the
matter of your presentation up again on our own
account." Monsieur Dumay, as is well known, was
not disposed to believe in the separation of Church
and State. He made me promise to write to Cardinal Mathieu, saying that this prelate could get anything he wanted. "But the question," he added, "is
to ascertain whether he will be favorably disposed."

On the 27th of October I wrote to the Cardinal,
whom I had chanced to see at the home of Monsieur
Paul Thureau-Dangin at Bellevue on the 17th of the
previous August. After announcing to him the presentation of my two volumes, *Gospel Studies* and
The Gospel and the Church, which were to appear a
few days later, and explaining the situation as to my
two-fold candidacy, I said:

So far as concerns myself, I am not quite sure whether
I prefer that one of these arrangements shall come to
something, or that both shall come to nothing. This
is how I estimate them. At the present moment, I have
wide open before me a highly honorable scientific career,
guaranteed against the malevolence of persons who, for
reasons which need not be discussed, have already once
or twice broken my life. On the other hand, I do not
disguise from myself that the progress of this career,
considering the subject of my studies, cannot be indifferent to the Church. There is, at present, among the

younger clergy, a growth of ideas which may become disturbing because there is no one to guide it, and which nevertheless one cannot dream of nipping in the bud, since it arises from conditions. In the situation created for me by measures that need not here be recalled, I am only an incitement to this movement, and cannot be a moderating influence. I have been placed in a purely scientific environment, and been obliged, so to speak, to shut myself in to criticism exclusively; and it is evident that, in pursuing these purposes, I am able indeed to promote Biblical science, but cannot work effectively at the conciliation of this progress with the Catholic faith and doctrine. With the best will in the world, I cannot make my lectures at the Sorbonne anything but a technical initiation into a science which all my hearers are probably not in a condition to grasp. Although everything possible has been done to prevent the attendance of ecclesiastics, my audience is abundantly recruited from among the clergy. If, then, my personal interest is to stay in Paris, I am not sure whether, from the standpoint of the general Catholic interest, it would not be more advantageous to place me elsewhere. I should work contentedly, with the sense of a different responsibility from that of the scholar, and my antecedents will prove sufficiently, I believe, that I am capable of understanding and practicing the obligations of a pastor of souls. In persistently suppressing my candidacy, it is not myself who may be harmed, but more likely the peace of the Church. As to the alternative of Monaco or a bishopric in France, I will not conceal from you, Monsignor, that I should much prefer the French bishopric if I did not have in mind the difficulties of the religious situation in our country, and especially the interest of peace of which I have just spoken. My health would also be better in Monaco. But I have decided not to go to Rome for the present to plead my cause. I do not wish to seem to care more for the episcopate than is really the case. No more do I intend to hold myself cheap, or to have the appearance of doing so. To the degree that it may be in my power, I shall be prudent and docile, but I do not wish to make commitments which will end in compromising the reputation that these last ten years have acquired for me in the learned world, in France and abroad, and that, after all, reflects honor upon the Church. I confide all these matters to your Eminence's discretion, and you are free to make any use of them that seems best to you. I do not ask you to speak in my behalf to the highest authority. Your Eminence may have reasons for not wishing to intervene. If you do so speak, Monsignor, I shall be very grateful. If you do not, I shall cherish no resentment against you.

Cardinal Mathieu was perhaps not exactly prepared to take my letter as it was meant. My first intention had been to make these confidences to a young layman, a former student of the *École de Rome,* high in favor with Cardinal Rampolla; the same who had handed him, in 1893, my letter of submission to the encyclical *Providentissimus Deus.* It transpired that this person, today a writer of repute, knew of the Monaco affair from another of the Prince's candidates. The manner in which he greeted my earliest overtures, without really knowing what was involved, did not encourage me to enter upon further explanations. He spoke as one having access to the thought of the Vatican, and that thought breathed neither confidence nor goodwill.

On November 20th, I received a friendly note from Cardinal Mathieu, who had attempted to support my candidacy. Cardinal Rampolla had simply replied to him that no one stood in the way of my showing myself "reassuring" in the position that I now occupied. This gave me a good opportunity for explaining to Cardinal Mathieu that the Vatican seemed to have a very limited comprehension of the obligations of a lecturer at the *École Pratique des Hautes Études,* and of the character of the movement alluded to in my former letter.

It would be a serious mistake to think that it (this movement) can be held back or hedged in by the exercise of mere authority, by pontifical encyclicals, or by decisions of the Biblical Commission (that lately instituted by Leo XIII). The movement cannot be controlled by decrees, but by the activity of persons capable of adding scientific competence to their ecclesiastical authority. The intellectual crisis in French Catholicism has long been at an acute stage. Is this perceived by the high personages to whom God has confided the care of His Church? . . . The "reassuring" type of man from their point of view is Abbé Vigouroux. Now everybody knows that Abbé Vigouroux's apologetic is scientifically worthless. I like to think that he himself believes in it, because he professes it. But it is "reassuring" only to people who are in the dark as to the real state of these questions. At the present time, the Catholic exegetes whose assent is worth having are unanimous in agreeing that the group of opinions which, for want of a better term, are called traditional, is in need of a fundamental overhauling. Only, aside from the inevitable divergences as to particular points, there are differences of general attitude. Some think that reform is as impossible as it is indispensable, and that the foremost consideration must be to make a success of one's own career by at least in appearance standing by tradition—these men are extremely "reassuring," and are all of them marked for posts of honor. Some there are who keep silence from timidity or prudence. And there are those who believe that conciliation is possible between what is truly traditional and what is truly scientific, and who speak out what they deem to be the truth, at the risk of arousing against themselves those who imagine that nothing new is to be said on the subject of religion and that nothing more is required to keep in touch with the incessant progress of science than to go on repeating the old theological formularies. For my own part, I have never been preoccupied with being "reassuring," but with being honest. I undertake, at the Sorbonne, to be loyal to the duties of the scholar; just as I should undertake to be a loyal defender of the Church if she would authorize me to speak in her name. But the present situation of Catholicism is too grave to admit of a scholar or an apologist sacrificing candor to the interest of his personal future. The lack of sincerity characteristic of the apologetics which obtains the *Imprimatur* is precisely what is revolting to cultivated minds. I do not complain of the refusal to give me episcopal responsibility in the midst of this crisis, which, as I see it, is frightful; much more serious than the political crisis. There is in me an old peasant who loves not change, and who would be horrified at having to move his household gods; a valetudinarian whom it would suit entirely to escape the labors of the apostolate; a student who would be delighted at being left alone with his historical researches; there is, as well, a priest who is wounded by unjust oppressions, yet who would be disposed to serve the Church to the best of his ability, according to his conscience. But as this priest is no great saint, and as he is not so fatuous as to believe himself necessary to the splendor of the episcopal body, he joins readily with the three others in celebrating the check to my candidacy, and we drink in Vichy water—all four of us!—a toast to the health of Pope Leo XIII and of his Eminence Cardinal Rampolla.

The outcome of this negotiation gave me positive relief. Whether I was wrong or right, it was clear that the views of Rome were altogether foreign to my own. The Prince of Monaco renewed his presentations in December, and they were definitively repulsed. I have always thought that the condemnation of *The Gospel and the Church* by Cardinal Richard, in January, 1903, was prescribed by the

Roman authorities, not only on account of the "errors" that the book might contain, but to make thenceforth impossible the presentation that was known to be among the intentions of our Director of Worship.

IV

When my *Gospel Studies* and *The Gospel and the Church* were placed on sale by the publishing house of Alphonse Picard and Son, at the beginning of November, I did not for a moment imagine that either of these books was destined to achieve any special success or to create any great sensation. The question in my mind was less whether or not they might escape condemnation, than whether they would have a good or bad effect on Cathol'c, and especially on ecclesiastical, opinion. On the 13th of October, 1902, I wrote in my journal:

Rarely have I been so uneasy about the moral effect of my publications as I am about the two volumes soon to appear. Both represent an effort to adapt the theory of Catholicism to the facts of history, and the practice of Catholicism to the realities of contemporary life. Is such an effort needed, and can it be fruitful? Taking things from one aspect, it may seem superfluous and even injurious. The real, the official Catholicism, that which exists and declares itself, protests rather against any such adaptation and declines to consider it. Many wonder, and not without reason, if in essaying to change it one is not contributing to its dissolution. It seems so completely bound up with a conception of the world, of life, and of human society which our time can no longer accept, that to invite it to change its mode of existence appears equivalent to suggesting a sort of suicide, which one cannot flatter himself is obtainable by persuasion.

Yet, on the other hand, there have been such far-reaching changes in the past, and the present need for some changes is so urgent, that it would be criminal to have nothing to say in face of such a situation. If the Church is wholly unsusceptible of amendment, she must be exterminated, as the great enemy of human progress. On the contrary, if she is still the chief moral resource of civilization, she must be sustained, defended and enlightened in all possible ways. Those who hold to the former alternative have only pretexts to go upon. For the present, I believe that the latter alternative is the true one.

Practically no notice was taken of *Gospel Studies*. This volume consisted of a dissertation on the parables contained in the First Three Gospels, being a summary of my lectures of 1902, and of several extracts from my commentary on the Fourth Gospel; with one exception, they had already been published in the *Revue d'Histoire et de Littérature Religieuses*. A brief introduction described the character of the evangelical records and that of the Christian tradition—"a living faith which, having its origin in the words and acts of Jesus, pursues its way across the centuries, explaining itself, and assimilating to itself for that purpose, whatever can aid it to a fuller consciousness of its inner force and to a further development." Being what it was, this book could hardly give occasion for vociferous opposition. I believe it was read by my friends; my enemies appear to have entirely ignored it.

I speak of my enemies, and without the least hesitation; for, in the uproar that gathered about *The Gospel and the Church,* a factor has to be reckoned with other than the eagerness of defenders of the faith flying to the rescue of an imperilled tradition. Back of the theologians and exciting their ardor, were persons who pretended to be the only ones who knew the aim I was seeking to accomplish by this little book, rather unusual in its makeup, which to all outward appearance was an apology for Catholicism, but which, according to their notion, had no other object than to disturb the faith of Catholics. The author, a proud mocker before the Eternal, wished to give himself the rare diversion of provoking a religious crisis. These insinuations, skilfully inserted in certain public journals, but spread in other ways as well, had a perceptible influence on the dispute. Care was taken to keep them in constant circulation, until Pius X had finally expelled me from the Church. On an earlier page I have estimated the merit of the individuals who provoked them, and assessed the value of their testimony. They hold in reserve a treasure of pious tears which they will pour out upon my tomb, deploring the tragic mischance that withheld me from rendering to Holy Mother Church the services of which I was capable.

What my intentions were, the reader will soon perceive, and the book itself demonstrates. I had seized the occasion offered by the interest awakened by Professor Harnack's Berlin lectures, published under the title, *"What Is Christianity?"* [1] but the substance of my work was taken, as I have already explained, from four chapters of the manuscript that

[1] *Das Wesen des Christentums*, Leipzig, 1900. The work was twice translated into French, the first translation appearing at the beginning of the year 1902.

I had brought with me from Neuilly. Professor Harnack's book was freely praised by Catholics, but its "essence of Christianity" appeared to me to be rather that of Liberal Protestantism.   I found it opportune to sketch the history of the Christian development, beginning with the Gospels, in order to show that its essence, in so far as it could be said to have any, had historically perpetuated itself in Catholic Christianity, and that its successive transformations had been, as a matter of fact, anything but a continuous decadence. Such was the chief aim of the book, and I hold that it was adequately presented; the two opening chapters, on the Kingdom of Heaven and the Son of God, fixing the historical point of departure for the evolution traced in the three later chapters on the Church, the Christian dogma and the Catholic worship. Subsidiary to this was a criticism of Liberal Protestantism, especially as regards its pretension to stand for the pure Gospel of Jesus, and this criticism is the part of my book that today appears to me as the most satisfying.

But this production contained two elements of a particularly delicate nature, concerning which orthodoxy might well bestir itself. On the one hand, my reasoning in opposition to Professor Harnack implied a criticism of the Gospel sources more radical at several points than that of the Protestant theologian; and, on the other hand, my defense of the Roman Church against certain judgments of the learned author implied at the same time the abandonment of those absolute theses which are professed by the Scholastic theology touching the formal institution of the Church and its sacraments by Christ, the immutability of its dogmas, and the nature of its ecclesiastical authority.   Thus I did not confine myself to a criticism of Professor Harnack, but paved the way, discreetly yet definitely, for an essential reform in Biblical exegesis, in the whole of theology, and even in Catholicism generally.   I was travelling in the steps of Firmin in the *Revue du Clergé Français,* which was no wonder, since I was merely publishing the sequel to his articles.   One half of my book could be accepted by all Catholics; the other half, notwithstanding my caution as to the language employed and the fact that it masqueraded, so to speak, under the cloak of the more apologetic portion, was calculated to awaken opposition.

It should be stated, nevertheless, that I did not dogmatize and did not undertake to impose on any one, still less on the Church than on my readers, any specific theoretical conclusion.   I set forth facts, from which it seemed to me that certain consequences must follow.,   I drew the attention of persons of good faith, as well as that of the Church, to the existing state of the texts and of the evidences. If I constituted myself the advocate of Catholicism against Protestantism, as regarded the Church herself I was only a witness, and I left to her the decisions to be taken relative to her teaching and practice.   My attitude was perfectly loyal, and I could have written at the end of my "little orange-colored book" as at the close of my article of 1893 on the Biblical Question: "A word of sincerity and of reconciliation is always in order; if true, it can only benefit all alike, while it is easy to correct whatever in it may be misleading." But the Catholic publicists, the theologians, and the Roman Church were not in the habit of thinking in these terms. Once admit that tradition is sacred and beyond the possibility of change, and any word directed against tradition becomes reprehensible.

Still, there was a moment of hesitation, as it were, among the zealots for orthodoxy. The apologetic part of the book made a good impression; even the philosophical and historical element was pleasing to certain minds. A papal bookseller proposed to me to publish an Italian translation in Rome. The scene instantly changed when the theologians began to utter themselves. Abbé Gayraud came out with a violent series of articles in the *Univers*. The clerical member of the House of Deputies must have been urged on in this affair by others more expert than himself. He knew nothing at all about criticism, but he wielded a trenchant pen, and was not even abashed when it was proved to him that he had taken citations from Harnack for the expression of my own ideas, and had refuted them in that capacity! The more or less learned Catholic Reviews joined in chorus with the clerical press. I did not read all that was written against me, and did not reply to any of it. I have stated in what manner the quarrel was speedily embittered. The feeling that all this tumult inspired in me was one of utter disgust. I can recall one article, quite sensible and moderate, in no way flattering, but written in a dignified manner by a man with whom I could have entered into a discussion; the article appeared in the *Études* for January 20th, 1903, and its author was Father L. de Grandmaison, a Jesuit.

Cardinal Richard signed, on January 17th, an ordinance [1] which was promulgated a few days later, and which reproved the book entitled *The Gospel and the Church* because it had been published without the *Imprimatur,* and because it was of "a nature gravely to trouble the faith of believers in the fundamental dogmas of the Catholic teaching." The Cardinal had not decided on this form of procedure on his own initiative. He would certainly have preferred to have the condemnation come from Rome, in order that it might carry greater weight. But Leo XIII did not trouble himself to intervene. The matter was handled at the Nunciature. It was arranged that the Archbishop of Paris should cause my book to be examined by a commission of theologians; that he was to condemn it following the report of this commission; that Cardinal Perraud would sustain this censure with his academic authority by publicly adhering to it and by proclaiming it in his diocese (which he did on January 28th); that the Apostolic Nuncio, Monsignor Lorenzelli, would recruit a number of other adherences from among the bishops. Thus it came about that *The Gospel and the Church* was condemned by the Archbishop of Cambrai, the Bishops of Angers, of Bayeux (now Archbishop of Paris), of Belley (now Archbishop of Rheims), of Nancy and of

[1] See Appendix IX.

Perpignan.   Several of these prelates abstained from even reading the book that they forbade to their flocks.   The ordinance of Perpignan in particular proves that its author knew only vaguely and by hearsay what it was all about.   Other bishops declined to act.

Not being disposed to enter upon an open conflict with Cardinal Richard, I held up the second edition of *The Gospel and the Church,* which was in the press.   At the same time, I suppressed an introduction of ninety-six pages which had been prepared for the third edition of my *Biblical Studies,* and was of a nature to stir up further polemics.   It was my intention to go no farther by way of concessions.   Just as I had kept silence under the condemnation brought against Firmin's articles in 1900, I had in mind now to say nothing in view of the censure put upon *The Gospel and the Church.*   This was the best attitude for me to take, and the sincerest, since within myself I had no positive feeling of respect for the archiepiscopal sentence, and I could make a "submission" to it only by accompanying this with reservations which would render it meaningless or equivocal.   However, learning on February 2d, by letter from Monsignor Mignot, Archbishop of Albi, that Leo XIII expected my formal adherence to Cardinal Richard's ordinance, I addressed to the latter the following lines:

Monsignor:
Your Eminence must already have been informed that, out of respect for the decision taken by yourself relative

to my book, *The Gospel and the Church,* I have withdrawn the second edition of that work, which was on
the point of being published.

I submit myself to the judgment which Your Eminence
has rendered according to your episcopal powers.

It goes without saying that I condemn and reprove
all the errors that others have been able to deduce from
my book by placing it, for purposes of interpretation, in
a totally different perspective from that in which I must
have placed myself, and actually did place myself, in
composing it.

This was not going very far, still it went much too
far. I did not bow very low, but it would now be
possible to require me to bow lower. Also, it was a
piece of rare impertinence on my part to impute
to the censors of my book the errors that the Cardinal had sought to proscribe. No doubt it was true
that I had not formulated any dogmatic conclusion,
and that my thought had been twisted by being
taken for a theory opposed to the Scholastic speculations. But the censure made no mention of errors,
and consequently I had no occasion to repel this
charge. The Cardinal had said that my work was
of "a nature gravely to trouble the faith of believers." It was to this point that I should have
replied, as I could have done without difficulty. My
book was not intended for the public at large, and it
was the clamor of my adversaries that had made it
known to "believers." The censure had thus been
framed with greater wisdom than my letter, since it
did not concern the substance of my book but only
the effect that reading it might produce on the
masses.

The unwisdom of my action at once became apparent. No sooner was my letter received than Cardinal Richard, who had interpreted it with more naïveté that I had written it, sent me a most amiable request to call upon him. The almost sickening unction of the good Cardinal in circumstances such as these never failed to exasperate me. I have previously spoken of the feeling that had been aroused in me by the polemics which led up to the condemnation of my book. There was no sign that these polemics were drawing to an end, or that the ecclesiastical authority was at any pains to stop them. I was afraid, furthermore, and with reason, that the Archbishop, having condemned my book for having been "published without the *Imprimatur* required by the laws of the Church," would endeavor to subject my writings to the control of the theologians, or even demand that I give up my course at the *Hautes Études* or else change its subject. Instead of presenting myself at the Cardinal's audience-room, I wrote him on February 5th:

Monsignor:
   In withdrawing my book from public sale, and in notifying Your Eminence that I have so withdrawn it, it has been my purpose to act in conformity with the ecclesiastical discipline; and in thus acting I assume that I am in accord with the wishes of the Sovereign Pontiff. But I reserve, assuredly, my personal judgment on all that has happened in relation to this book of history in which an effort has been made to find errors in theology. Your Eminence will excuse me from responding at the present time to the invitation which you have been so kind as to send me. Under existing circumstances, the interview proposed by Your Eminence would prove too painful for me and, I am afraid, also for yourself.

This letter restored to its rightful proportions—that is, to naught—the foregoing "submission." It reached the Archbishop's palace too late to effect any modification in the official note dealing with this latter which appeared in the *Semaine Religieuse* of the diocese of Paris in the number for February 7th. The note, by a skilful suppression, omitting the closing lines of my first letter, made it appear that the author of *The Gospel and the Church* had himself repudiated the errors which others "had been able to deduce from his book."

Only to outward appearance was the affair at an end. The Bishop of La Rochelle, Monsignor Le Camus, a combatant overflowing with good intentions, published his refutation of my volume, under the title *True and False Exegesis*. He wrote me naïvely that his purpose in combating me was to prevent my being condemned. Nothing was simpler to refute than his refutation, and later on I let him see this very clearly. The *Univers* of February 6th contained a letter by Cardinal Perraud to one of his former classmates at the *École Normale,* in which the distinguished prelate and member of the French Academy undertook to resolve all the problems of exegesis with two sentences used by Bossuet against Richard Simon. The Bishop of Autun had drawn upon his own resources only for a figure of speech in questionable taste: "Shall I say . . . that the wabblings of the author of *The Gospel and the Church* produce in the reader something like seasickness? You see a disturbance, you are nauseated, you feel bad inside, and have all the other symptoms." Just about that time, it came to me from a reliable source that my "little book" and *Gospel Studies* had been referred to the Congregation of the Index. The idea of a defense of *The Gospel and the Church,* in the form of dialogues or of letters, began to shape itself in my mind. By the end of March, 1903, the first sketch of *Concerning a Little Book* was practically complete, but it seemed to me opportune to postpone its publication until October, when my volume on *The Fourth Gospel* was to appear. Toward the end of June, I learned that Leo XIII had refused to sanction the placing of *Gospel Studies* upon the Catalogue of the Index. The old Pope died on the 20th of July.

V

One of my English friends, who was in Rome during the conclave at which Pius X was chosen, wrote me that all the leading candidates for the Papacy, with the single exception of Cardinal Zvampa who has since died, were noted "extinguishers." I find in my journal, under date of July 28:

The most pressing duty of the new Pope will be to put my books upon the Index. This pontiff's individuality will not count as much as that of Leo XIII, and he will be obliged to reckon with the machine. New machines are always machines, that is to say, brutal. Only, at the present moment, there is a potent trend of opinion and of truth against the machine.—Advance without fear, speak without anger, act sanely.

The campaign prosecuted against *The Gospel and the Church,* the actions of the episcopate, and what I knew, from private communications, concerning the intentions of Cardinal Richard, proved conclusively to my mind that the aim of the ecclesiastical authority and of its auxiliaries was to reduce me to silence or, what to me would be even more insupportable, to the régime of the *Imprimatur*. I was resolved to maintain at any cost my scientific freedom, and it goes without saying that I knew no better way of doing this than to make full use of it. It was for this reason, notwithstanding the condemnation of *The Gospel and the Church,* that I had begun the printing, in the early months of 1903, of my big book on *The Fourth Gospel,* in which are formulated conclusions unheard of among Catholic exegetes: the unauthenticity of the book, which it is impossible to attribute to the Apostle John; the symbolical and fictitious character of the narratives, in harmony with the theology of the discourses, which are not a part of the actual teaching of Jesus; finally that the Fourth Gospel is a product of Christian faith, and in no sense a biography of Jesus Christ. At the same time, I determined to publish an explanation of *The Gospel and the Church,* as well as a defense against the condemnations with which it had been greeted, and certain criticisms emanating from high personages, whose competency scarcely equalled their pretensions. Also I reissued the condemned volume, completing it by adding a chapter on "The Gospel Sources." As this book was not prohibited in the diocese of Versailles, the second edition no longer bore the name of my Parisian publisher, and the place of publication was given as the home of the author at Bellevue.   The attacks not having let up since the month of January, I did not consider myself under obligation to adjourn indefinitely this second edition which I had "withdrawn" out of respect to the censure by Cardinal Richard.   A commentary on *The Sermon on the Mount* formed the fourth volume of this new library, which purported to exist simply in its own right.

The most daring among these products of the printing press was the apology for *The Gospel and the Church* which I entitled: *Concerning a Little Book*.   In the preface, I affirmed my privilege of writing on my own responsibility, without ecclesiastical authorization, on topics relating to religious history.   "The primary condition of scientific production is freedom.   The primary duty of the scholar, Catholic or non-Catholic, is sincerity."   And under the régime of the *Imprimatur* I believed neither freedom nor sincerity to be possible.   I could not "be sorry for not having stultified myself to conform to an authority which seems to be conscious only of its power, and not even to surmise the situation created for exegesis, for apologetics, and for Catholic theology generally by the progress of Scriptural research and the broad movement of modern knowledge."   After a reference to the vicissitudes of my personal career, I was so bold as to write: "Ideas are not killed by a stroke of the crozier."   Possibly I was not enough mindful that there are some truths too obvious to be useful when spoken!

The body of the book consisted of seven chapters, in the form of letters addressed to persons whose names were not given, but who were for the most part easily recognizable. The first letter to a rural dean, Abbé Ludot, my former professor in philosophy at the Châlons seminary, dealt with the origin and purpose of *The Gospel and the Church*. Not a few persons may perhaps have been scandalized to learn from it that "God is not a historical personage," and that "it was as a man, not as a God, that Jesus came into the history of mankind."

The second letter, on the Biblical Question, had for its recipient "a Cardinal," Monsignor Perraud, to whom I explained this question, which truly he had passed over with a too superb presumption, and I used terms so explicit that he had no excuse this time for his former "seasickness." Perhaps the sarcasm of my opening sentence may seem excessive: "All the glories of the Congregation, restored in the Nineteenth Century by Father Pététot under the name of the Oratory, pale before the noble and serene figure of the ex-Oratorian, Richard Simon, the father of Biblical criticism and the victim of the great Bossuet." Monsignor Perraud was the greatest glory of the restored Oratory, and I question whether he found my comparison flattering.

Monsignor Le Camus, Bishop of La Rochelle, was accorded the honor of the third letter, on the criticism of the Gospels and particularly on the Gospel according to John. This prelate piqued himself on his scientific acquirements and on his broadmindedness. In exegesis, he allowed himself to take minor liberties in a way that had an air of simple self-admiration. "When one avails himself of criticism," said I to him, "one must be cautious not to avail himself of too much of it, and perhaps it would be wiser not to meddle with it at all than to make so little use of it." As the letter to Cardinal Perraud was a general introduction to Biblical criticism, so this introduced the reader particularly to the criticism of the Gospels, summarizing, with the supporting proofs, the principal conclusions of my commentaries. This letter supplemented, by its discussion of the Gospel sources, the chapters dealing with Jesus in *The Gospel and the Church*. In it I set forth how and why the contents of the Gospels, even of the first three, cannot be accepted unreservedly as literal history. All this was, at least in part, new to Monsignor Le Camus, and was bound to seem outrageously venturesome to the orthodox theologians.

The Archbishop to whom the fourth letter went was Monsignor Mignot, who had asked me to give my readers some enlightenment on the divinity of Jesus Christ. I was unable to satisfy the learned prelate, who was hoping for a demonstration of the divinity of Christ from the testimony of the Gospels. I explained rather, in brief, how the Christological dogma had acquired form and fixity, proceeding from the early faith in Jesus as the Messiah, by a gradual adaptation of that faith to the mentality of converts brought in from Paganism. It was, of all the themes that I could venture upon, the one most full of peril. Who can guarantee to us that Christ was God if he never gave himself out as such, if even he displayed no consciousness whatever of being divine? It was all well enough for me to write:

"The historical Christ, in the humility of his 'service' is great enough to justify the Christology, and the Christology does not need to depend for its truth upon having been expressly taught by Christ himself." These propositions were wholly incompatible with the Scholastic conception of dogma, and with the personal and absolute divinity of Jesus. They were intelligible only in relation to a theory, more or less "symbolist" in character, of religious belief and of the universal immanence of God in humanity.

The Catholic apologist, Abbé Felix Klein, an excellent man whom, quite unintentionally, I was the means of seriously embarrassing, was the recipient of the more than half playful dedication of the fifth letter, on the foundation and authority of the Church. Not long before, Abbé Klein had planned to give, in the Church of the Carmelites, a series of lectures on the religious "phenomenon," studied by the method of observation; and he had had as a result a bone to pick with the Papal Nuncio, Monsignor Lorenzelli, who found it passing strange that religion should be regarded by anyone as a "phenomenon." The preacher had been obliged to change his title, and discourse rather of the religious "fact." The opening lines of my letter contained a good-natured allusion to this incident: "You are a doctor in Israel; you study the religious fact by the method of observation, which is indeed the best of methods for the study of facts, even those of religion." This innocent-looking sentence contained also an ironical allusion to the theologians, who study facts by another method. But what proved embarrassing for Abbé Klein was the mention, on the same page, of "our walks together for the benefit of our health in the forest of Meudon." It should be recalled that Abbé Klein was taken for the father, or at least the guardian, of a phantom heresy named "Americanism," which was condemned by Leo XIII, and of which it has been impossible to discover, in either the Old or the New World, a single authentic representative.

Great was the uproar in the Catholic press when it was known that this professor, already somewhat under suspicion, had taken frequent walks with me in a wood. Abbé Klein was obliged to establish his orthodoxy by a public letter, in which he proved, by citations from his writings, that he breathed nothing but the pure doctrine of the Church and pure love for her. Certain bishops began to bestir themselves because he was a professor in the Catholic Institute. Happily, the then Rector, Abbé Péchenard, was a man of firm and upright character, and no real harm ensued to my correspondent. It is quite certain that, on our walks, we talked of other matters than the weather; but it is no less certain, and Abbé Klein was in the habit of avowing this in our discussions, that he was able to think his religious ideas only by making use of the traditional categories.

This fact did not prevent the chapter on the Church from being a disagreeable mouthful for the theologians. In it I showed how, in the Gospels, the foundation of the Church is attributed to the risen Christ; therefore the Church was not instituted by Jesus during his lifetime, but was born of faith in the glorified Christ. I dwelt on the nature of authority, as being, in the Church, as elsewhere, nothing but a form of service:

The time has arrived when the Church, having done everything possible to make her own authority secure, should undertake to guarantee as effectively the right of the simple Christian to concern himself with what she owes to him, and what she owes to humanity. Nineteen centuries of Christianity have had for their outcome the solemn proclamation of the Roman primacy and of Papal infallibility. Is it so very venturesome to assume that such cannot have been the ultimate end of the institution of Christianity, and that the Pope cannot have been invested with so great a power for any other purpose than to enable a unified Church to realize with all the more promptness and ease all the reform and all the progress required by the passage of time? Does it take more than common sense to perceive that so formidable a force can subsist only by serving as an organ for the aspirations of the Christian world, by seeking its living supports in a multitude of loyal, sincere believers, and by distributing itself, so to speak, and decentralizing itself for effective action, and by making itself all things to all men, instead of trying to absorb everything into itself?

The young scholar, to whom the sixth letter, on the origin and authority of dogmas, was destined, was Monsieur François Thureau-Dangin, my former pupil in Hebrew and Assyriology at the Catholic Institute, already become eminent as an Assyriologist. This letter reproduced the greater part of the ideas formerly ventilated by Firmin on the character of revelation, that is to say, on religious knowledge, and these it supplemented by considerations on the current crisis in apologetics, in theology, and in the faith generally.

What has been called revelation cannot be anything else than the consciousness acquired by man of his relations with God. The theoretical notion of an immutable dogma is powerless to efface the history of these dogmas themselves. It would be easy to demonstrate that the fundamental truth of religion, faith in God, has had a history of infinite complexity, and that the idea of the Divine has not ceased to undergo modifications even within Christianity. History attests the relative insufficiency and perfectibility of the dogmatic formulas. There is a sort of latent incompatibility, which speedily becomes conscious in a large number of individuals, between the general knowledge of the universe and of man which is acquired today in the common schools, and that which dominates, or one may better say which penetrates, the Catholic doctrine. A radical evolution in that doctrine would be out of the question and is not required; what is essential is chiefly a change in spirit and attitude toward the intellectual movement of our day.

This closing remark was not wanting in sagacity. Only superficial minds can insist that the Church shall from day to day remodel, in the spirit of science, a creed whose object is in no way scientific. But what we have a right to ask, and what would be to her interest as well, is that she shall not impose her theology as an obstacle to the normal growth of human knowledge.

The last of the seven letters, and in its content the least original, on the institution of the sacraments, was the one that most irritated the orthodox theologians, because it was the one they could most readily understand. The superior of a seminary to whom it was addressed was Abbé Monier. This venerable Sulpician was goodness personified. Strongly attached, for his own part, to the theological tradition, he was considerate of the ideas of others. He himself reported to me a conversation which he had with Cardinal Perraud after the publication of *Concerning a Little Book*. The Cardinal had read as far as the seventh letter without encountering the heresy that simply must be there. The light dawned on his intelligence almost at the last page, when he read this obvious statement concerning the sacrament of ordination: "In proportion as the Eucharist took on the character of a liturgical act, those who regularly presided over it acquired the standing of priests." "So they did not, then, have it from the beginning!" he cried. And this monstrous assertion, contrary to the definitions of Trent, enabled him retrospectively to find plenty of other errors in the volume.

Minds less preoccupied with their own ideas must have been aware from the outset that the letter had for its sole purpose to make evident the disaccord between the decrees of Trent and the historical evidences concerning the origin of the sacraments. The Council attributed the institution of the seven Catholic sacraments to the personal initiative of Jesus. My seventh letter showed that even the two rites practiced by the earliest Christian communities —baptism and the Last Supper—were not instituted by Christ himself. "The general idea of the institution of the sacraments, as it is announced in the decrees of the Council of Trent, is not a historical representation of what Jesus did or of what the Apostolic Church thought, but an authentic interpretation—I mean one authorized by faith—of the traditional fact."

Thus, without directly opposing a single dogma, I established, along the whole line of Catholic beliefs, the position of the historical facts and witnesses as they confront the official formulas, drawing the obvious conclusion that a new and broader interpretation of these formulas, when they were in contradiction to reality, was indispensable. But all the contradictions that I had signalized were susceptible of being interpreted by the theologians as so many doctrinal errors professed by myself in opposition to the Catholic faith—as if I were responsible for the facts which I brought to the attention of the Church and of her theologians, and as if I must feel constrained to present them otherwise than as I saw them. I regarded it as extremely probable that my manifesto would thus be tortured out of its plain meaning, and I had decided on my course beforehand. Either my new books—a very improbable hypothesis—would escape censure altogether, and I could thenceforth pursue my scientific researches untrammelled; or my conclusions as a historian would be condemned as heretical, in which case I meant to insure my freedom of initiative by the door of excommunication.

VI

Concerning a Little Book and *The Fourth Gospel* were placed on sale in Paris by Alphonse Picard and Son, the publishers, on the 6th of October, 1903. Before the end of the month, Cardinal Richard was in Rome, and it became known forthwith that he would not return until he had been assured of my condemnation by the tribunals of the Index and the Holy Office. The Cardinal was over eighty years old, but his zeal heightened his vitality, and he was now encouraged by the prospect of success. Leo XIII, whose policy he did not sustain with any degree of cordiality, esteemed his virtues above his intelligence. His credit stood higher with Pius X, who strongly resembled him. The Catholic press made some stir over my new publications; possibly there was more anger than after *The Gospel and the Church*, but no detailed refutation was attempted. The incisiveness with which I had posed certain problems made the task of the apologist more exigent. Moreover, any polemic was thought to be superfluous, since Rome at length was on the march, and on the very point of proclaiming "the Truth!"

After repeated hesitations as to the form that should be given to the promulgation of this "Truth," so impatiently awaited by the Ultramontane theologians, Rome at length produced it, but under conditions that still left it profoundly obscure, and that again gave evidence of a marked reluctance to have the Papal responsibility in any way implicated in this affair. At first, it appears, the idea had been to publish a *Syllabus* of propositions extracted from my writings by the Holy Office and condemned without naming their author. In fact such a collection of condemned propositions must have been prepared, and it is safe to assume that it played a considerable part in the framing of the decree *Lamentabili,* which the Roman Inquisition put forth in 1907. But undoubtedly it was felt that this procedure, the least disturbing to myself, had the disadvantage of not directly involving either my writings or my person, and also of promulgating a doctrinal decision whose consequences might not be entirely happy. The prudence which characterized Leo XIII had at this time only half abandoned the counsels of the Vatican.

On December 16th, the Congregation of the Holy Office simply decreed that five of my works should be placed upon the catalogue of the Index: *The Religion of Israel, Gospel Studies, The Gospel and the Church, Concerning a Little Book* and *The Fourth Gospel.* In addition, to mark the special importance and to make clear the motives of this decision, the Congregation charged the Cardinal Secretary of State to write a letter of explanation to the Cardinal Archbishop of Paris. Pius X gave his approval to these actions on the 17th, and Cardinal Merry del Val wrote his letter on the 19th of December.[1] The desire to corroborate by means of the Roman authority the condemnations previously pronounced by Cardinal Richard appeared in the mention of *The Religion of Israel,* a pamphlet which at that time was non-existent, since it had never been publicly issued; and also in a kind of deliberate parallelism between the letter of the Cardinal Secretary of State and the censure brought by the Archbishop of Paris against *The Gospel and the Church.*

[1] See Appendix X.

But this time there was specific mention of my errors. "The extremely grave errors which fill these volumes to repletion," said Monsignor Merry del Val, "concern chiefly the primitive revelation, the authenticity of the Gospel facts and teachings, the divinity and the supernatural knowledge of Christ, the resurrection (doubtless that of Jesus is meant), the divine institution of the Church and the sacraments." It was on account of these errors that my books were condemned by the Holy Office.

Although the terms of the letter were vigorous and explicit enough, it could not escape the most inexperienced canonist that, while it contained an official notification of the judgment of the Holy Office, yet it in no way constituted of itself a judgment of that tribunal. The Inquisition had merely ordained that my writings should be placed upon the Index of Prohibited Books; it had not specifically condemned any errors. The sentence which Cardinal Richard had so insistently demanded, and which had so impressive a sound, was in reality nothing so very formidable. It had been conceived and framed in such fashion as to involve on the part of the Roman authority a minimum of responsibility, while at the same time permitting the exaction from the condemned author of a maximum of submission.

For reasons unknown to myself, Cardinal Richard did not at once publish the documents which he had received. The Parisian press got wind of them about Christmas Day. They were distributed to the parish priests of the city toward the end of December, with a brief note from Vicar-General Fages, directing the pastors to communicate them to their subordinate clergy, but not to read them from the pulpit.   Probably it was felt that noise enough had already been made over the affair, and that the best course was to end it, if possible, quietly.   The Cardinal sent me the official texts on December 30th, with a truly kind autograph letter.   "I hope," he wrote, "that you will very soon give us the consolation of being able to say: *auctor laudabiliter se subjecit*.   If you care to see me, I am entirely at your disposal."

I had no thought whatever of seeing the Cardinal, having too clear a recollection of our earlier conversations.   But I was not insensible to his moderation in handling the matter.   If one wishes to measure the difference between a bishop conscientiously performing what he deems to be a duty pertaining to his office, in order to guard the integrity of the faith, and a prelate who seeks any and every occasion to display his zeal and exhibit his rhetoric, and so merit an archbishopric or the cardinalate, one need only compare the acts of the venerable Archbishop of Paris, or even the pastoral letter written at this time by Cardinal Perraud on *The Errors of Abbé Loisy Condemned by the Holy See*, with the violent pamphlet brought out by Monsignor Latty, Bishop of Châlons,[1] when he thought that my definitive con-

---

[1] *Instruction et ordonnance de Mgr. Latty, concernant les deux derniers écrits de M. l'abbé Loisy.*   The bishop of Châlons was cognizant only of *The Gospel and the Church* and *Concerning a Little Book*.   His instruction bears date of December 27, 1903, but it did not appear in the *Semaine Religieuse* of the diocese of Châlons until sometime in January.   Monsignor Latty has since been made Archbishop of Avignon.

demnation gave him the opportunity to play, in all security, the part of a Bossuet avenging orthodoxy against a feeble successor of Richard Simon.

The wisest course for me to have taken at this juncture, as after the condemnation of *The Gospel and the Church,* would have been to remain silent for a time, to say nothing at all in advance of a summons from the ecclesiastical authorities, and then merely to explain my attitude in reference to their decisions. But from the outset I had resolved to perform an act of respectful submission, with the express reservations which sincerity dictated. I had not taken sufficient account of the difference in the disposition manifested toward myself in the letter from Cardinal Merry del Val to Cardinal Richard from that shown in the one addressed to me by the Archbishop of Paris himself. Besides, I wanted to believe that my candor could not be imputed to me as a crime by the Holy See. Thus I wrote, on January 5th, 1904, to Cardinal Richard, thanking him for the kindness he had manifested in my behalf, and informing him that I proposed "to send immediately to His Eminence, the Cardinal Secretary of State, my act of adherence to the judgment of the Sacred Congregations." On the 11th, I forwarded to Monsignor Merry del Val the following letter:

Monsignor:

By a letter from His Eminence, Cardinal Richard, Archbishop of Paris, I have been informed of the decrees of the Sacred Congregation of the Holy Office and of the Sacred Congregation of the Index concerning five of my works, and have received a copy of the letter from

Your Eminence which accompanied and explained these decrees.

I receive with respect the judgment of the Sacred Congregations, and I myself condemn whatever may be found in my writings that is reprehensible.

I must add, nevertheless, that my adherence to the sentence of the Sacred Congregations is purely disciplinary in character. I reserve the right of my own conscience, and I do not intend, in inclining myself before the judgment rendered by the Sacred Congregation of the Holy Office, either to abandon or to retract the opinions which I have uttered in my capacity of historian and of critical exegete. Not that I attach to these opinions a certitude that their character does not admit of; as I have never ceased to complete and to correct them, to the best of my ability, during many years of labor, I am assured that they will be completed or corrected, by myself or by others, in the future. But in the existing state of my knowledge, and in default of more complete and more solid information, they constitute the only form in which I can represent to myself the history of the sacred books and that of religion.

It is certain that this "submission" did not exact of me anything beyond a respectful silence toward the condemnation. Few authors would be so fatuous as not to be willing to condemn in their writings "whatever may be found in them that is reprehensible." The formula: "I reserve the right of my own conscience," might not be congenial to Roman ears. Is there any right of conscience contrary to the duty of obedience? He who wrote: "I do not intend either to abandon or to retract my opinions as a historian," was hardly on his knees before the Holy Office. Monsignor Merry del Val was soon to declare of this letter that it did not have "even the tone of a humble and sincere submission." I do not think, however, that its tone was objectionable. I had meant to make it dignified, and had very deliberately avoided the obsequious, unctuous, swelling phraseology that is usual in such cases.

My error lay in supposing that I stood any chance whatsoever, no matter how slight, of being understood. From the Roman, Scholastic, theological point of view, the truth is simply a formula which the Papal authority frames for reasons of its own; which has to be assented to without question by all the members of the Church, when it has once for all been determined upon by the competent power; which one can have no trouble about submitting to, provided one is possessed of the intellectual humility and docility that are obligatory upon every believer. Those who share this mentality have no conception of what it means to arrive at an experimental knowledge of facts and events by the methods of scientific or historical criticism. The heads of the Church must needs have considered me as puffed up with a boundless self-conceit, and this is the view that Pope Pius X always took of me. My letter said, it is true, that I did not attach to my opinions "a certitude that their character does not admit of"; but here self-pride seemed to mingle with want of logic. If these opinions are not assured, why seek to defend them against the Church, which claims a certitude of her own, since she speaks in the name of God? But no one took the pains to discover, by reading my books, that this certitude was, for me, no more binding, to say the least, than that of scientific opinions generally and that in comparison with these opinions it was of no account. My letter could not serve to dissipate the fundamental misunderstanding which exists between the Church, founded on the unreal principle of its absolute authority, and the modern mind, with its untrammelled quest of truth. It could only be the occasion of a series of confused negotiations, at the end of which was bound to come, soon or late, the excommunication that I had anticipated when I launched *Concerning a Little Book.*

On January 22nd, Cardinal Richard's secretary invited me to come the next day to the Archbishop's palace, there to be made acquainted with "an important communication received from the Holy Office." On the 23rd, at ten in the morning, I was on hand at the *Rue de Grenelle,* and heard from the Cardinal's own lips the reading of a letter written by Monsignor Merry del Val. This letter was extremely violent; it insisted upon the instantaneous retractation, without any reserve, of the five condemned volumes and their contents, in default of which the Holy Office would proceed against me *ad ulteriora,*— in other words, I was to be excommunicated. I replied frankly to Cardinal Richard that any such retractation was quite impossible for me, and that I must stand by my letter of January 11th. The Cardinal admitted that he had not expected a retractation from me, and Cardinal Merry del Val's letter showed plainly that Rome was no more hopeful of it, and indeed did not desire it. "He is condemned; let him get out," the Papal Nuncio, Monsignor Lorenzelli, said about this time.

Meanwhile, Cardinal Richard explained to me the conditions on which I could continue in the Church. Independently of the retractation required, I must renounce my course at the *Hautes Études* and retire to some religious institution where I could refashion for myself a Catholic mentality. I carefully avoided discussing these conditions, but remarked to the Cardinal that he had at last accomplished the end he had pursued for ten years past—to reduce me to a nonentity, or to drive me out of the Church—and that he was at liberty to enjoy his triumph. Some malicious gossip had reached his ears libelling my private conduct, and he insinuated that the hardihood of my thinking was possibly connected with certain liberties of a different order. Two words from me were enough to immobilize him in his armchair, and to rid him of any inclination to return to that particular subject, regarding which he clearly saw that he had been misinformed. In the course of this conversation, he said some things to me that, on any other occasion, would have greatly amused me. "The interpretation of historical documents," said he, "depends on the attitude of the interpreter. The principle of your criticism—to enter into the thought of an author or of a text—is erroneous to begin with. One does not enter into the thought of an author; one finds in him what one brings to him. That is why it is essential to interpret Holy Scripture in the spirit of the Church." And in his most majestic manner, lifting his hand impressively, he said: *"You are a subjectivist!"* His logic was better when he assured me that, if the resurrection of Christ is not a historical fact, the demonstration of the truth of Christianity lacks a foundation. Reliable persons had told him that the apologetic arguments in *The Gospel and the Church* were very weak, and this he repeated to me. I did not in the least deny it, for I knew better than he why the apology for official Catholicism in *The Gospel and the Church* was so inadequate.

At home once more, I thought there might be some advantage in defining my sentiments in a fresh letter to Cardinal Merry del Val. On the 24th, I wrote to Cardinal Richard's secretary to ask him to request that prelate to furnish me a copy of the document that had been read to me on the 23d. On the 26th, having received no answer from the Archbishop's palace, I wrote in these terms to the Cardinal Secretary of State:

Monsignor:

His Eminence, Cardinal Richard, Archbishop of Paris, communicated to me on Saturday, January 23rd, the letter written to him by Your Eminence concerning myself.

It is a matter of deep regret to me that the Holy Father did not deem sufficient the adherence given by myself to the decrees of the Sacred Congregations of the Holy Office and of the Index. I should have been remiss in the obligation of sincerity if I had not made express reservation of my opinions as a historian and a critical exegete. It did not enter my mind that anyone could expect of me the pure and simple retractation of a whole body of ideas, forming the substance of my works, trenching upon various orders of knowledge over which the magistracy of the Church has no direct control.

I accept, Monsignor, all the dogmas of the Church, and if in expounding their history in the books which have just been condemned I have, unwittingly, uttered opinions contrary to the faith, I have said and I repeat that I myself condemn in these books whatever in them may be found reprehensible from the point of view of the faith.

This letter was not merely superfluous; it further accentuated the equivocation in which I found myself entangled in my relations with the Church. It reaffirmed my reservations, indeed, in respectful and measured terms. But the expression, "I accept," was expressly chosen that I might not have to say, "I believe"; and the "faith" that I might have unwittingly opposed was not the faith of the Church as expressed in its official creeds. As a matter of fact, I might say to myself that those who were requiring of me the retractation of my five books did not know themselves what they were asking, or else they were not serious in asking it; and neither of these hypotheses was wholly beside the mark. Still, what led me to proceed in this manner was that, however resigned I might be to leaving the Church, I did not yet want to leave it, and that I felt it to be my duty neither to bring about the rupture myself, nor to do anything to provoke it.

On the 29th of January, Monsieur Clément, Cardinal Richard's secretary, replied to my letter of the 24th; but, in place of sending me the desired copy of the letter from Rome, the Cardinal tendered me an audience for Saturday, the 30th. There being no object in this further interview, I failed to keep the appointment; upon which the Cardinal had me notified, on the 2nd of February, that he desired to see me on the 4th or the 6th. On the 5th, I replied to Monsieur Clément that I saw no reason for this meeting and that, if the Cardinal had any communication to make, he could send it in writing. Cardinal Richard never suspected that the things he said were for me a veritable torture. I was unable to control all the movements of impatience or of indignation that his tone and attitude aroused. I respected this old man, who was worthy of respect; but he did not himself impose it upon me, and I do not know if there is anyone in the world to whom I have expressed myself with more utter freedom, I may almost say with more brutal frankness. It was repugnant to me to multiply these nerve-racking sessions which revealed the Church to me with all its disguises thrown off, and showed, as well, how vain was my purpose to remain in it.

As was to have been expected, my second letter to Monsignor Merry del Val was no more acceptable than the first had been. Cardinal Richard informed me of this in a note on February 8th. Rome persisted in demanding a retractation pure and simple, adding the threat of excommunication in the event of my refusal. The Cardinal tendered me an audience for the 11th; on the 10th I responded that I still held firmly to the position stated in my two letters written to the Cardinal Secretary of State. On the 21st, Cardinal Richard wrote again at considerable length, exhorting me to obedience; it was the Pope himself, he said, who had charged him with this mission. The Archbishop's letter, paternal and full of unction, showed how entirely its author failed to enter into my state of mind. "There has never been," he wrote, "and there could not be, any thought of requiring of you an action that was insincere on your part. But I have difficulty in understanding how, after having prayed to God, and examined everything from the supernatural point of view, you could fail to recognize for yourself the duty of submitting without any qualifications." My letter of February 23rd simply reiterated what I had written him on the 10th.

Excommunication thus seemed inevitable, and there is every reason for believing that sentence was actually passed by the Holy Office on March 2nd, to be published by Cardinal Richard in the manner which the latter might judge most auspicious. For my part, I had ready at hand the letter that I should send to the Archbishop of Paris when the excommunication was made known to me or otherwise published. The arguments that I elaborated in it against the Roman demands still appear to me valid. Why did the Holy Office wish to force me to disavow errors which it did not clearly define, and bring against me a judgment in which it was plainly to be seen that the Congregation was anxious not to compromise itself? Was it that the entire contents of my books were equally fallacious? What kind of a notion can the Congregation have formed for itself of its power over historical evidence and historical data? In what kind of a light must appear the arbitrary action whereby I was to be made to substitute, in the twinkling of an eye, for the entire body of knowledge acquired by the toil of more than twenty years, the sole conviction that my intelligence

was darkened by errors of every kind? Was it really
in my power to admit, on the good faith of Pius X
and Cardinal Richard alone, that the narratives of
Genesis, the Garden of Eden and the flood, were
historical facts, that the accounts of the Gospel were
true exactly as written, that those of the resurrection of Jesus were consistent and demonstrative, that
the Christian Church, the dogma of the divinity of
Christ, and the sacraments could be traced back to
the preaching of Jesus himself? I could have gone
on much farther in this direction, and have proved
peremptorily that the retractation demanded of me
was an utter absurdity, that it was impossible that
it could be sincere, and also, for good measure, that
I was no longer a Catholic. Excommunication would
have put me in my rightful place, which was outside the Church; and my mistake on this occasion,
after all the experiences I had undergone, was in not
adequately realizing this. As a result of new overtures which I made at the eleventh hour, the sentence of excommunication was not launched, and I
gained for myself four more years of anxiety, of
unrest, of deadly weariness, only to arrive in March,
1908, at the solution which I had avoided in
March, 1904.

VII

During the last part of February, while I was in
daily expectation of the judgment which was to ex-
clude me from the Roman communion, my physical
strength, of which I had never had an overabundant
supply, suddenly collapsed, and this circumstance

unquestionably had its influence on the course I then determined upon. It seemed to me, and it was true, that with the coming of the excommunication, and amid the public excitement that was bound to result from it, my health would not allow of my going on with my writing and teaching. Already the lecture-room at the *École Pratique des Hautes Études* was invaded by a veritable mob, friendly enough, for that matter, or at least respectful, but whose very presence was to an amazing degree fatiguing. It was not to these crowds of curiosity-seekers that I wished to lecture; and so far from dispersing them, my excommunication would only add to their number. An equal embarrassment in my own eyes was that the Section on the Science of Religion, which had not thought it worth while to elect me a permanent member in 1901, might be disposed to take this step in 1904, and it did not appeal to me to seem to be seeking by way of excommunication an honor that at first had been refused me. Moreover, I could not help being concerned as to the consequences that, under certain conditions, my departure from the Church might have for those, in high places or low, who had followed, encouraged, sustained or protected me. I was worn out by the tumult raging around me, and felt an overwhelming need for quiet and repose of spirit. I did not in any sense deceive myself as to the serious check to the tentative I had undertaken for the emancipation of Catholic thought. Those who had grasped my meaning were singularly few. With the rarest exceptions, nothing could have been more superficial than the judg-

ments printed by the newspapers concerning a debate which was, at bottom, at least as tragical for
the Church as for myself. I had a sense of peculiar
isolation, placed as I was between the Church, preparing to expel me as a dangerous innovator, and the
age, willing to find a few days' entertainment in
watching the duel between a mere abbé and the
whole Catholic hierarchy.

It was in this frame of mind that, on the 27th of
February, without having consulted any of my
friends, and without the idea having been suggested
to me by any one, I decided upon the following line
of conduct: to let the excommunication come; then
when sentence had once been rendered, to write to
the Pope, making protestation of the uprightness of
my intentions, declaring that I could not honestly
have abstained from making the reservations indicated in my two letters to the Cardinal Secretary
of State, and testifying to my good will for the
pacification of spirits by agreeing to abandon the
instruction which I was giving in Paris; after that,
His Holiness could judge whether or not to maintain in its rigor the censure that had been brought
against me.

Two of my friends, to whom I confided this plan
—a priest and a layman—were united in feeling that
I had better make my intentions known to the Pope
in advance of the excommunication; the course of
action I was contemplating might check the force
and turn the edge of the decree, but would not ensure
its recall. They were right in so judging, but for all
that my first plan was wiser than theirs. The essen-

tial thing on my part was not to escape excommunication, but to safeguard my moral integrity in face of the demands of authority. By entering upon the path of yielding concessions, I could be drawn farther than I had any intention of going. Finally, I could stay in the Church only by persisting in the equivocation from which I had tried to free myself by the publication of *Concerning a Little Book*. Excommunication had the advantage of providing a way out, and the accommodation dreamed of by my friends proved to be merely an *impasse*. Nevertheless, it seemed to me that they had logic and good sense on their side, and I agreed to their suggestion. The priest—he was a monk who has since left the Church—promised to write to Father Lepidi, whose pupil he had formerly been in Rome; and the layman—Monsieur François Thureau-Dangin—received from my hands on Sunday, February 28th, to mail from Paris, a letter addressed directly to His Holiness, Pius X. I wrote to the Pope:

Most Holy Father:

I well know Your Holiness's goodness of heart, and it is to your heart that I now address myself.

I wish to live and die in the communion of the Catholic Church. I do not wish to contribute to the ruin of the faith in France.

It is beyond my power to destroy in myself the result of my labors.

So far as in me lies, I submit myself to the judgment brought against my writings by the Congregation of the Holy Office.

To give evidence of my good faith, and for the pacification of spirits, I am prepared to abandon the teaching chair which I occupy in Paris, and at the same time to suspend my scientific publications now under way.

This letter, as I was speedily to learn, was at a considerable remove from the customary style of humble submissions, but it voiced my sincere sentiments. Its most serious fault consisted in the fact that it was destined for persons who were incapable of understanding it, and that it strove to conciliate what the Pope himself deemed irreconcilable—the profession of a Catholic and that of a scholar as I had trained myself to conceive it. Another friend, a rather lukewarm layman, who came to see me on the 2nd of March, said, on learning what I had just done: "You have retreated only to make a further leap." It was he who had the right of it.

Would my letter be favorably regarded by Pius X? I was inclined to think so. Abbé Monier was of the same opinion. The Archbishop of Albi, whom I saw on March 4th in the presbytery of Saint Médard, felt assured of it. However, Cardinal Richard, informed by Abbé Monier of what I had written to the Pope, and asked by him to intervene with Pius X so that I might be unmolested, had contented himself with replying that the affair was in the hands of Providence. And a rumor began to circulate in the press that excommunication had been decreed against me by the Holy Office.

On Saturday, March 12th, I received this note from Cardinal Richard:

My dear Monsieur Loisy:
I am just in receipt of a letter from the Holy Father in reply to that which you wrote to him on February 28th. With a truly fatherly goodness, he charges me to transmit his point of view to you with the least possible delay.

I do not know who can have given this morning's papers the news that the Holy Office had pronounced excommunication against you. This news finds no justification in the Pope's letter, which I am charged to convey to you.

The news was in contradiction to the Pope's letter, nevertheless it may very well have been accurate. The pains which the Cardinal took to deny it, and the omission of a portion of the Papal missive as he read it to me, gave me grounds for thinking that Pius X had used this means either of setting aside the excommunication or of empowering the Cardinal to do so. In any case, on the morning of the same day I presented myself at the Archbishop's palace to learn what had been determined upon by the Pope's "fatherly goodness."

That goodness, which seems to have so impressed Cardinal Richard, was scarcely apparent in the words of Pius X himself. After reproducing my letter of February 28th, for the purpose of acquainting the Archbishop with its contents, Pius X declared that this letter, addressed to his heart, was not written from the heart, since it failed to contain the act of obedience which had been required of me. The Pope was favorably impressed by my declaration regarding the abandonment of my chair at the *Hautes Études,* but added immediately that the satisfactory part of my letter had been spoiled by the sentence: "It is beyond my power to destroy in myself the result of my labors." He insisted anew on an absolute retractation, and concluded by saying: "Assuredly, he is not asked to write no more, but to write in defense of tradition, in conformity with the words of St. Remy to Clovis: 'Adore what you once burned, and burn what you once adored.' " During the reading of this stupefying epistle, the tumult of conflicting feelings within me was beyond all description. I desired greatly to see the text, and asked the Cardinal to allow me to make a copy. He pretended not to hear, and read to me over again the most important passages.

When the opening words greeted my ears, something gave way within me. The Head of that Church to which I had devoted my life, for which I had so abundantly labored for thirty years past, which I had loved and could not help loving still, outside of which I had neither ambition nor hope of any kind, when I had responded to absurd demands by offering a supreme sacrifice, could find nothing else to say to me than the harsh words: "That letter, addressed to my heart, was not written from the heart." But it was, all the same! It had pressed into it the last drop of feeling left in my Catholic soul for the distress from which the Church was suffering, in some small degree through what I had done, but in no sense from any fault of mine. And because I asked to be allowed to die peaceably in that Church of my baptism, without being constrained to prevaricate in order to remain in it, I had to be taken for a person insincerely posing as a martyr, for an individual so insanely conceited as to wish to appear a victim (this, verily, was the idea of Pius X), and to affect a renunciation of something for which he cared not at all, when what was asked of him was simply nothing, or next to nothing: namely, to uphold as true what he perfectly well knew to be false, and, reciprocally, to reject as false what he clearly knew in his heart to be true! Still other experiences were required to bring me to the point of no longer even wishing to be a Catholic; but this one was decisive above all others. When, in August, 1910, the Pope condemned *Le Sillon,* the organ of social democracy in the French Catholic Church, I said to my friends: "The Roman Church is utterly heartless." I had been convinced of this, in a degree, ever since the 12th of March, 1904. Cardinal Richard would have done well to brand me then with the decree of excommunication which lay in one of his desk drawers. It could not have lacerated my feelings more than what he did do, and on the other hand would have done me a very great service.

Our interview, probably the longest and also the last that we ever had, was likewise the most agitated. I was unable to control my indignation, nor the Cardinal—wholly out of sympathy with my viewpoint as he was—his irritation. He reproached me openly with "the pride of learning." "There is also," I rejoined, "a pride of ignorance." And I felt constrained to say to him that all who knew me were aware that I was as little infatuated with my acquirements, and as little preoccupied with urging my private opinions, as anyone alive. He insisted, taking on a tragical tone—which was also comical, since it was plainly assumed—as he reiterated: "Self-pride is lurking at the bottom of your difficulty." "I beg you to spare me this humiliation," was my answer, "Your Eminence is gravely in error." Upon which the orthodox old man, misapprehending the nature of the error to which I was referring, and thinking my allusion to be to the simplicity of his personal faith, responded: "If I err, I err in company with the Church!"

He brought up again the learned personages who had refuted me, notably Cardinal Perraud in his pastoral letter. "That," said I, "is a veritable tissue of contradictions." In fact, the Bishop of Autun had thought it enough to demonstrate that my historical results were irreconcilable with the definitions of the Councils of Trent and of the Vatican; and he, like all the rest, took those conclusions of historical research for dogmatic propositions which deserved censure because they came into conflict with the official theology. I endeavored to make clear to the Cardinal how it was that I could condemn the errors found in my books, and the false theology attributed to me; an oversubtle distinction of which I had made use in *The Gospel and the Church,* and of which I was further to avail myself, most unadvisedly. It was true that the theologians were not on the right track; but it was also true that they took the definitions of the Councils for data of history, in such wise that their false history was most assuredly in contradiction with what I was presenting as the true. If their wrong data constituted orthodoxy, then mine were clearly heresy.

In conducting me to the door, at the close of our conversation, the Cardinal once again brought up the considerable number and weight of authority of those who had opposed me. "Eminence," said I, laying my hand familiarly on his arm, "those who are most ardent in their refutations of me are persons who know perfectly well, in their own hearts, that I am in the right of it." At which he beat a hasty retreat into his private office, and I departed in a state of profound uncertainty as to what it was best for me to do. The summary of the interview, written in my journal, ends thus: "All that is most deplorable. It will be a misfortune for me, as well as for others, if I am driven, provisionally or definitively, out of the Church. Still, it is plain that my place is outside, and that inside there is for me no longer either sincerity or dignity or protection."

Notwithstanding all that had occurred, before the day was over I sent to Cardinal Richard the following lines:

Monsignor:

I declare to Your Eminence that, in a spirit of obedience toward the Holy See, I condemn the errors which the Holy Office has already condemned in my writings.

I wish that it lay in my power to expunge that note from the record! If I was able to bring myself to send it to the Archbishop of Paris, the reason was that it was associated in my own thought, and must necessarily be in that of Cardinal Richard, with the long discussion between us of that morning on the subject of Cardinal Perraud's pamphlet. What had passed between us would serve as a commentary on what I had written. But, as has been said, there was not wanting a certain equivocation in this same discussion; and moreover, my declaration would have to be forwarded to Rome, of course unaccompanied by any oral exposition. There it would naturally be taken in a far more extended sense than I had meant to give it, and in future would serve as point of departure for an accusation, on the first occasion that might present itself, of bad faith on my part. Also, it would there be regarded as meaningless, since the Holy Office, in point of fact, had not condemned any particular error but whole volumes which I was expected to disavow in their entirety, and which I had no intention of disavowing at all.

In the time which had elapsed between my letter to the Pope and Pius X's reply, I had foreseen that in case my proposal failed of acceptance I should be in a position to make the declaration just cited, adding expressly that the errors I was reproving consisted rather in the system imputed to me than in the opinions which I had actually sustained as a historian. This was the formula that I was proposing to send to Cardinal Richard, and I was in a position to do so because it represented my state of mind at the time; though assuredly it would have been better not to write at all. Some of my friends—in such cases one's friends ought to be exceedingly chary of their advice—led me to feel that any explicit reservation on my part would take all the meaning out of the tender of my submission, and that either I should refrain altogether from sending it or should send it without express limitation, since Rome would probably not find any other form of statement acceptable. In so thinking, they were clearly in the wrong. I was even more in the wrong to accept their advice, and I have always deeply regretted having added those four miserable lines to what I had written on February 28th; the response made to this letter by Pius X being worthy only of silence.

Fortunately for myself, Rome understood quite clearly that my new statement belonged in the same category with the former ones, and signified nothing beyond my wish to remain in the Church, as in my letter to the Pope, and without any disavowal of my opinions as a historian, as in my two letters to Cardinal Merry del Val. The Holy Office did me the great kindness not to make my submission a matter of record, doubtless because there was no belief in its genuineness. Excommunication was not ventured upon; it may even be that Cardinal Richard insisted that I should not be excommunicated. So the threat of excommunication remained hanging over my head, like a sword of Damocles. Nothing could have been more nicely calculated to accustom me to the idea of having it descend upon me.

CHAPTER V

ON THE FRONTIER OF THE CHURCH

I

AFTER that ill-starred 12th of March, for a number of days I remained in a state of acute mental anguish. There were moments when I felt a strong inclination to write once more to the Cardinal, assuring him explicitly that my latest declaration had not been a retractation, since it was forever impossible that I should "destroy in myself the result of my labors." Could I only have known that my letter had not even left his possession—so just an estimate had the Cardinal placed upon it, and so little vital significance had he attached to it—I might have been more at ease. Monsignor Richard wrote me, on March 17th, that he was on the point of forwarding it to Rome. So there was no possible haste about it! The fact that the Cardinal wrote this last time solely with a view to persuading me to send to the Pope the letter of "full and filial submission" which Pius X was still awaiting, is proof enough that my note was deemed of small account. So it had not been felt to constitute a "full submission." Precisely this had been my purpose, and it mattered little to me now that it was not considered "filial." I wrote neither to the Pope nor to the Cardinal, nor did I hear again from the one or the other. On March 26th, I learned from a woman friend who was in Rome that the Holy Office had for the time being abandoned any further action against me, and this was confirmed by certain high ecclesiastics connected with the Roman congregations. Beyond this, I had no further information.

It was under these circumstances that I proceeded with the preparations for my retirement from public teaching. On March 27th, I wrote to Professor Albert Réville, Director of the Section of the Science of Religion at the *École Pratique des Hautes Études,* announcing to him that I should not resume my lectures after Easter, and at the same time I sent to Monsieur Philippe Berger my resignation as assistant in the work of the *Corpus Inscriptionum Semiticarum.* Monsieur François Thureau-Dangin had placed at my disposal a small cottage located on his property, Marmousse, in the village of Garnay, not far from Dreux. There it was that I was proposing to pass the rest of my days in solitude, and first of all to build up my strength so as to be able to exist at all.

The spring and early summer were occupied in making ready for my new domicile. On April 9th I wrote in my journal:

I have given myself a lot of trouble in this world with small result. I took my own life and the Church seriously, and the consequence is that I have wasted the one and disturbed the other. The search for truth is not a trade by which a man can support himself; for a priest it is a supreme peril. For a long time now I have not really been a Catholic in the official sense of the word. I have strewn my intelligence and my activity to the four winds of an empty ideal. That has made for me an aimless life, a career that has led nowhere. I am gathering up my fragments of life and strength to carry them to Marmousse, old before my time, suspected by the Church, abandoned by the world, destined to quick oblivion. After high-soaring dreams, comes anticipation of the grave. Whatever may be the future fate of Catholicism, I can have no part in it. What is to be the religion of the future I do not know. Roman Catholicism, as such, is bound to perish, and it deserves no regrets. It might endure by transforming itself, but it is not willing. It does not pertain to me to wish this in its stead. Let me have peace! Henceforward, nothing would be more out of place than to throw myself into theological squabbles. I have no further responsibility in the Church, and I have the right to organize what remains to me of existence to suit my own tastes.

The proof that I was not quite so far gone as I had the appearance of believing is that I wrote, on April 11th, "Tomorrow I shall probably finish my commentary on the Synoptic Gospels. All that will be left to do is to prepare the Introduction." This Introduction was to be my principal task at Garnay. I finished it in March, 1905, after which the revision of both the Commentary and the Introduction occupied me until the end of 1906.

During all these months my inclination progressed steadily in the direction of a complete secularization of my occupation and of my manner of life. The following extracts from my journal will throw light on my inner disposition and on the progress of events.

May 10, 1904.—This morning, in reciting the prayers from the Missal, I felt almost a desire that it might be

for the last time. Do I still believe enough to call myself
a Catholic, and is what I believe Catholic truth?   I
remain in the Church from motives which do not accord
with the Catholic faith, but are motives of moral oppor-
tunism. It would take little, very little, to make it
impossible for me to persist honestly in my calling as a
priest. If this little happens, I shall not be surprised
at it, and I believe I shall not even regret it.

May 12.—I am in acute distress of mind. There are
moments when I fall to wishing for something definite to
happen to put me out of the Church. But I must not
count on being liberated by the progress of events.
Events do not liberate those who submit to them, but
those who succeed in dominating them. I should have
done better to let the excommunication come, and then
to have taken the steps I have taken since. I am staying
in the Church so as not to trouble certain souls, but I
am exquisitely troubling my own! If I believe in anything, I do not believe in what the Church teaches, and
the Church shows no disposition whatever to teach what
I believe. Can I honestly remain in it?

May 28.—An unfriendly physician might very well
explain my conduct since the 27th of last February as
having been due to a crisis of neurasthenia.

May 31.—What I have just been reading of Abbé
Laberthonnière's new book on *The Realism of Christianity and the Idealism of Greek Philosophy* is not so
bad. What it demonstrates is that faith is faith, and
science is science, not that one of these is truer than the
other, nor, above all—as the author would like to have it
—that faith is justified in postulating, in despite of
history, the physical and material reality of events like
the virgin birth and the resurrection of Jesus. Moreover, the system of Laberthonnière, who is Maurice
Blondel translated into French and purged of his magisterial manner, is everywhere penetrated by Protestant
illuminism. His system involves the fundamental negation of the theological dogma which tradition has handed
down to us, and of the authority of the Church which is
its sovereign guarantor. Men such as he believe in all
the dogmas of the Church, but they do not believe in

the usual literal manner, resting on an objective revelation and on the testimony of the Church. They find their source of authority in their inner experience, just as do the Protestants; they are "subjectivists," they are not orthodox. Nobody is orthodox! Orthodoxy is the chimera of persons who are incapable of doing any thinking. *Psittacorum genus.* It is apparent to everyone that the system of Roman absolutism, in the full rigor of its pretensions, is absurd, impracticable and immoral. All the same, that is the system which now constitutes Catholicism, and is it possible to be a Catholic in these days in despite of Rome and the Pope?

June 7.—If I wake up to find myself outside the Church, it will not be to act the part of a much-abused doctor, waiting for the door to reopen and let him back within the fold. I propose to live the life of a lay scholar, concerned with the higher life of humanity, and to die in the same capacity. I cannot very well conceive of myself as reconciled *in extremis* by an explicit profession of faith in the virgin birth and the bodily resurrection of Christ, in the absolute validity of traditional dogma and in the despotic power of the Pope over the intelligence and the will.

I am well aware of inconsistencies in my feeble thinking. But for all that, I do not feel any need of blindly subjecting myself to those organs of the Holy Spirit who happen to be named .Pius X and Francis Richard. I feel myself in close enough communion with the intelligent and moral portion of mankind in these days to desire no other support. It will get me nowhere to believe firmly that Jesus Christ descended into hell and that he rose again to the skies. Neither do I find any spiritual solace in thinking that there are really three persons in God, or in considering Him a person at all. For a long while I have not found it possible to pray to God as one beseeches an individual from whom some favor is anticipated. My prayers consist of retiring into the depths of my own consciousness and there gathering my best impulses together to determine what for me is right and lawful.

June 25.—There is an infantile aspect to the ordinary

notion of a future life, that is not highly moral, and is even immoral. To represent another life as the direct continuation of this one is childish; for, if we persist in any fashion, it can only be quite otherwise than here. To conceive of eternal happiness as a reward gained for a definite service, which is worth sacrificing a good deal not to miss, is to put ourselves on the level of a dog who retrieves the game in order to save himself from being whipped and to enjoy his rightful portion. And yet I am far from certain that the dog's morality is not higher, and that he does not do his work in the end to be pleasing to his master, thus in his way practicing pure, all-forgetful love. Oh, it is odious to pay poor human creatures with tickets to Paradise, as though the eternal hope must be prostituted to become the conservative guarantor and guardian of all the abuses, inequalities and miseries of this present existence!

Taking things from the standpoint of experience, there is no more reason for admitting the immortality of men than that of fleas, of ants, of snakes and of donkeys. All these are earth's vermin, proceeding from it, returning to it, dust of its dust, following the progress of its evolution, as the earth doubtless follows the evolution of the sun, and the sun that of the stellar system to which it belongs. It presupposes a singular naïveté and an insensate pride in man for him to imagine that he is entitled to special attentions from the Eternal, and that God is counting on him to adorn His heaven. It is even a gross exaggeration of man's value as a moral being, or so it appears to me, to want him to be immortal on this score. Whatever he may do in this world, he has his due reward when he leaves it. The life of a man is phenomenal, like the life of a plant; and to say that a man is immortal amounts to saying that this phenomenon lasts on when it has already ceased to be. . . .

Whoever has known, even if only for an instant, and notwithstanding the inherent limitations, and the tendency to illusion, of all our perceptions—whoever, I repeat, has known the ideal under the form of the true, the good, and the beautiful, who has known the joy, more or less pure and perfect, of knowledge and of love, has already entered eternity, has seen God face to face, and can die without a qualm; for he has lived enough to live forever; he has inscribed himself, in characters never to be effaced, in the consciousness of the living God.

.   .   .   .

October 2, 1905.—It appears that Pius X, immediately after the promulgation of the law on the separation of Church and State, will publish an encyclical to which will be annexed the doctrinal *Syllabus* that has been rumored for the past year to be imminent. That also will be the time for turning me out of the Church; for which I shall have no regrets.

November 27.—I do not deem it my duty to break the tie that attaches me to the Church, but if the Church dissolves it I shall be very much relieved. Under these circumstances, no protest from me will be in order, but I can contribute, if an opportunity should come, enlightenment to the public on the antecedents and the manner of my condemnation.

December 8.—The separation was definitively voted day before yesterday by the French Senate. Now let us wait for the sequel.

It seems to me that troublous times are ahead, in which there will be a chance for me to do something. But what? Physically I have not much to go on, and morally I am pretty desolate. Still, I think I see the way to take, the way of emancipation on which I shall go forward tremblingly, and on which others will be able to follow me more safely.

December 23.—The less I have to write by way of self-justification, the better it will be. For that matter, truth to tell, there has been nothing in my conduct requiring defense or justification. All my sins have been in the realm of ideas. I shall have only questions of doctrine to handle, not private affairs. Even my exit from the Church, if it is brought about, hangs on the question of the intellectual régime of the Catholic Church; that is to say, on whether the idea of an absolute authority, as ignorant as absolute, in all the different orders of knowledge, is not something absurd, and whether the inward and outward submission which this authority demands is not something impossible and immoral.

December 30.—I foresee clearly the kind of judgment that will put me outside the Catholic Church. My only protest is against the personal abuse and vilification that will probably accompany, and will doubtless follow, it. The Church is not in the habit of respecting the feelings of those whom she chooses to regard as her adversaries.

. . . .

January 6, 1906.—Taking all things into consideration, it has been by a kind of auto-suggestion that I have come to conceive of my secession as just now indispensable. In itself it is no more so than two years ago, at the height of the rumpus, when I was not able to decide upon it. But my present persuasion is none the less a result of concurrent circumstances, working together with the inner process of which it is the outcome. If it is true that inwardly I am more distressed by what there is of falsity, of equivocation, and of insincerity in my position, it is true also that outwardly I cannot utter a word without throwing myself in the path of that system of repression which is in a way to become the law of the Church in France. Not only am I no longer Catholic in myself, but I cannot even appear to be so except by keeping an unbroken silence. Still even this will not suffice. I shall be required to speak in condemnation of my thought as it was formerly made public. I see but one solution compatible with common honesty. Only arguments of worldly conformity, without moral value, can hold me back now.

January 9.—I have need of my freedom, but I have no need for combating the Church.

On April 22nd, 1906, I wrote to a friend who had questioned me concerning the fundamental problems of religion:

The proofs for the existence of God do not seem to me conclusive, at least as to the existence of a God who is eternal, immutable, omniscient, omnipotent, etc. Something is, therefore something always has been. But that the impelling principle of evolution in the universe is not immanent in it, that it is transcendent to the point of possessing the infinite totality of its being independently of the universe which it has created by a caprice very imperfectly benevolent, this is what reason cannot demonstrate, and what even begins to be conceived with increasing difficulty. Nor does the scientific observation of nature reveal to us any better "the glory of God" in the Psalmist's sense; what appears is an immensity of force, a vast ocean of being, but not as if ruled by a will external to its own mass. It has, as it were, a sort of will diffused throughout itself, like a mind latent in each atom, carrying its law within itself; and we may even say that it makes that law and submits to it at one and the same time.

There remains the testimony of the moral consciousness. Our dear X—— holds that while the reason may lead us into monism, the heart is sufficient to prove God. That species of dualism is hard to accept. Conscience can no more impose a God upon reason than the latter can find one for itself. Is not this God of our excellent friend, which bears a striking resemblance to that of Harnack, merely a survival, in minds otherwise emancipated, of a subjective notion which has now lost its former points of attachment and is upheld provisionally by feeling, by a mystical bent of soul, and by inherited habit? How many men of good-will entirely lack that direct perception of God! The intimate experience from which it is supposed to be derived—is that secure from all illusion?

It seems obvious to me that the notion of God has never been anything but a kind of ideal projection, a reflection upward of the human personality, and that theology never has been and never can be anything but a more and more purified mythology. God is like a higher self who watches over a lower self with which we remain identified; and, the individual consciousness being also a social consciousness, this higher self is equally the personification, in a transcendental sense, of society or of humanity. This entire fabric of religious thought is no more shot through with illusion than is that of scientific thought, whose advance consists, in the main, of a series of conjectures. The good is equally real with the true, and with life itself. These all are not things existing in some metaphysical fashion outside of and above ourselves, but things very really existing in us, and being daily made by us. And the Infinite and Eternal Energy from which all things proceed, by which all things subsist—although it is not "a great Spirit in three persons, enthroned in the highest heaven"—must be something more marvellous, more august, and more beneficent than we are able to conceive. We only minimize this Power in supposing it to be always and uniquely occupied with ourselves. The fact is, nevertheless, that it is not a stranger to us, and that we are not indifferent to it. We are a part of its very being. Invoking it by prayer is no doubt a rather antiquated fashion of participating in its energy. Whoever seeks, loves, and does the true and the good, prays to it in the right spirit.

II

Such was my general state of mind from the time of my installation in the hermitage at Garnay, toward the end of July, 1904. My life there was much secluded, varied only by the care of my little garden and my few fowls, and by walks in the park of Marmousse. At long intervals, one or two friends would come to visit me. I should have been perfectly content, however, if it had not been for constant uncertainty as to my ecclesiastical situation. I continued my writing of book reviews for the *Revue Critique,* and my notices of new publications, as well as my exegetical articles, in the *Revue d'Histoire et de Littérature Religieuses.* These latter were taken from my forthcoming commentary on the

Synoptic Gospels, but from the parts dealing with the teaching of Jesus, a region having fewer pitfalls than the narratives of his career.   At the same time, I was repeatedly informed that inquisitors—who, of course, wished me well!—were following whatever I published and regularly denouncing it, either to the authorities in Paris or to those in Rome.   I was even told that Pius X had been horribly shocked by an article on the message sent by John the Baptist to Jesus (Matthew xi, 2-19) which was not at all venturesome.   At least, it must have been evident to my readers generally that the censures of the Church had not led to any change in my mode of treating Biblical questions, nor in the opinions I had professed in the condemned volumes.   It was doubtless on this account that, late in the year 1906, a measure was taken against me which, without attracting public notice, quietly relieved me of the exercise of my priestly functions.

I have already related how, in October, 1899, I had obtained from Rome an *indult* authorizing me, for a term of seven years, to say the daily mass in my own room.   That *indult* expired on October 17th, 1906. On my arrival at Garnay, it had been countersigned without hesitation by Abbé Legué, the Vicar-General of the diocese, the Bishopric of Chartres being then vacant.   I was not especially anxious to have the *indult* renewed; but, as I did not yet look on it as a duty to separate myself from the Church, since I was resolved to leave to the Church herself the initiative in any separation, I decided to take the necessary steps to secure its renewal.   The success of the undertaking was extremely doubtful, but at least it would reveal the present disposition toward me of the ecclesiastical authorities.

Thus, on September 23, 1906, I wrote to the new Bishop of Chartres, Monsignor Bouquet, as the intermediary through whom my request must be transmitted to Rome. On October 3rd, the general secretary of the diocese replied, asking me for the original *indult* together with my last *celebret* (i.e. the certificate of a bishop attesting that a priest is within the canonical conditions requisite for the authorization to say mass.) These papers would have to be forwarded in support of my new request. I sent them forthwith; but, on October 10th, I was advised by the secretary that the *celebret* was insufficient. It was the one delivered to me in October, 1899, by Abbé Odelin, Vicar-General of Paris, when I was preparing to leave Neuilly to take up my residence at Bellevue. What was required, I was told, was a *celebret* from my bishop, the bishop of the diocese in which I had received ordination, i.e. the Bishop of Châlons-sur-Marne. The attitude taken toward me by Monsignor Latty after the condemnation of my books by the Holy Office has already been described. It was very distasteful to me to have to write to this personage, and I therefore wrote instead to one of his vicars-general on October 10th. Well aware that he would be entirely secure in making a mock of me, Monsignor Latty returned at once the following attestation:

I, the undersigned, Vicar-General of Monsignor, the Bishop of Châlons, certify that Abbé Loisy left the diocese of Châlons in 1881, with the consent of Monsignor Meignan, Bishop of the diocese, and consequently that at the above date the diocesan authority judged him worthy of celebrating Holy Mass.

Châlons-sur-Marne, October 12th, 1906.

(Signed)   A. JACQUET,
Vicar-General.

The secretary-general of Chartres, like the honest man that he was, judged this proceeding of Monsignor Latty as it deserved. On receipt of this ridiculous document, he wrote me not only that he could do nothing, which was only too obvious, but that Monsignor Latty had no right thus to refuse me the certificate which I had requested from him.

Since I had gone so far as to begin these negotiations, it seemed to me I must now carry them through; so I wrote again to Abbé Jacquet on October 20th, insisting that the Bishop either give the *celebret* or explain the canonical reasons for his refusal. The reply, cold and haughty, reached me on October 31st. Monsignor Latty, by the hand of his Vicar-General, declared that he had no personal knowledge of me, because I had left his diocese twenty-five years before, and further that I had neglected to adhere to the pastoral instruction which he had published against my doctrines in 1904: nevertheless he would grant me the *celebret* asked for, provided the Cardinal Archbishop of Paris was willing to give me one first—a most unusual condition, since I had left the diocese of Paris as well seven years before, had resided for five years in that of Versailles, and more recently for two years in that of Chartres, where I still was. But Monsignor

Latty, of course, knew perfectly well that Cardinal Richard was made the special channel for the intentions of the Roman authorities toward me; and in sheltering himself thus behind the Archbishop of Paris, he was merely guarding himself from taking any step that might make a wrong impression at the Vatican.

So, on the same day, I wrote to Cardinal Richard's secretary, describing my fruitless resort to the provincial bishops, and praying His Eminence to examine whether Paris could concede the *celebret* which Châlons did not wish to take the initiative in granting. My patience was pretty well exhausted. My letter to Monsieur Clément took the form of a simple request for information. Cardinal Richard, like the other prelates, needed time to think the matter over. In a letter dated November 11th, Monsieur Clément informed me that His Eminence could not respond at once to my request, but that he would do so "in the near future." No reply ever came, and I did not feel disposed to insist further for the sake of obtaining it.

I have no doubt whatever that the postponement of Cardinal Richard's answer was agreed upon in concert with Rome. By a similar artifice, George Tyrrell was prevented from saying mass after his expulsion from the Society of Jesus. What end the authorities proposed to themselves in employing this roundabout method in my case, I have never known. Possibly it was only a way of putting me out of the Church without the publicity of an open excommunication; or perhaps it was calculated that, for the sake

of obtaining the authorization that I appeared to
desire, I might be inclined to enter upon negotiations
which would at last afford an opportunity to obtain
from me some substantial concession. If this latter
supposition is the true one, it rested on a total misapprehension of my actual purposes. My desire was
that the *indult* should be refused, as I foresaw that
it would be. But, apparently, Rome was not ready
to take the responsibility for the refusal, or at least
chose not to have to say so openly, and had instructed Cardinal Richard to refuse the sending of
the *celebret,* so that the *indult* could not even be
asked for. It would have been more dignified, I
think, to have replied that I could no longer be
authorized to say mass because I had ceased to be
considered as belonging to the Catholic Church. It
was my wish that this declaration, which would
restore to me my liberty so far as concerned the
Church, should be made by the Church herself;
and in the end I was successful in wrenching it
from her.

Already, by the time Monsieur Clément's letter
arrived, I had ceased to say mass. A serious indis-
position had made it impossible for me to say it on
November 2nd and the next few days. When my
condition improved, I continued the omission. My
last mass, therefore, was celebrated on November 1st,
1906; my first had been on June 30th, 1879. This
act had not altogether lost its religious import for
me; but latterly it had become burdensome, because
it had seemed to imply an adherence to the official
Catholicism. In renouncing it, I took one step more

toward the complete secularizing of my existence. Not for one moment did the idea occur to me of persisting, without *indult* or *celebret,* in the performance of this sacerdotal act. The notion of attempting to remain a Catholic priest outside the Roman Communion, or a Catholic despite the Pope, could not even enter my head.

III

Just at this moment, external happenings conspired to destroy the last vestiges of the deep attachment that I had felt for the Church. I followed with the liveliest interest the legislative debates in Paris over the separation of Church and State, the measures taken to enforce the law, and the resistance offered to it by Pius X and the French episcopate. The attitude imposed by the Pope on our unhappy clergy revolted my very soul. When I saw that the whole policy of the Roman diplomats tended exclusively to stir up an agitation among us that might easily degenerate into a civil war, and this in no way in furtherance of the Catholic faith in France, but purely to save the miserable political prestige of the Roman Papacy, then, I avow, I came to despair of the future of Catholicism in our country, and deemed myself fortunate to be no longer Roman, that I might be ever, and yet more patriotically, and with my whole soul a Frenchman.

I even took, without its being noticed, an infinitesimal part in these mighty struggles, by publishing anonymously short pieces directed against the clerical manifestoes. This was at the instigation of Monsieur Paul Desjardins, in the publication issued by the *Union for Truth*. It has already been stated, and it goes without saying, that my articles were unsigned, and I do not imagine they were widely read. The first consisted of Reflections upon the letter addressed by the five French cardinals, assuredly by direction of the Pope, to the President of the Republic, protesting against the proposed legislation. The following extract from the latter part of my article may serve to show that, coming from a wholly inexperienced political observer, as I am, it was not so far from doing me credit.

This letter shows, better than anything else could show, both the imperativeness of the separation and the necessity for our lawmakers to see to it that the Church shall not take unfair advantage, against the governing authority and even against the nation itself, of the freedom conferred upon her under the new law. The entire strategy of the Roman Church is revealed in this single sentence: "The project of separation leads straight to religious persecution, and is not an expression of the real will of the nation." From the moment when the Church can no longer dominate, she begins to claim that she is not free. In refusing to conform to the law, duly enacted, she will force the civil power to suppress the acts of insubordination which, precisely by reason of this attitude on her part, will break out among Catholic partisans, and then she will assert that she is being persecuted. Moreover, she will insist on interpreting as the real will of the nation the dissatisfaction that she herself will have deliberately aroused.

It may seem to short-sighted politicians that the separation will plunge us into a series of difficulties which it would be more sensible to avoid by retaining the

Concordat. This latter choice, even if it were still open to us, could serve only to perpetuate another sort of distress and embarrassment, involving still graver peril to liberty, or to every legitimate form of it, and to religious peace in our country. The future of France can only be secured as the outcome of a struggle in which the victory shall rest with the lay element in society, with the secular arm; provided that the law-making power and the government show themselves at once strong and moderate, resolute opponents of clerical domination and exempt from anti-religious fanaticism; capable of framing a law combining freedom with justice, and able to make that law respected. They will thus succeed in setting a notable example to European civilization.[1]

The year following I commented upon the encyclical of August 10th, 1906, in which Pius X, contrary to the express desire of the majority of the French bishops, condemned the associations for public worship:

The Liberal Catholics and the liberal non-Catholics have once again been mightily deceived in the Holy See. Judging by common sense, they were persuaded that the Catholic Church could not fail to conform to a law regularly voted by the Chambers, a law whose observance did not imply the disavowal of any religious principle. And now the Pope declares that he cannot conscientiously authorize the formation of Catholic associations for public worship, under the conditions provided by Article 4 of the law concerning the separation of Church and State.

Their surprise would be less and their disappointment not so poignant if they had attentively read and clearly understood the first encyclical,[2] in which Pius X, in virtue of his apostolic office, reproved the law elaborated by our legislative Chambers. They would then have perceived that a deep-seated antagonism exists be-

[1] *Union for Moral Action* (Open Forum), June, 1905, p. 451.
[2] Of February 19th, 1906.

tween the Catholic Church—I mean in its official representatives—and contemporary society. This antagonism is what would first of all have impressed them, and without a doubt they would have seen that no agreement between Catholicism and modern civilization can be other than verbal, and of the nature of a compromise. They would have realized beforehand that the Church would never accept the law, but that of necessity she would submit to it with a more or less bad grace. . . . They would have felt that between the two adversaries it is a question of life and death, the Church abdicating none of those pretensions which contemporary society cannot admit without self-destruction; and contemporary society pursuing, more or less consciously, a single aim— the complete extermination of the Roman theocracy by means of the primacy of reason and of experience.

It is amazing that so few persons apparently have remarked the huge anachronism committed by Pope Pius X in condemning and seeking to annul a law framed, voted and promulgated by our government. . . . The Pope arrogates to himself the right to judge, to condemn, and to dissolve the laws set up by the governing powers, every time they run counter to the Church and its doctrines. And, since no existing law fails so to do, Pope Pius X assumes to himself the same authority over the powers of this world as a Gregory VII, an Innocent III, or a Boniface VIII: he lends a little more caution to the form of his demands,—and yet!

I cannot refrain from asking how many Catholics there are today, even fervent and practicing Catholics, who admit any such power in the Pope? As to the vast majority of Frenchmen, it is needless to speak. Pius X seems to us like a contemporary of Saint Louis who has lived on into the present, and to whom the history of the past six centuries has conveyed absolutely no lesson. The Pope does not realize that he has ceased to be the tutor of peoples and of kings; that the constitution of modern States leaves no room for the intervention of his authority in political affairs; that the worst laws can be amended only by their responsible authors; that a spiritual power such as he exerts can still act upon public opinion by means of persuasion, but that its absolute condemnations, the very basis of which is not admitted by those chiefly concerned, have about them something at once monstrous and absurd. He does not see that everything in his attitude is artificial and fictitious, the good faith and sincerity of his act being naturally excepted.

I pass over certain points of detail. It appears certain, notwithstanding the public statement of His Holiness, that his decision does not accord with the sentiment expressed by the majority of the bishops of France at their meeting held at the end of May in the archbishop's palace in Paris. Neither do I pause to inquire whether behind the great display of reliance on principle there lurks anything more than the purely political interest of the Holy See, whose prestige will suffer if the other Catholic countries follow the example of France. . . .

In the name of a power which they (the French people) do not take the trouble to oppose, so clearly do they realize their perfect independence of it, the Head of the Church, annulling a law whose effects he cannot prevent, addresses himself to a Catholic France that long ago ceased to exist, as if he were unaware of the existence of a new France which is beyond the reach of his anathemas. Words fail properly to characterize this strange phenomenon of attempted domination by old ideas and old formulas, to which the masses no longer pay the slightest attention, and which by instinct they repel. . . .

It signifies nothing that the Pope shows himself disposed to regard as valid this law which he has tried to annul—provided the disposition is to interpret it in such wise as to guarantee positively "the divine constitution of the Church, the unalterable rights of the Roman Pontiff and of the bishops, as well as their authority over the essential possessions of the Church." Neither Monsieur Jaurés, nor Monsieur Briand, nor Monsieur Clemenceau, nor even Monsieur Ribot, have any notion of going as far as that. Monsieur Denys Coçhin will be forced to do so; but, unless I am vastly mistaken, it will be with the utmost hesitation and the most profound apprehension that even he will see a parliamentary majority concede the wish of the Pope and consummate a triumph so tremendous, so unlooked-for, and so perilous to the Catholic establishment.

The separation has not been secured for the purpose of introducing among our laws the decrees of the Vatican touching the absolute authority and infallibility of the Roman Pontiff. It has for its sole object the substitution, for the religion of the Concordat, of a religion of the State.[1]

Thus the pretensions of Pius X to interfere in political matters seemed to me as illegitimate and as disturbing as his pretensions to dominate in the realm of scholarship. Only, here the practical consequences appeared immediately, and it was a vital interest of France that was involved. And the bishops simply obeyed orders, repeating as if they were their own the declarations that came ready-made from the Vatican. All this underhanded policy, these impotent efforts to arouse the country for the benefit of a cause that plainly was not that of religion, impressed me chiefly by their anti-French character. In this capacity they made me more indignant, and irritated me more deeply, than the acts of ecclesiastical power by which I myself had been oppressed in the past. It was with matters at this pass that, in September, after the bishops, constrained by Rome, had resolved to place themselves outside the sphere of the law, I prepared a short manifesto in which I passed summary judgment upon the Roman absolutism and the beliefs on which it is founded. Here is the beginning of this ve-

[1] *Union for Truth*, Correspondence, No. 2, 1906, pp. 162-175.

hement *pronunciamento,* which was addressed directly to the bishops:

The deed, then, is done, and the bishops of France, obedient to the Pope of Rome, have proclaimed the end of French Catholicism! A law regularly voted and officially promulgated by the government of the Republic gave to our religion the privilege of perpetuating itself under the same conditions as the other forms of worship, together with the major part of its formerly acquired possessions. The Pope has willed, and the bishops have decided, that Catholics should not conform to this law and that the Church should treat it as non-existent. But since the law holds good, it has the opposite effect of treating the Catholic Church as non-existent. Behold your work, my lords bishops! One does not care to insult you by asserting that you have failed to anticipate these results. You have acted under duress, and if there is one thing you have failed to grasp, it is the obligation you were under to follow your own lights and your own consciences, not an authority which, for the crime that it has forced you to commit, lacked even the excuse of any interest whatever of religious faith in our land; it is, as well, perhaps, to what extent the principles that you obey, intelligible to yourselves, have ceased to be so for your contemporaries.

The remainder of the document was couched in the same tone. Paul Desjardins, to whom I forwarded my philippic, thought best not to print it, as I should inevitably have been recognized as its author. A kindred expression of my strong feeling over this issue will be found in a letter, since published, which I wrote on December 20th to an English publicist who had questioned me on the subject.[1] This letter ended thus:

[1] See *Some Letters,* pp. 54-58.

I wish I might be self-deceived, but it is to be feared that the Church in France will never recover from the disgraceful, equivocal, tormented position in which Pius X has just placed it, and that the present crisis merely presages the approaching end of Catholicism among us.   And it will not have been the State, it will not have been the bishops—unless by their supine obedience to the Pope—it will have been the Roman absolutism which, in order to save its face, has wrecked whatever remained of the Church in which shone Saint Bernard, Saint Louis, and Fénelon.

So far as concerned the "approaching end," I was clearly in error. But I was entirely justified in being indignant; I am so still.

IV

Under the conditions created for me by the Church itself, I did not consider that I had any ground for delaying the publication of my work on the *First Three Gospels*. The state of my health, after November, 1906, also inclined me to hasten. I took certain measures to assure the publication in case I should die before the printing was completed; but the best precaution was to see to the correction of the proofs for myself, so far as I might be able. The work began in January, 1907, and lasted a whole year, until the beginning of January, 1908. There could be no doubt as to the reception the Church would give to my two volumes; but, this time, what the Church might think was indifferent to me, and what action it might take against me was no longer disquieting.

The hemorrhages that had occurred in November, 1906, were repeated in January, 1907, and while they did not for the moment endanger my life, they could not but make me anxious. And it appeared that others than myself felt concerned, for the good Abbé Monier came down from Paris to see me. I do not know that he had talked previously with Cardinal Richard, but he knew his attitude and assured me that, in the affair of the *indult*, the Cardinal would have been willing to grant me the *celebret*, if Rome had not forbidden it. Abbé Monier came provided, in view of eventualities, with an authorization from the Bishop of Chartres to hear my confession, should opportunity offer. We had a very long and very friendly talk, in no wise lugubrious, although it chiefly dwelt upon my approaching end.

My former Director had come to set me right with the Church, thinking or knowing that Rome considered me as good as excommunicated, and that ecclesiastical burial would be refused me if I happened to die without having made the retractation which had been insisted upon in 1904. His purpose was, in fact, to obtain from me a written declaration in which, while protesting my good faith and the uprightness of my intentions as concerned the past, so far as need be, I should submit all my writings without reservation to the infallible judgment of the Church.

I was obliged to remonstrate that I had ceased to believe in the infallibility of the Church, and was not prepared to submit myself to its judgment. For the rest, the Church was free to appreciate my writings in any fashion that might be congenial to it, and for this it needed no permission from me; nor had I any further need of its approbation.

I did not conceal from Abbé Monier that I had taken resolves exactly contrary to those which he was soliciting; that I purposed, living or dead, to assure the publication of my *Synoptic Gospels,* and that this purely scientific work would be found in more flagrant contradiction with the traditional theology than anything that I had previously written.

I do not know whether or not my venerable interlocutor anticipated a more favorable issue for his undertaking, but he did not seem greatly surprised. Kind-hearted as he was, he seemed happy, rather, to find me not so near death as he had feared. He talked freely to me, with all the confidence of earlier days, of ecclesiastical matters, of the Papal policy, whose developments he was following with more anxiety than admiration, and of the fears which he felt for his dear Society of Saint Sulpice. He went away promising to return, but I was never to see him again.

An eminent physician whom I consulted at Paris in March, 1907, advised me not to remain at Garnay, where I was completely alone during one-half of the year, but to live nearer my family. He found me enfeebled rather than really ill; my sole infirmity consisted in being a great deal older than my actual age. My mother having died early in 1901, I decided to live with my sister; and by the end of April I was installed at Ceffonds, near Montier-en-Der.

V

At first, I did not find there the peace I had come to seek. Having arranged the situation of the Church in France to his liking, Pius X was entering with vigor upon his campaign against the so-called "Modernist" movement, and a series of pontifical and episcopal measures followed one after another which more or less directly concerned myself. Not that these acts alarmed me in the least. I was determined not to speak one word more for the sake of being retained in the Church, though I was ready to speak more than one to let the ecclesiastical authorities know what I thought of the measures in question.

I was well aware that, at the end of these explanations, the "salutary" excommunication, as Tyrrell called it, would arrive; but I held to my purpose of forcing the Church herself to notify me that I no longer belonged to her.

This will explain the nature of my correspondence with divers personages in the course of this period. When these letters came to be published, some judges who considered themselves penetrating were astonished that I should have so misconceived the mentality of those to whom my communications were addressed. That mentality I understood absolutely, having suffered enough from it to know it as well as any man living; but I was resolved not to submit to it and I let it know mine in return, without bravado, yet without undue tenderness, so that the authorities might know very clearly what they had to do and what they had to expect, or rather what they had not to expect, from me.

From the beginning of May, I knew that the *Revue d'Histoire et de Littérature Religieuses*, in which I had continued to publish my articles, was threatened, that Rome was about to order its condemnation by the Bishops of France, and to prohibit all priests from giving it their collaboration. On April 17th, in the course of a consistory called for the creation of new cardinals, Pius X had denounced "those rebels who profess and repeat monstrous errors, under skilful disguises, . . . without definitely revolting, in order not to be expelled, but nevertheless without submission, in order not to be faithless to their own convictions," and "that assault which does not constitute merely a heresy, but the summary and the poisonous essence of all the heresies which tend to undermine the foundations of the faith and to destroy Christianity." On April 29th, Cardinal Steinhuber, prefect of the Index, wrote to the Archbishop of Milan against the progressive review, *Il Rinnovamento,* published in that city, calling the editors "self-styled Catholics," who "in their self-pride pose as masters and doctors of the Church," and designating by name Fogazzaro, Tyrrell, von Hügel, and Murri.

Since the plan of the anti-Modernist campaign was already completely formed, it is not to be doubted that the Pope, while having more especially in view in his allocution certain Italian Modernists whom he knew close at hand, did not fail to include the entire Modernist movement, so-called, and its principal leaders, among whom he had always done me the honor of counting myself. It was for this reason that I took the liberty of addressing to my former correspondent, Cardinal Merry del Val, on the 12th of May, some comments on the allocution of Pius X. Recalling the incidents of the year 1904, I said:

> Your Eminence then insisted upon so extensive a retractation that I was unable to conceive even the possibility of it. This insistence has always seemed to me to go far beyond the legitimate bearing of the judgment rendered. . . . But it would be both false and unjust to say that I did not then revolt for the reason that I was fearful of being expelled. I did not revolt for the reason that I had no conscientious grounds for breaking with the Church, and that I believed myself to have such grounds for remaining in the profession of Catholicism. The threats that have been employed against me are not what has influenced my conduct. And although that conduct has not been understood, I do not regret the sacrifices which I made three years ago for the sake of contributing as much as lay in my power to the pacification of spirits.

I had been so outraged by the injury done to Baron von Hügel, the least wilfully proud of men, that I could not avoid writing also on the same day to Cardinal Steinhuber to tell him of my astonishment and distress. And as one of the editors of the *Univers,* perhaps in obedience to instructions received from higher up, had made aspersions upon the *Revue d'Histoire et de Littérature Religieuses,* I sent also on the same date—for the first time in my life, although opportunity had not been wanting me for more than fifteen years—a letter of rectification to a newspaper.

It was an experiment that I wished to undertake. The attacks of the "kept press" had never inspired in me anything but contempt, but I was not sorry to study its methods a little more in detail.   I was gratified to my heart's content.   The editor to whom my letter was addressed thought he could use it to my disadvantage.   He published it with a commentary of his own kind, and I followed it with others of which he published only fragments or incorrect abstracts.   In a word, I had a chance to measure the resources of sincerity and impartiality which a Catholic journalist has at his disposal when he is dealing with an unbeliever.   The public was at a loss to understand it all, and some of my friends questioned why I should risk, without apparent reason and under such unfavorable conditions, the expression of certain radical conclusions upon the formation of the Gospels, the virgin birth of Christ, and the accounts of the resurrection.   The reason was that I had no fear of compromising myself, and that the replies of my opponents—for the lay journalist called in the aid, in these matters of special knowledge, of a Benedictine monk and that of a priest crowned by the French Academy—which did not convey to me any information on the merit of these questions, none the less were of interest to me in various connections.   I might, it is true, have employed the time given to the polemical encounter, to better advantage.[1]

[1] The texts of this correspondence may be found in *Some Letters*.   The same collection contains likewise the letters sent to Cardinals Merry del Val and Richard, and the others referred to in the rest of the present chapter.

On May 28th, Cardinal Richard signed his ordinance against the *Revue d'Histoire et de Littérature Religieuses*. So far as I can recollect, the majority of the French bishops promulgated it in their respective dioceses. By order of the higher authorities, it was read from the pulpit in the church of Montier-en-Der. The ordinance confined itself to prohibiting the collaboration of all priests of the Church in a review which, as it said, had recently published "in addition to certain disrespectful, hardy and dangerous notices of books on the Bible, a number of articles notoriously contrary to the Catholic dogma, namely, three articles on the Trinity signed 'Dupin,' and an article on the virgin birth of Christ signed 'Herzog.'" The author of these reviews of books on the Bible was not named, and it was a mere affectation to name "Dupin" and "Herzog," by way of insinuating—in conformity with the fact—that these were pseudonyms. Who were, or who are, these two, "Dupin" and "Herzog" is not known officially to this day. But kindly disposed persons had taken pains to say that I was the author in question, and the archiepiscopal decree lent itself to this interpretation. I hastened to instruct the Cardinal, on June 2nd, that if it had been his intention to imply this he was self-deceived, or some one had misled him. I had not written over a pseudonym since the affair of the *Revue du Clergé Français* in October, 1900; and I profited by the opportunity to explain to Cardinal Richard what was the true character of a publication like the *Revue d'Histoire et de Littérature Religieuses*.

That review, I said to him, is not an organ for the propagation of dogma, with a doctrinal program on which all its collaborators are agreed. It is a medium for the publication of scientific studies, concerning which no further requirement is made than that they shall be truly scientific. Thus they must needs be judged each on its own merits. . . . There is no place here for the application of vicarious merit. My articles, if they are weak and inadequate, cannot do injury to the magnificent study that Monsignor Duchesne published recently in the Review, on the origins of the temporal power of the Papacy. Reciprocally, that study does not communicate any shadow of prestige to whatever may proceed from a less masterly hand. I may venture to add that it is the same with regard to the more or less exact conformity with the recognized teachings of Catholic theologians which these articles may exhibit. Our readers are generally intelligent enough to understand that my radicalism—or what is taken for such—does not convey any taint of heresy to Fathers Van den Gheyn and Griselle, S.J., who have contributed to the Review; and they also know that the orthodoxy of these Jesuit Fathers is in no sense a guarantee of harmony between my conclusions and the decrees of the Papal Commission on Biblical Studies. If Your Eminence should apply consistently to the end the principle which you have thought well to employ in our case, there is not a review of truly scientific standing with which you could allow the collaboration of your clergy.

Ink and arguments wasted! At the close of 1900, a campaign was launched in the Catholic press against a priest who was, like myself, a regular contributor to the *Revue Critique,* edited by Professor Chuquet, my colleague at the *Collège de France.* The ecclesiastical authorities enjoined him to abandon further collaboration. To tell the whole story, I must add that the same authorities also forbade him to meet me at the table of a mutual friend.

We no longer had any right to meet, except by accident on the street; and I am not quite sure that we would be allowed to bow, even in that event!

On the 29th of May, Pius X ratified a decision by the Papal Commission on Biblical Studies, upholding the authenticity and historicity of the Fourth Gospel. Cardinal Merry del Val being a member of this Commission, and consequently being concerned—or being supposed to be concerned—with the questions of exegesis, I took occasion to send him a brief memorial on the subject, in which I asked, in the first place—not very discreetly, indeed, —whether the Papal Commission flattered itself that it was a learned society, in which case its decrees were superfluous, "the very nature of science excluding any such prescriptions"; or whether it was, instead, a theological tribunal making a mere pretense of being a scientific committee. I argued at some length against the decree of the Commission, saying in conclusion:

The new decree simply leaves the Johannine question precisely where it was before. All that has been altered is the position of those Catholic professors and scholars who hold official teaching chairs, and who now find themselves constrained to put forward, as true and established opinions, what many of them believe to be false, or at least extremely doubtful. It is inconceivable to me how an exegete who does not profess to speak in the name of the Church, and who is moved solely by scientific considerations, can be required to accept those opinions, to declare them his own, and to defend them as such.

It is needless to add that the Cardinal Secretary of State never acknowledged the receipt of this letter.

Among the bishops who circulated Cardinal Richard's ordinance in their dioceses, there were some who did not content themselves with its mere publication. I took the liberty to criticize somewhat ironically, in a letter sent to him on June 23rd, the vague and oratorical formulas in which Monsignor Bougonin, Bishop of Périgueux, took refuge in this connection; and more respectfully what was written by Monsignor Dadolle, Bishop of Dijon, a man of parts and a former student under Abbé Duchesne at the Catholic Institute in Paris. This prelate, without being altogether sure of his ground, had affirmed that true history and true criticism had "nothing in common" with what appeared "but too often" in the *Revue d'Histoire et de Littérature Religieuses*. In retrospect, these controversial sallies appear rather futile. I was not sorry, however, before quitting the Church, to make it known to the bishops who had condemned me without mercy, and of whom several had taken an unfair advantage of my silence, that I was quite capable of defending myself if I cared to do so, and that my moderation had been due to something besides impotence.

VI

On Thursday, July 4th, 1907, Pope Pius X gave his approval to the decree *Lamentabili sane exitu,* rendered the day before by the Holy Office. It was the *Syllabus* frequently announced in the Catholic press following the condemnation of my writings in December, 1903. It contained sixty-five propositions which were "reproved and proscribed," without their character being otherwise indicated; that is to say, without its being specified by the Inquisition whether this or that proposition was to be deemed heretical, or erroneous, or simply hazardous in nature. Thus the Holy Office made use of a measure of caution, requiring complete obedience, while it avoided committing its authority irrevocably. What struck me most forcibly in this collection of propositions considered to be objectionable was the large number of them that had been extracted from my own books, especially from *The Gospel and the Church* and from *Concerning a Little Book,* and moreover the alterations that had been made in some of them from their original form. It seemed obvious that, in certain cases, the censors had failed to grasp my meaning; and that in others they had, whether intentionally or not, more or less modified the sense of what I had written in order to extract from it an error that they might condemn. Their manner of procedure seemed to me curious enough to deserve some study, and accordingly I prepared a series of critical notes on the sixty-five propositions, pointing out the sources of the condemned opinions and explaining their relations to the passages from which they had been derived.

It was only in the latter half of July that the decree was promulgated. In my particular honor, the ecclesiastical authorities again required its reading entire from the pulpit of the church at Montier-en-Der on a certain Sunday. Those present were scarcely qualified to know what it was all about. The same result might have been obtained by having the decrees of the Councils of Trent and of the Vatican read in its place!

Passing over this detail, the purpose of the Roman authorities was perfectly evident, and a personage who must have had his information regarding this at first hand, Monsignor Baudrillart, Rector of the Catholic Institute in Paris, interpreted this intent with precision in the *Croix* newspaper of July 23rd.

The errors which the Church now condemns . . . had led astray certain minds preoccupied wholly by a theory or dominated by a passion for systematizing, and the influence of these minds had become very baneful. The Church was obliged to speak out. . . . We may venture to hope . . . that those who have been misled while seeking truth in all good faith will at once and unreservedly submit. The others have no choice but to leave the Church; it is too bad, but it was high time that all equivocation should come to an end, so that one can no longer affirm himself a Catholic and at the same time uphold Protestant and rationalistic opinions.

As a matter of fact, it may well be doubted whether the authors of the condemned propositions were any more preoccupied with a point of view or with a system than was Monsignor Baudrillart himself with the orthodox doctrine. It was also a misuse of terms to denounce them as Protestants and as rationalists. But, above all, I was shocked by the cheerful promptness with which one of my former students—for Monsignor Baudrillart had taken my lectures at the Catholic Institute in 1892 and 1893; I had thought highly of him, and he had shown signs of reciprocating the feeling—without being in the least called upon to do so by his official station, undertook to show me to the door of the Church. I wrote to him with some heat, and a correspondence ensued between us in which I took occasion to define the character of my apologetic writings, concerning which Monsignor Baudrillart asserted that so far as he knew they had converted nobody, but on the contrary had troubled the faith of more than one believer. I replied:

What you tell me of your experiences does not surprise me. My books of apologetics are in no sense adequate to bring unbelievers and non-Catholics into the fold; they can do no more than dissipate their prejudices against the Catholic idea and, in a certain measure, against the Church. They represent my own endeavor to continue within Catholicism, notwithstanding the impossibility which I found of retaining in their literal sense the bulk of those ideas which constitute Catholic teaching. My writings, therefore, could be of use only to readers who were in a situation more or less analogous to my own. It may be that they have prevented some few desertions; no doubt, as you observe, they have not brought about any conversions, properly speaking. And it is inevitable that they should have disturbed a good many minds that had, as yet, no suspicion of the difficulties that exist. But you will at least grant that these minds could hardly escape being disturbed some day or other.

The crisis of faith, whether we regard it as for good or for ill, was not induced by my publications. I am its victim far more than its agent. Knowing it to be unavoidable, I have tried to moderate it, and it is perhaps that presumption on my part which has destroyed the peace of my existence. If I had been willing to shut myself up in Orientalism, I should still be today teaching Hebrew and Assyriology by your side; the Rector of the Catholic Institute would sing my praises in his annual reports to the Assembly of Bishops; I should be cited as an example of the accord between science and faith, precisely because I had concerned myself exclusively with science and had never spoken of faith. Probably I should be an honorary canon of Notre Dame. And that is how I missed being happy in this world!

As was to have been expected, the decree *Lamentabili* was followed by the important encyclical, *Pascendi dominici gregis,* "against the errors of the Modernists," which is dated September 8th, 1907. That encyclical for the first time solemnly denounced the Modernist system, which at the same time it invented for the purpose; that system, in the form in which the encyclical constituted it, never having been professed by anyone. Also, it created, in order to extirpate the error, the inquisitorial police which still terrorizes the Catholic Church, at least in certain countries, especially France and Italy.

With the philosophy of Messieurs Blondel and Laberthonnière, penetrated to some extent by Kantian conceptions; with the theology of Tyrrell, who was in close sympathy with Protestant individualism and illuminism; and with my books, in which historical criticism was predominant, the theologians of His Holiness had constructed a sort of encyclopædic doctrine with agnosticism as its foundation, and this they declared to have inspired the whole strategy of the Modernists. Pius X and his co-workers assuredly were within their rights in indicating the logical connections that might exist between the different phases of the pretended Modernism. They could likewise, if they thought it worth while, exhibit the ultimate consequences of the ideas which they were opposing. But what they had no right to do was to present as an actual form of teaching, which had been privately accepted or publicly professed by all the individuals whom they were pleased to include under the name of Modernists, the artificial construction which they themselves had elaborated. The negative philosophy that they claimed was at the bottom of the Modernist movement was a mere caricature of the ideas of Blondel and Laberthonnière, who are positive believers if there are any such, and more remote from agnosticism, that is, from the doctrine which consists in ranging God under the category of the Unknowable and there leaving Him, than the most orthodox of Scholastic theologians. On the other hand, my Biblical criticism was as completely independent of agnosticism as it was of the traditional theology; and the manner in which the framers of the encyclical undertook to ridicule the methods of historical exegesis—by putting forward as the affirmations of purblind theorists the most obvious facts, such as the development and gradual transformation of the first-hand memories of the apostles in the progress of the gospel tradition—was itself nothing short of absurd. The encyclical had been intended as a solemn act of the ecclesiastical magistracy; but instead it had taken the form of an anti-Modernist pamphlet. Even the persons of the innovators were not left unscathed by it. They were monsters of conceit, who fancied themselves to be "the sole possessors of wisdom, entirely pre-

occupied with reforming others, and utterly lacking
in respect for their ecclesiastical superiors."

In truth, the pretended Modernism had never
been the doctrine of a few prominent individuals,
but rather the more or less conscious tendency of a
multitude. Even in the writings of those who were
looked upon as the leaders of the movement, this
tendency appeared in a form so subtle and volatile
that it was impossible either to define it or to make
it explicit without grossly materializing it. In
order to make a heresy out of it, the Papal theologians transformed it into a completely rounded
system, of such a character that it became susceptible of every kind of condemnation. But what had
really existed was not a synthesis of doctrine which
those who held it would have wished to substitute
for the traditional beliefs. It was a somewhat dif-
fuse, but for all that intense, endeavor—far less
blind and chimerical than may now appear to superficial observers merely because it failed—to moderate
the rigor of Roman absolutism and of theological
dogmatism. There was no more need for it to set
one fixed form of doctrine over against another than
there was for it to establish a new Church over
against the old. The Church as it actually existed
was the point of departure, as it was the objective,
of the Modernist agitation. The purpose was not
to force it to adopt a new creed or to repudiate its
centuries-old organization; but to induce it to relax
somewhat its tyrannical attitude, to permit discussion of the problems that must be faced at the present time, and to attempt in good faith their solution,

with the aid of the enlightenment and good-will that were actually at its disposal. Looked at from this point of view, which is that of sober reality, Modernism was not altogether utopian and was in no sense a conspiracy. Possibly, even, it might be argued that with less of pure intellectuality and more of religious enthusiasm it would have been a stronger force; and that it would have stood a better chance of imposing itself to some extent upon the Church, or that at least it would have stood out against it longer and more effectively, if there had been, among its adherents, that common understanding and concerted action of which they never had the faintest idea.

Once again it seemed to me opportune to convey to Cardinal Merry del Val the outstanding reflections and feelings suggested to me by the pontifical document. My letter was dated September 29, 1907, and it began thus:

It is with a feeling of the deepest depression that I have read the recent encyclical of His Holiness against the errors of the Modernists. In it I find not merely a solemn denunciation of opinions which, in essential respects, are not those of the persons to whom they are imputed, but also a personal defamation of them of a kind that, in not a few passages, seems as if inspired by positive malevolence towards certain individuals at whom it is especially directed. I am no more able to recognize my doctrine in the Modernist system, than I am able to recognize myself in the portrait of the alleged exponents of that system. A defense would be futile, and I may even venture to say that the character of the encyclical excuses me from attempting one. The lines which I allow myself to address to Your Eminence have no other purpose than to inform the Holy Father of my present attitude of mind.

My answer to the charge of agnosticism followed, and also to "the description" of the work of criticism in dealing with Christian origins "satirically sketched by the theologians of His Holiness"; and I ended by protesting against the imputation of bad faith contained in one passage of the encyclical.

The policy of repression went forward none the less. A *motu proprio* of Pius X, dated November 18, 1907, pronounced excommunication against those who should be "so audacious as to defend any one of the propositions, opinions and doctrines reproved" in the decree *Lamentabili* and in the encyclical *Pascendi*. The circle of disciplinary measures was thus complete; either the Modernist heresy was on the way to being suppressed, or the Modernists would be forced to leave the Church. The outcome showed, nevertheless, that measures of even this severity did not suffice, and in 1910 there was added the imposition of the anti-Modernist oath, by which all ecclesiastics exercising any sort of ministry in the Church are required to reprove explicitly and in detail the chief errors of Modernism. It is not easy to ascertain to what extent all this inquisitorial apparatus has proven efficacious. But it cannot fail to be so in the long run, if its rigorous application is persisted in.

VII

While Pius X was organizing his police, I was carrying through the printing of my *Synoptic Gos-*

pels, and also of my critical reflections on the decree *Lamentabili* and the encyclical *Pascendi,* their publication occurring simultaneously at the end of January, 1908. Early in this month, I received a letter from Abbé Monier, inviting me in urgent fashion to submit myself explicitly to the Papal requirements. According to him, I had maintained a respectful silence toward the latest acts of Pius X; and it would cost me little to give to them a positive adherence, which would reconcile me with the Church and ensure the peace of my existence. I replied to the venerable Sulpician that he had misread the meaning of my silence, and that I was intending to break it within a few weeks. Abbé Monier's initiative was explained to me a few days later. The admonition from the Bishop of Langres which came to me on January 12th must have been first of all entrusted to Cardinal Richard, who had declined to transmit it since I was beyond his jurisdiction, and the old Archbishop had encouraged Abbé Monier to make one further attempt to induce me, if possible, to submit.

The Bishop of Langres, following instructions sent from Rome, ordered me to present myself before him, having need, as he said, to talk with me "for a few moments on a very serious matter that affected myself." For me the matter now had no seriousness at all. It was in the depths of winter, and between Ceffonds and Langres lay almost the whole length of the Department of Haute-Marne. I excused myself on the ground of my health, requesting Monsignor Herscher to be so good as to make his communication in writing. A week passed by, during which no doubt the Bishop consulted Rome. On the 18th he wrote me a long letter, very kind and not unworthy in tone, which traversed exactly the same ground as that of Abbé Monier. I had taken a prominent part in the movement of ideas reproved by the Papal acts of 1907; as to these acts I had maintained silence; but my silence alone did not suffice to reassure the Pope or to edify the Church. It was on this account that Cardinal Merry del Val, in the name of the Pope, had charged the bishop of the diocese in which I resided to require of me a full and complete adherence to the condemnations brought against Modernism.

The style of the Cardinal Secretary of State, whose instructions the Bishop proceeded to quote to me, was less fatherly:

Abbé Loisy must declare without restriction that he condemns all and every one of the propositions condemned by the decree *Lamentabili* as confirmed by the *motu proprio Prœstantia,* as Holy Church condemns them, and that he condemns Modernism as the Holy Father has condemned it in the encyclical *Pascendi* Your Grace will forbid him moreover to publish in future any writing or article similar to those which have already been the objects of reprobation by the Holy See. May God grant that Monsieur Loisy will respond to this final appeal of grace, and that he will have regard to his own soul, that the Holy Father may not be obliged to take the measures necessary to terminate the scandal which his continuance in the Church creates.

I replied to Monsignor Herscher, on January 19th, as best I could: my letters to Cardinal Merry del Val must have informed Pius X of my state of mind.

As to subscribing to the Papal acts, I could not do it in sincerity. I might be able to condemn certain propositions or doctrines that these acts had distorted in the process of extracting them from my books; but I did not conceal from myself that my actual opinions were proscribed, in and together with those that I might be able to disavow.

This being the case, to adhere purely and simply to the condemnation of Modernism, precisely as it has been condemned by the Papal encyclical, would be to admit that I no longer find within myself a single consistent thought, and that I am at the present time as remote from all reason as the encyclical proclaims that until now I have been remote from all faith. An avowal of this sort would not bring me to orthodoxy, but to the utter extinction of mind and conscience. . . . My intellect would be no more able to survive in the atmosphere of the decree *Lamentabili*, and of the encyclical *Pascendi*, than my lungs would be capable of breathing in the depths of the sea. . . . It is needless to add that, as regards my publications, I cannot engage myself to follow explicitly the pontifical directions. It is hardly possible to put forth a single page of Biblical criticism without controverting, in one fashion or another, those directions.

And I announced "the intention of bringing out shortly a commentary on the First Three Gospels" whose principal conclusions were in conformity with those of my previous writings. Also I should publish "at an opportune moment" my views of the relation between my opinions and those which had been censured by the Holy Father. The notice thus given of my intentions probably had the effect of retarding the sentence of excommunication, which was not launched until after the publication of my forthcoming volumes.

It is to be noted that, on this occasion, Rome accorded me more favorable conditions than in 1904. It was not required of me now to condemn my own books, to retract formally the opinions I had professed, or to recognize as mine the doctrines and propositions reproved by Pius X; but solely to reject these as Pius X rejected them. The difference was not unimportant; but, as I stated in my letter to the Bishop of Langres, it was merely superficial, and did not suffice to make my adherence possible. I strongly question whether Rome had any desire or expectation of thus retaining me. Nevertheless, it may be that the relative moderation of my attitude, as compared with the vehement polemic that Tyrrell began at this time to launch against the acts of Pius X, had brought about the change of temper toward myself. But if Tyrrell was an insurgent against the Roman Church, this was because he still felt a passionate concern for the interests of the Catholic religion, while if I did not conduct myself after his manner, it was because the affairs of the Church were no longer any concern of mine.

The Synoptic Gospels and *Simple Reflections on the Decree Lamentabili and on the Encyclical Pascendi* appeared at the end of January. I have never quite understood why the public fastened itself upon the little volume of *Reflections* as it might have done upon some blazing manifesto. It was not perceived until after the earlier onslaught, when I was obliged to put out a second edition on the heels of the first, that the book was tedious. It was only a comparative study of texts, for the purpose of showing how the Papal theologians had put together the decree and the encyclical. The real aim of this discussion was not generally grasped; what appeared was simply that I had no intention of submitting to the pontifical commands; and this stand, which for that matter had nothing of the violent or the unexpected about it, was what attracted momentary attention. A flood of episcopal condemnations served merely to advertise it yet further.

Cardinal Richard died on January 28th. His successor, Monsignor Amette, by an ordinance [1] dated February 14, 1908, forbade the reading of my books "under peril not only of mortal sin, but of the excommunication expressly reserved to the Sovereign Pontiff," the same censure affecting those who had these in their possession, published them, or undertook their defense. Monsignor Herscher followed on February 17th, 1908, and all the bishops in France did likewise.

On February 22nd, a final summons reached me from Rome, with the Bishop of Langres acting as intermediary. Monsignor Merry del Val had written him on the 19th:

The Holy Father, wishing to make proof of the greatest forbearance towards Abbé Alfred Loisy, in order if possible to save a soul, charges me to pray Your Grace to send to Monsieur Loisy a new and final warning, formal and peremptory, in the sense of the preceding. At the same time, you will notify Monsieur Loisy explicitly that, if he does not place his submission in the hands of Your Grace within ten days, counting from that on which he receives your notice, the Holy See will proceed without further warning to his excommunication by name.

[1] See Appendix, No. XI.

Monsignor Herscher accompanied this comminatory summons with a pathetic commentary. I could only reply, on the 23rd: "The formal menace of excommunication cannot effect the slightest change in a state of things which I suppose myself to have explained sufficiently in my letter of January 19th, and which does not depend on any will of mine." It will be noticed that Monsignor Merry del Val made no mention of my recently published works. It was not on account of these writings, but because of refusal to submit to the pontifical acts relative to Modernism, that I was excommunicated.

Why was it that, in November, 1893, the Assembly of Bishops having supervision over the Catholic Institute, as well as Pope Leo XIII and Cardinal Rampolla, could not have said to me: "You have the temperament of a lay scholar. The Church renders back to you the promise you have made to her. Go, she will not misuse you; do not misuse her, on your part." How much I should then have had cause to bless her! In 1908, too many painful years had elapsed. My life had been taken from me to no purpose, and then the dismissal had come with harshness. I could not be particularly grateful.

CHAPTER VI

EXCOMMUNICATED!

I

THE sentence of excommunication was decreed by the Holy Office on March 7th, 1908, and announced on the same day to the city and to the world at large.[1] It was never officially communicated to me, but I read the news of it in the newspapers of the 8th. My first impression, which is not yet altogether effaced, was one of inexpressible relief. The Church restored to me—after no end of fracas, in the guise of disgrace and condemnation, by way of ostracism, and so far as possible by means of my extermination—nevertheless at last she restored to me the liberty which I had been so ill-advised as to alienate to her thirty years before. Despite herself, but effectually, she gave me back into my own keeping, and I was almost ready to bless her for it.

There was no clemency of purpose in the act of Pius X. Rome did all that lay in her power to see to it that the command issued to Catholics everywhere to break off all social relations with me did not remain a mere dead letter. By her orders, assuredly, and not by the initiative of Monsignor Herscher himself, the inquisitorial judgment was posted in the

[1] See Appendix, No. XII.

318

churches of the diocese of Langres, especially in those at Ceffonds and Montier-en-Der. But the faithful either did not, or would not, comprehend. On the contrary, it was thought entirely fitting that I should put off the clerical dress, since I no longer had the right to wear it. The citizens of Ceffonds, two months later, even gave me spontaneously seventy-eight votes for the municipal council; three more would have elected me. Success was not the point. The evidence of their good-will was the significant thing, and I am grateful to the honest neighbors who offered me this token.

In the excommunication which thus set me free I found but a single defect; it had arrived twenty years too late! I was only fifty-one years old, but how many of my years had counted double! My aim in retiring to Ceffonds had been to end my days among my own people. I had no further expectations in life, and the excommunication did not arouse in me any fresh hopes. It merely assured me, or had the promise of assuring me, a tranquil close for my days. My inner peace was entire. To go back in memory to a like serenity of spirit, I should have had to recall that period in my early youth when, with no concern about the future, with no disquiet of mind or conscience, I had assisted my mother in the care of her fowls and of her garden. Once again, I was in the country and back amid that simple life and those simple duties which I have always loved. My purpose was to go on with my New Testament studies, to write a commentary on the Acts of the Apostles and on the Epistles of

Saint Paul, and to crown the series of my published works with a book on the founding of the Christian Church. Provisionally, and while the foolish prattle over my affairs in the newspapers was slowly wearing itself out, I was in the full enjoyment of the satisfaction of no longer belonging to the Church, and of possessing in some slight degree my own soul.

During this interim, I felt that I owed to the thoughtful public certain explanations concerning myself, since it appeared to me that many were in danger of being misled, the newspaper polemics serving chiefly to obscure the whole matter. On the one hand, a number of Catholic writers depicted me as an impostor, obstinately bent on the ruin of the Church, whom Pius X, with aid from the Holy Spirit and from certain very penetrating doctors of theology, had had the great merit of unmasking. On the other hand, I am not sure that, in certain circles, I was not being taken for a popular agitator, or a fanatic, anxious principally to get myself talked about. Just then, nevertheless, I felt the greatest repugnance to publishing anything directly in my own defense, and persuaded myself that it would be a waste of time. As a substitute, I decided to collect in a small volume, entitled *Some Letters,* my correspondence, covering the period between the condemnation of my books toward the end of 1903, and my recent excommunication by the Holy Office. The following will indicate how I explained my purpose in making this collection, in a letter addressed on March 26, 1908, to Abbé Albert Houtin:

Dear Sir:

If I had not preferred to leave to my readers the task of forming their own impression of the whole, the little book that I am sending you might have been entitled: *An Equivocation Disentangled.* Some readers, unquestionably, will be struck by the apparent contradiction between the earlier letters, in which I express myself as accepting the dogmas of the Church, and the later ones, where I profess my inability to adhere to the literal sense of these same dogmas. It must be avowed, however, that a contradiction there really is, and that either my attitude must have changed radically in the last four years or I must have disguised my real feelings to begin with.

There is only one point on which I have altered. I still believed, in the early part of the year 1904, that the Holy See did not aim at the total extermination of criticism, but that its purpose was rather to restrain a movement, certain of whose manifestations might be deemed disquieting. This being my conviction, I was able to content myself for the time being with conciliatory phrases which, without directly attacking the official teaching of the Church, made due reservation of my own freedom of conscience and that of scientific research. In asserting that I *accepted* the dogmas of the Church, I did not pledge myself to interpret them in the same sense as the theologians of the Holy Office; and in condemning in my own writings whatever might be found reprehensible in them, I refrained from reproving such of their correct conclusions as might be contrary to the doctrines of the later Councils, while rejecting whatever my writings might contain that was offensive to the truth as it now finds expression in Christian consciences. In view of my explicit reservations, and my utter outspokenness in *Concerning a Little Book*, it could not be maintained that the authorities were misled as to my tendencies. If, then, they tolerated me, I was justified in the inference that they were no more disposed to draw the extreme conclusions from their principles than I was determined, for my part, to go to the full limit of my freedom.

But the species of Concordat, under protection of which the progressive enlargement of the Catholic system might have been effected, did not get itself established. Rome displayed from the beginning the intention of carrying things to extremes. My excommunication was decided on in the month of March, 1904. The sacrifices that I then made simply postponed it, because they did not dare crush me out of hand. Meanwhile the Pope's reply to my letter of February 28th, 1904, was for me a frightful experience. I may say that, on the day when Cardinal Richard read me that reply, something broke within me; I saw that Pius X would not stop with half-way measures, and that my fixed intention to remain in the Church was illusory, since it was not destined to meet with any answering sympathy.

Thus I embarked without hope on the program of abstention that I had outlined; and I freed myself from it in proportion as the Holy See began to multiply its acts of opposition to the scientific movement, and, one may add, to the legitimate development of modern civilization, as well as to the maintenance and progress of religion in our country. All that it did on the side of reaction drove me in the direction of freedom—the decisions of the Biblical Commission, the diplomatic policy in the matter of the Separation, the decree *Lamentabili*, and the encyclical *Pascendi*. The measures taken by Rome following the Separation Law aroused my greatest indignation, as those relating to questions of exegesis or theology, or even to my own person, had not. You are aware, also, that I had requested the renewal of my *indult*, permitting me to say my mass in private, in the autumn of 1906, in order to absolve my conscience, almost wishing at the same time to be denied it. My situation as regards the Church was fixed by the refusal of the *celebret*. After that, I concluded that my sole obligation was to make known to the public in all sincerity the result of my labors and of my reflections. The events that have just taken place are the natural climax of an open break that has now lasted four years. And this conclusion may be taken as having been arrived at, in effect, as early as March, 1904. It has done nothing more than put both sides where logically their position and their attitude of mind had already placed them.

It may be that certain journalists, who suppose themselves well-informed, will pretend that my departure from the *Hautes Études*, at Easter, 1904, was not spontaneous, as I claimed, but that the ecclesiastical authorities had required it from the first. No such demand was ever officially promulgated. When Cardinal Merry del Val returned my letter to him as unsatisfactory, he required nothing beyond a complete retractation of my books and of their contents. Cardinal Richard alone gave me to understand that the required retractation must have as a consequence the abandonment of my instruction and of my publications; he even added— what the reporters never knew—my retreat into a religious establishment, where the excellence of my surroundings might restore me to a Catholic mentality. But nothing of all that took on the character of a condition imposed under threat of excommunication. It was the retractation exclusively that was thus presented; and it was of this alone that there was any question in the sequel. On this account I have not spoken of anything else. There was no occasion then to make known to the public the details of my interviews with Cardinal Richard.

The better-informed journalists did not protest my presentation of my case. Plenty of devoutly disposed persons had probably already made up their minds that I ought to be considered as good as defunct. Some few were astounded that I should have shown myself so little respectful toward that distinguished prelate, and graduate of the *École Normale Supérieure*, Monsignor Alfred Baudrillart. One anti-clerical writer for the press found it surprising, both that I was in no way exasperated against those who had excommunicated me, and that I was still capable of using the word "God" in several of my letters. There was an increasing weariness of this interminable squabble, in which a good many saw nothing but a parochial row. Possibly, too, my letters were not well suited to the object that I had proposed to myself in publishing them, and it may be that they needed the elucidation of a commentary. In any case, silence very soon fell around this book, which attracted practically no general attention.

II

In May, 1908, the chair of the History of Religions in the *Collège de France* fell vacant owing to the sudden death of its occupant, Professor Jean Réville, who had filled it scarcely a year. Jean Réville was of almost exactly my own age, and had possessed a rugged constitution. It had simply never entered my thoughts that I could, by any possibility, be his successor. The news of his death threw me into a species of panic. I foresaw just what would probably happen; well-intentioned friends would urge me to apply for his position, which at first blush did not attract me in the least. As it turned out, Jean Réville was barely in his grave when I was invited by the authorities of the *École Pratique des Hautes Études* to present myself for the other chair, of the history of Christian origins, which he had retained in that institution, combining it with his duties at the *Collège de France;* and at the same time, several of the professors of the *Collège* urged me to present myself as a candidate for the chair of the History of Religions.

The question, from my point of view, was not one of choosing between these two proposals, but of considering whether I cared to accept either of them. I was not inclined to resume a public career, but I said to myself that perhaps I had no right to follow my own private inclination. If I could render a service to the cause of national education, was not my duty made evident by the opportunity that now presented itself? My health was not very dependable; but had it ever been so, and yet, had it not left me always plenty of ability to work? Had I any compelling motive for declining the support of those eminent men of learning who deemed me worthy to become their colleague?

I was still in this mood of hesitation when the rumor of my possible candidacy at the *Collège de France* began to spread through the press. The reception which it met from a certain quarter was what determined me. Because the Pope had solemnly declared that I no longer belonged to his Church, it seemed to be assumed that my name on a list of professors in the service of the State would be an injury to the faith of Catholics. The secular arm not lending its support any longer to inquisitorial proceedings, as in the times when John Huss, Joan of Arc, and Savonarola were burned, it was none the less intended that I should be morally annihilated. As I did not deem myself in any sense disqualified for any function whatever in the service of my country; as I was no more considered to be disqualified by impartial men who were informed regarding my writings and my career; as it was inadmissible that a purely theological and ecclesiastical judgment should lay down the law for the *Collège de France;* as I was fully determined to maintain for myself the right to exist, the right to work, and the right to teach; as, finally, a liberty was being taken toward me, whether intentionally or not—I entered upon the rôle prepared for me by this opposition, and I have remained in it ever since.

Thus it happened that I became a candidate for the chair of the History of Religions. I was proposed by the *Collège de France* for nomination by the Minister of Public Instruction, and I was duly named. Those who elected me can testify that no candidate ever importuned them less. I relied solely on their wisdom and their justice, and up to the last moment, in the depths of my soul, I was more resigned to defeat than to success. The latter inspired in me no other feeling than that of the responsibilities which my new position imposed upon me.

Renan had given me an exalted conception of the *Collège de France,* and of the place that it occupies, and should occupy, in our higher education. I have spoken earlier of the profit which I derived from his course in Hebrew, but it was especially in his writings that Renan had made me acquainted with his idea of the *Collège.* I had read repeatedly his inaugural lecture, which had resulted in his temporary retirement, and the explanations on this point which he published; also the articles in which he depicted the early glories of the institution of which he was himself an ornament, and set forth the ideal he had of it. I am not equally satisfied with everything in Renan's literary production, but his historical works have a great deal more of solidity in them than many of those even who profess to be his admirers are in the habit of admitting. Let us not blame him too severely for having been a marvellous stylist no less than a profound scholar. There will always be plenty of erudite persons who write abominably! Renan was truly my master, though I had never talked with him in person. I read him with a view to criticizing; but I learned much in the process. It was somewhat under his ægis that I ventured to enter the institution he had adorned.

In no respect did I pretend to be his successor; but in many respects he served as a useful example to follow. Leaving aside the smiling skepticism and the good-natured irony that Renan affected by a kind of intellectual coquetry, he esteemed religion, respected religious emotion, and retained a deep gratitude towards the Church for the moral good he had derived from her. This was not the attitude of a commonplace mind, and it appeals to one who finds himself in an analogous situation, as regards the Church, to that of Renan. As a philosopher, Renan considered that the most valuable part of religion is the moral ideal that it upholds, and that this ideal, forever perfectible, is eternal. That, too, is a lesson which it may be well not to overlook.

And this author of so many eloquent books and striking phrases had said, in his *Souvenirs of Childhood and Youth,* a word that was now an encouragement to me: "Saint Sulpice knows from experience what Christianity is; the Polytechnic School does not know this." He could probably have been persuaded without long solicitation to add that other schools not less illustrious know hardly better than the Polytechnic School what Christianity is, and in general what religion itself is. I am not unaware that, in the context of the expression just cited, what Renan has in view are his questionings and his problems in exegesis, of which Gratry had no comprehension. But such sentences are constructed for the purpose of being enlarged upon by commentators, and it is no distortion of the thought of Renan, in this passage or elsewhere, to hold him to mean that an experience in religious matters is a great resource toward the historical understanding of the various religions.

In my inaugural lecture, I explained how I interpreted the instruction entrusted to me. What seemed to me most needful in the general studies to which the title of my chair invited me was not the framing of a synthesis of the history of religions, or even of an important epoch in that history—for example, the fortunes of Christianity and its victory over the other religions within the Roman Empire —but to direct my attention to the essential elements of all living religions, and to analyze the nature and form of these elements in the diverse cults, in order to penetrate to the inner soul, not merely of each separate religion, but of all religions and of religion universally. The elements in question are sacrifice, divination and prophecy, prayer, religious morality, and the beliefs, the priesthoods, and the reforming endeavors from which arise those religions called universal, as opposed to the cults of tribes or peoples. I began with sacrifice, the ritual acts being the most consistent element in all religions, as well as the most enduring, and that in which the spirit of each cult is most clearly apparent.

My program was not in the least sensational, or constructed for the sake of impressing the imagination of my hearers. Its apparent simplicity might even lead to its being thought a trifle commonplace, and perhaps not quite worthy of the illustrious spot to which I was bringing it. Twenty years earlier when, an utterly unknown priest, I had essayed to introduce among Catholics the use of critical methods in the study of the Bible, I had likewise outlined a plan of work which the most enlightened spirits around me had thought almost puerile; yet I had evolved from it a great deal more than was expected or required of me. It was no longer now a matter of upholding the rights of criticism, but rather perhaps of directing it and practicing it correctly.

In recent years, the outstanding problem had been assumed to be that of the method to pursue in treating the history of religions; as if the method of historical investigation and critical observation still remained to be discovered. Any self-respecting historian of religion felt compelled to excogitate some new method, and the idea seemed to prevail that the method itself, apart from its results, sufficed to recommend its author. Hypotheses, as general as they were absolute, on the origins of religion, had their day. My originality, if I may venture to say so, was in thinking that the true method in history is one of seeing aright, of penetrating as completely and as intimately as possible into the meaning of testimony and of data; and also there was an element of novelty in not propounding any theory which was considered exhaustive of the meaning of the history that it was my business to explore. There was abundant erudition at work, engaged in research into the different religions; what was most lacking, in my humble judgment, was due comprehension of the realities that constitute the life of religions and of religion itself. It was for this reason that I failed to offer any revelation in methodology to the crowd, animated by good-will as well as by mere curiosity, that filled the lecture room at the *Collège de France,* on May 3rd, 1909, to hear my inaugural lecture.

It could not be either my hope or my expectation to fill out completely my general program of instruction. When, in the enumeration of the subjects that I should have to treat, I assigned the last place to the great founders of religions, I did not thereby pledge myself to postpone speaking of them —especially of certain of them who have a quite particular interest for us, such as Jesus and Saint Paul—until after dealing with everything that had preceded them. Christianity, indeed, is not the key to universal history; but, in so far as it is useful to us to know the history of religions at all, in certain respects and relatively to ourselves, Christianity is its center. The history of Christianity helps in the understanding of that of the other religions, and *vice versa*. In my investigation of sacrifice, after having studied this rite—or rather this system of rites—in the religions of the antique world, I have been led to examine the place of sacrifice in Christian worship; and that place has come to appear to me in a wholly different light than in the days when I studied the Biblical texts and the Christian origins apart by themselves, without disturbing myself very much about the environment in which Christianity had its birth. From my excursions into the wider field of the religions of the world, I now come back to this central fact of Christianity, to determine more exactly its meaning and value. If I am permitted to complete my study of sacrifice, which will have led me into the heart of most of the religions that have existed, it is more than likely that I shall discuss anew the genesis of Christianity—the metamorphosis of the gospel preached by Jesus into a religion which was neither Judaism nor Paganism, but which borrowed from the one and from the other whatever it needed to impress itself upon the Mediterranean civilization.

This undertaking is not a mere superfluity. The serene and impartial study of the religious past of humanity is not without its definite bearing upon the solution of those grave difficulties which are stirring at the heart of contemporary society. To it, I propose to devote the strength and the time that may yet be vouchsafed me, in the service of France, in her ancient *Collège,* now become my secure retreat, my supreme honor and my abiding affection.

APPENDICES

I

Extract from a letter by Monsignor Meignan to Monsignor d'Hulst, of May 15th, 1882, published by Monsignor Baudrillart, *Life of Mgr. d'Hulst,* I, pp. 474-475.

A vacancy has occurred in my Seminary, and I am obliged to appoint a professor of general theology. My Council has unanimously voted to nominate Abbé Loisy for this chair. I have let it be known that you had given me to understand that you would request of me this ecclesiastic for the Seminary of higher studies, at the Carmelites'. . . . Will you be good enough to settle the question? Monsieur Loisy may not render quite the kind of service you anticipate, notwithstanding his good-will. His health is feeble, and furthermore I believe he will not be sorry to return to us.

Monsignor d'Hulst, having insisted, Monsignor Meignan sent him, on May 20th, his final consent. He wrote to me on the same day:

My good little Loisy:
It is apparent to me, after your letter and that of Monsignor d'Hulst, that it is the will of Providence that you should part from us here. I say this with real regret, but I assent.

You will go to Germany and to the Orient, and become a genuine exegete, an apologist for Holy Church.

So be it. It only remains to a father, under such circumstances, to give good counsel to his son. It is a heavy and wearing task on which you are entering, in the midst of grave perils to both soul and body. Your health is not of the best; and it is at the price of wearinesses and of watchings that one attains true knowledge. And if travelling at the present day is without material obstacles, it is not without its dangerous distractions. Science has its temptations; it puffs up the mind. *Scientia inflat.* Holy Scripture, which affords so vast a field of investigation, and demands at the present time many a new elucidation, has to be approached with a profound humility, with a profound distrust of self and of all neologisms. More than one Protestant, even, has lost whatever was left to him of faith in the course of thorough study. More than once they have made painful avowals to me of this mishap. May God preserve to you your own faith in all its delicacy!

Never forget your native diocese; ever think kindly of us. You were, you know it well, a Benjamin to our good Monsieur Roussel: he did not desire for you either Paris or the laurels of the higher learning. But would he have held you back now that your professors and the fascinations of study call you far from us? In any event, never forget that true friend of your youth, nor the Bishop of Châlons, who loved to hear him speak of you with the accent of a father, full of hope and of affection; and never forget what I have counselled you. If you read this letter over after your travels,[1] and some years of foreign study, you will discern in it the voice of experience. It is the voice of your Bishop who, on his part, has travelled, has studied, and who thanks God every day for having protected him in study and travel.

When you come to Châlons, do not forget that the Bishop's palace is to be your hotel. We will talk exegesis together!

Faithfully yours, in Our Lord,
✠ WILLIAM, BISHOP OF CHÂLONS.

II

Circular letter addressed by Monsignor d'Hulst, August 13th, 1893, to the Bishops charged with

[1] These travels were never more than a vague plan of Monsignor d'Hulst, who gave no further thought to its realization.

oversight of the Catholic Institute, reproduced from the before-mentioned work of Monsignor Baudrillart, I, p. 484. (I italicize certain passages to attract the reader's special attention.)

Even before the recent controversies had arisen regarding latitudinarian tendencies in matters of Biblical interpretation, and *still more since these controversies,* you have doubtless been aware of reproaches addressed to our young and learned professor, Monsieur Loisy, regarding *his too advanced ideas touching the inspiration of the sacred books.* I am not called upon to enter into the merits of the teachings, traces of which are thought to have been found in his lectures and his writings; but *the reputation which has been given him by determined and influential opponents cannot but be injurious to our Faculty of Theology and to our Institute altogether.* Cardinal Richard, Cardinal Langénieux, Monsignor the Bishop of Bayeux, and several others among the Bishops Founders, with whom we have had occasion to confer about the matter during the past twelve-month, were of the opinion that something must be done about it. *Eminent personages at Rome, last April, spoke to me in like tenor.* To dismiss Abbé Loisy from the Faculty appeared to us too radical a measure, far too severe for this young priest of so unusual and precocious a talent, as well as of a complete devoutness, and doubly disadvantageous to our undertaking *because it would cast blame upon our past,* and also deprive us of an honorable and most desirable assistant. I have felt it to be my duty to propose to Cardinal Richard a compromise measure, which has obtained his approval and which I submit to yours: namely, to invite Monsieur Loisy to confine himself henceforward to exclusively philological instruction, in the Hebrew, Assyrian and Chaldaic (?) languages, in which he excels, and to request Monsieur Icard to lend us, as professor of Biblical exegesis, Abbé Fillion, well known for his admirable edition of the Bible and his other Scriptural commentaries. To this, Monsieur Icard has assented. We shall thus have an additional professor. *Monsieur Loisy will have no occasion to deal directly with thorny questions, and he has given me his promise not to handle them indirectly in his language courses.*[1] The Biblical instruction will thus be divided between two professors who inspire complete confidence, Messieurs Vigouroux and Fillion, both of the Society of St. Sulpice. *Finally, if it is true that the Holy See is on the point of issuing a pronouncement on Biblical questions, we shall have given assurances of prudence and of orthodoxy in advance.* These several measures can be *announced as a development in our theological instruction.* It would seem desirable to bring them promptly to the notice of the clergy. But meanwhile it is our wish to learn the judgment of Your Eminence.

III

Extract from the minutes of the Assembly of Bishops, having oversight of the Catholic Institute, November 15, 1893, quoted from Baudrillart, I, p. 487:

The Rector recalled the circumstances which had led him to address during the vacation a circular to their Lordships, the Bishops, suggesting the introduction of Abbé Fillion into the professorial body of the Faculty of Theology . . . and to *confine* Abbé Loisy to instruction in Oriental languages. *Since then, a grave incident had occurred.* In the little periodical conducted by him, Monsieur Loisy had printed a doctrinal article *on the nature of inspiration,* an article which had seemed to the Cardinal-archbishop of Paris so seriously to involve the responsibility of the Faculty that measures must be taken to remove the danger of a type of instruction *under suspicion.*

The speaker paid tribute to the exceptional ability of the young professor, who is already a scholar of note, highly esteemed abroad, and who is moreover a man of exceptional force of character. *He proposed to offer*

[1] On this statement, see above, p. 153.

Monsieur Loisy an option between the suppression of his periodical and dismissal; if he would agree to confine himself to instruction in languages, he might continue, and we could retain a professor who is dear to us and who does us credit.

Monsignor, the Bishop of Chartres, found this measure inadequate. The Cardinal of Paris was likewise of this opinion. *It would be dangerous for the Faculty to retain this professor among its members. Already, various seminaries were refusing, on account of him, to send us their students of theology.* The two Cardinals of Rheims and Paris declared his dismissal to be essential; both pronouncing for the gentlest form of expulsion, one disguised under a voluntary resignation. . . .[1] Several Bishops voiced their sympathy for the professor. With practical unanimity, on the roll being called, the counsel of the two Cardinals was adopted.

IV

Notice sent to the subscribers to *Enseignement Biblique* in December, 1893:

Enseignement Biblique will not appear in 1894. In filial submission to the latest instructions of the Sovereign Pontiff, Leo XIII, the editor of this review feels the need of retiring for a time into a work of silence. He is grateful to all his subscribers for the generous co-operation that they have given him in a difficult undertaking which may not have been entirely without profit.

V

Letter from Cardinal Richard, December 1, 1893:

My dear Monsieur Loisy:

I have just read attentively the Encyclical of the Sovereign Pontiff on the Biblical Question. We are

---

[1] The omission is Mgr. Baudrillart's. I do not know what the omitted portion may have said,—possibly expulsion, pure and simple, in case I refused to offer my resignation.

assured that further instructions regarding its detailed application will soon be received from the Holy Office.[1]

Under these circumstances, my dear Monsieur Loisy, it will be necessary for you to suspend the publication of your Biblical review until we are in receipt of the announced instructions,[2] to which you must and certainly will submit yourself.

Meanwhile, I am at your disposal and ready to listen to any comment you may wish to make to me on the course of conduct which I am outlining to you.

VI

Letter to Pope Leo XIII, December 7, 1893:

Most Holy Father:

Humbly prostrating myself at the feet of Your Holiness, I beg you to accept the profoundly respectful and sincere witness that, under the existing circumstances, I conceive it my duty to proffer you as to my fidelity to the instructions of the Church and especially to those which are contained in the encyclical, *De studiis Scripturae sacrae.* Called, four years ago, to occupy the chair of Biblical exegesis in the Faculty of Theology at Paris, I have wished to pursue in my lectures the accord between faith and science in the field of Scripture. As regards the theological doctrine of inspiration, I have always maintained, as my writings will prove, that the Bible is inspired in its every part, and inspired that it may be true. I have held those systems to be false which tend to limit the scope of this inspiration, and which the Encyclical has condemned. On those points wherein the Scripture is in apparent contradiction with the natural sciences, I have declared that the Biblical authors spoke in the language of their time and that, for this very reason, they were in the right relatively to the knowledge then acquired; the science of our day not being entitled, moreover, to assume that it has found the ultimate solution of everything, or to serve as an absolute standard

[1] Those instructions never came, so far as I know.

[2] A very curious notion of the way a periodical has to be issued!

to control, even in these matters, the testimony offered by the sacred books. In questions of history, I have sought to resolve, by an attentive scrutiny of the means employed by the sacred writers and of the end which they had in view, the contradictions which seem to exist among them. *It appeared to me necessary, in response to the needs of the present time, to make a prudent application of the critical method, so far as might be legitimate, to the study of Holy Scripture, and thus to meet the adversaries of the Bible with their own weapons.* The apparent novelty of my method of exegesis has aroused objections. A short time previous to the publication of the Encyclical *Providentissimus Deus*, I was required to resign the chair which had been confided to me.

It is a severe trial for a priest whose life has long been devoted to Biblical studies to find himself thus held up to general reprobation as a disseminator of dangerous opinions, in advance of any judgment by the Apostolic See. But I now find much consolation in attesting to the Vicar of Jesus Christ, in all simplicity of soul, my most entire submission to the doctrine promulgated in the Encyclical on the Study of Holy Scripture.

The objections which the enemies of the Church already raise against this admirable document have suggested the idea of a memorial, addressed in lowly homage to Your Holiness, as a witness to my perfect submission to the instructions of the Holy See, to the good-will with which I have hitherto served the Church, and to my hope of further service in conformity to all the directions of the magnanimous Pontiff, Leo XIII.

VII

Extract from the Encyclical of Leo XIII to the clergy of France, on September 8, 1899:

On the subject of the Holy Scriptures, we call your attention once again, Venerable Brethren, to the instructions given by us in our Encyclical *Providentissimus Deus*, regarding which we desire that all professors shall instruct their scholars, adding whatever explanations may be necessary. They will put them on their guard especially against those disquieting tendencies which are trying to crowd themselves into the interpretation of the Bible, and which if they should accomplish this would not stop short of destroying its inspiration and its supernatural character. *Under the specious pretext of snatching from adversaries of the Revealed Word the advantage of arguments which seem irrefutable against the authenticity and veracity of the sacred books, some Catholic writers have thought to display their skill by turning these arguments to their own account.*[1] In virtue of this strange and perilous expedient, they have toiled with their own hands to make breaches in the walls of that citadel which it was their mission to defend. In our Encyclical beforementioned, . . . we have done justice to these dangerous innovations.

VIII

Letter from Cardinal Richard to Abbé Bricout, secretary of the *Revue du Clergé Français,* October 23, 1900:

My dear Mr. Secretary:

The *Revue du Clergé Français* published, in its number for October 15th, an article entitled: "The Religion of Israel; Its Origins," and bearing the foot-note: "To be continued."

This article is in contradiction with the constitution *Dei Filius,* promulgated by the Vatican Council; it is likewise in contradiction with the rules laid down by the Sovereign Pontiff, Leo XIII, for the interpretation of the books of Holy Scripture in the Encyclical *Providentissimus Deus.*

We prohibit the publication of any sequel in the *Revue du Clergé Français.*

You are required to print this letter on the first page of your number of November 1.

[1] Compare the passage italicized in the preceding document.

IX

Ordinance of Cardinal Richard, dated January 17th, 1903, in condemnation of *The Gospel and the Church:*

François-Marie-Benjamin Richard, by the grace of God and of the apostolic Holy See, Cardinal-priest of the Holy Roman Church, titulary of *Santa Maria in via,* Archbishop of Paris—

After having taken cognizance of the conclusions of the report submitted to us by the Commission instituted by us to examine the book of Abbé Loisy, entitled *The Gospel and the Church;*

Considering:

(1) That it has been published without the *Imprimatur* required by the laws of the Church;

(2) That it is of a nature gravely to disturb the faith of believers in the fundamental dogmas of the Catholic teaching, notably on the authority of the Scriptures and of tradition, on the divinity of Jesus Christ, on his infallible knowledge, on the redemption operated by his death, on his resurrection, on the Eucharist, and on the divine institution of the Sovereign Pontificate and of the episcopate;

We reprobate this book, and we forbid the clergy and the faithful of our diocese to read it.

X

Decree of the Holy Office and letter from Cardinal Merry del Val to Cardinal Richard (official translation):

In the congregation of Wednesday, the 16th instant,[1] upon receipt of a report upon various works of Abbé A. Loisy, former professor in Paris, the most reverend and most eminent cardinals, the inquisitors general, after mature consideration, have rendered the following decree,

[1] December 16, 1903.

approved by the Holy Father at his audience of the next day:

The works of Abbé A. Loisy, entitled: *The Religion of Israel, Gospel Studies, The Gospel and the Church, Concerning a Little Book,* and *The Fourth Gospel,* shall be inscribed on the Index of forbidden books,[1] in virtue of the decree of this date, and the decree shall be communicated to His Eminence, the Cardinal-archbishop of Paris by His Eminence, the Cardinal Secretary of State, charged to make known the contents of this decree.

(Signed)   J. B. LUGARI,
Assessor of the Holy Office.

Most Eminent and Most Reverend Lord Cardinal:

By order of the Holy Father, I am charged to make known to Your Eminence the measures which His Holiness has decided to take on the matter of the works of Abbé Alfred Loisy. The extremely grave errors which fill these volumes to repletion [2] concern principally: the primitive revelation, the authenticity of the facts and teachings of the gospels, the divinity and perfect knowledge of Christ, the resurrection, the divine institution of the Church, and the sacraments.

The Holy Father, profoundly afflicted and sorrowfully preoccupied by the disastrous results that writings of this character do and will continue to produce, desired to submit them to examination by the supreme tribunal of the Holy Office. This tribunal, after mature reflection and a prolonged study, has formally condemned the works of Abbé Loisy, by a decree of the 16th instant, which decree the Holy Father has fully approved at the audience of the next day, the 17th instant.

I am charged to transmit to Your Eminence an authentic copy of this document, whose grave importance cannot possibly escape you.

(Signed)   MERRY DEL VAL.

Rome, December 19, 1903.

[1] The decree of the Index was rendered on December 23rd, 1903. The same decree condemned two volumes by Abbé Albert Houtin: *The Biblical Question in its Relation to French Catholics in the XIXth Century,* and *My Difficulties with My Bishop.*

[2] The Italian text reads: *Gli errori gravissimi che regurgitano in quei volumi.*

XI

Extract from the ordinance by Monsignor Amette, under date of February 14th, 1908, condemning *The Synoptic Gospels* and *Simple Reflections:*

We, Léon-Adolphe Amette, by the grace of God and of the apostolic Holy See, Archbishop of Paris . . .

In view of the *motu proprio* of His Holiness, Pope Pius X, dated November 10, 1907, declaring and decree-ing that 'if anyone should be so audacious as to defend 'any of the propositions, opinions or doctrines reproved 'in the decree of the Holy Office, *Lamentabili sane exitu,* 'and in the Encyclical *Pascendi dominici gregis*, he will 'fall *ipso facto* under the censure inflicted in the chapter '*Docentes* of the constitution *Apostolicae Sedis*, namely, 'under the first of the excommunications *latae sententiae,* 'expressly reserved to the Sovereign Pontiff';

In view of the mention contained in the same *motu proprio* and declaring that 'this excommunication shall 'not prejudice in any respect the penalties which may be 'incurred by those who infringe in any way upon the 'above documents, either as propagators or as defenders 'of heresies, when their opinions or doctrines are properly 'heretical';

In view of the article of the constitution *Apostolicae Sedis* which visits an excommunication expressly reserved to the Sovereign Pontiff upon 'those who, knowingly and 'without authorization from the Apostolic See, read the 'books of apostates and heretics sustaining heresy, and 'those who have possession of these books, print them, or 'defend them in any manner whatsoever';

Considering that the works entitled *The Synoptic Gospels*, by Alfred Loisy, and *Simple Reflections on the Decree of the Holy Office 'Lamentabili sane exitu,' and on the Encyclical 'Pascendi dominici gregis,'* by the same author, put on sale in Paris, besides defending the doc-trines forbidden in the two above-mentioned pontifical documents, in addition attack and deny several funda-mental dogmas of Christianity, among others the divinity of Jesus Christ, his mission as Redeemer, the divine origin and infallible authority of the Church, and the divine origin of the sacraments;

The holy name of God having been invoked, after having conferred in the matter with the members of our Council of Doctrinal Vigilance;

Have ordained and do ordain the following: . . .

We declare condemned the works of Monsieur Alfred Loisy entitled: *The Synoptic Gospels* and *Simple Reflections, etc.;* the clergy and faithful of our diocese are forbidden, under penalty not only of mortal sin but also of excommunication expressly reserved to the Supreme Pontiff, to read them, to have them in their possession, to print them, or to undertake their defense.

XII

Decree of excommunication pronounced by the Sacred Congregation of the Holy Office:

Decretum Sacrae Romanae et Universalis Inquisitionis
Sacerdotem ALFREDUM LOISY, in dioecesi Lingonensi in praesens commorantem, plura et verbo docuisse et scripto in vulgus edidisse quae ipsamet fidei christianae potissima fundamenta subvertunt, iam ubique compertum est. Spes tamen affulgebat eum, novitatis magis amore quam animi pravitate fortasse deceptum, recentibus in eiusmodi materia Sanctae Sedis declarationibus et praescriptionibus se conformaturum; ideoque a gravioribus canonicis sanctionibus hucusque temperatum fuit. Sed contra accidit: nam, spretis omnibus, non solum errores suos non eiuravit, quin imo, et novis scriptis et datis ad Superiores litteris, eos pervicaciter confirmare veritus non est. Quum plane igitur constet de eius post formales canonicas monitiones obfirmata contumacia, Suprema haec Sacrae Romanae et Universalis Inquisitionis Congregatio, ne muneri suo deficiat, de expresso SSmi Domini Nostri PII PP. X mandato, sententiam maioris excommunicationis in sacerdotem ALFREDUM LOISY *nominatim ac personaliter* pronunciat, eumque omnibus plecti poenis publice excommunica-

torum, ac proinde *vitandum esse* atque ab omnibus *vitari debere* solemniter declarat.

Datum Romae ex Ædibus S. Officii die 7 Martii 1908.

L. ✠ S. Petrus Palombelli,

S. R. et Univ. Inquisitionis *Notarius.*

Translation:

Decree of the Holy Roman and Catholic Inquisition

It is now generally known that the priest, Alfred Loisy, sojourning for the present in the diocese of Langres, has both by word of mouth taught and in his writings published doctrines which undermine the fundamental tenets of the Christian faith. There existed, however, the hope that he might possibly have been deceived more through fondness for novelty than through evil intent and that he would comply with the recent declarations and precepts of the Holy See upon a subject of this nature; for this reason the severer canonical decrees have up to the present time been held in abeyance. The result has been the opposite: for scorning them all, he has not only failed to recant his errors, nay, in further writings and in letters addressed to his Superiors he has not feared stubbornly to maintain them. Since, therefore, his obdurate defiance following the formal canonical warnings is established, this Supreme Congregation of the Holy Roman and Catholic Inquisition, that it may not fail in its duty, does, according to the proclaimed mandate of Our Most Holy Master Pope Pius X pronounce the sentence of major excommunication upon the priest, Alfred Loisy, expressly and individually named, and solemnly declares that he is visited with all the penalties of those publicly excommunicated, and henceforth is to be and must be dutifully shunned by all.

Given at Rome at the Holy Office the seventh day of March, 1908.

L. ✠ S. Peter Palombelli,

Clerk of the Holy Roman and Catholic Inquisition.

INDEX